BUENOS AIRES
...LIKE A LOCAL

D1343345

C333408626

BUENOS AIRES...LIKE A LOCAL

Chief Contributing Editor	Peter Greenberg
Editorial Director	Cynthia Clayton Ochterbeck
Editorial Manager	Jonathan P. Gilbert
Editor	Rachel Mills
Principal Writers	Vicky Baker, Matt Chesterton
Production Manager	Natasha G. George
Cartography	Géraldine Deplante, Michèle Cana, Stéphane Anton, Andrew Thompson
Photo Editor	Yoshimi Kanazawa
Photo Researcher	Chris Bell
Proofreader	Liz Jones
Interior Design	Chris Bell
Layout	Michelin Travel and Lifestyle North America, Natasha G. George
Cover Design	Chris Bell
Cover Layout	Michelin Travel and Lifestyle North America
Peter Greenberg Editorial Team	Lily J. Kosner, Sarika Chawla, Alyssa Caverley, Adriana Padilla
Contact Us	Michelin Travel and Lifestyle North America One Parkway South Greenville, SC 29615 USA travel.lifestyle@us.michelin.com www.michelintravel.com
	Michelin Travel Partner Hannay House 39 Clarendon Road Watford, Herts WD17 1JA, UK ✆01923 205240 travelpubsales@uk.michelin.com www.ViaMichelin.com
Special Sales	For information regarding bulk sales, customized editions and premium sales, please contact us at Travel.Lifestyle@us.michelin.com www.michelintravel.com

HOW TO USE THIS GUIDE

INTRODUCTION
The Introduction section at the front of the guide explores the city today, history, architecture, art, performing arts and nature. It includes a section of full-color photographs representative of the city's neighborhoods and excursions.

PLANNING YOUR TRIP
The Planning Your Trip section gives you ideas for your trip and practical information to help you organize it. You'll find tours, practical information, a host of outdoor activities, a calendar of events, information on shopping, sightseeing, kids' activities and more.

DISCOVERING
The Discovering section presents Principal Sights by neighborhood, featuring the most interesting local Sights, Walking Tours, and nearby Excursions. Admission prices shown are normally for a single adult.

ADDRESSES
We've selected the best hotels, restaurants, cafes, shops, nightlife and entertainment to fit all budgets. See the Legend on the cover flap for an explanation of the price categories.

STAR RATINGS★★★
Michelin has given star ratings for more than 100 years. If you're pressed for time, we recommend you visit the ★★★, or ★★ Sights first:
★★★ **Highly recommended**
★★ **Recommended**
★ **Interesting**

MAPS
🕲 Principal Sights map.
🕲 Town maps.
All maps in this guide are oriented north, unless otherwise indicated by a directional arrow. A complete list of the maps found in the guide appears at the back of this book.

LIKE A LOCAL... FEATURES
Full page features give you the low-down on the best little things that make each neighborhood of Buenos Aires special.

ASK PETER...
One-on-one Q&A sessions with Peter answer your worries so that you can enjoy your visit.

Travel Tips: Peter's Travel Tips give you the inside track on local deals, tricks and techniques that you might otherwise miss.

SIDEBARS
Throughout this guide you will find short sidebars with lively anecdotes, detailed history and background information.

C 333408626

CONTENTS

BUENOS AIRES IN PICTURES

WELCOME TO BUENOS AIRES

PLANNING YOUR TRIP

DISCOVERING BUENOS AIRES

YOUR STAY IN BUENOS AIRES

MONSERRAT

Named in honor of the Virgin of Montserrat, this neighborhood at the heart of the city is thinly populated but rich in history and importance. It was here that Juan de Garay re-established the city—really just an armed camp at that time—in 1580, and while the original forts and churches built by the colonists are long gone, Monserrat's status as the city's, and indeed the country's, power center endures. The *barrio*'s ecclesiastical heritage is strong too: you should make time to visit the Basílica de San Francisco and the Iglesia de San Ignacio as well as Plaza de Mayo's Catedral Metropolitana.

1 Catedral Metropolitana. Built in stages between 1754 and 1910, this cream-toned Neoclassical construction is the sixth cathedral to be built on the site. Liberation hero General San Martín is interred here. *See p110.*

2 Edificio La Prensa/Casa de Cultura. This Beaux-Arts landmark from 1898 was originally the headquarters of the once-mighty *La Prensa* newspaper. It now houses the city government's Casa de la Cultura cultural center. *See p111.*

3 Plaza de Mayo.
Laid out by city father Juan de Garay in the 1580s, this world-famous square was remodeled by landscaper Carlos Thays in the 1890s. The Pirámide de Mayo was added in 1911. *See p108.*

4 Café Tortoni.
With its sumptuous wooden panels, marble-topped tables, stained-glass windows and tuxedoed staff, the Tortoni has barely changed since it was founded in 1858. *See p111.*

5 Casa Rosada.
Built between 1862 and 1885 and officially known as the Casa de Gobierno or Government House, the Pink House acquired its famous hue during the presidency of Domingo Sarmiento (1668-74). *See p109.*

1 Palacio del Congreso.
Not coincidentally resembling the US Capitol Building, this monumental Neoclassical construction was inaugurated in 1906. Overlooking Plaza del Congreso, it is the seat of Argentina's national legislature. *See p126.*

2 Galerías Pacífico. Located on pedestrianized Calle Florida, this is a shopping mall like any other—save for one splendid feature: the ceiling murals from 1946 that were executed by artists including Antonio Berni and Juan Carlos Castagnino. *See p121.*

3 Confitería Ideal. Atmospheric, charming and slightly dilapidated, the Ideal opened in 1912 and has since become a downtown institution and one of the city's officially protected bars. A great place to watch, learn or dance tango. *See p252, 253.*

4 Teatro Colón. Opened in 1908 following two decades of construction, the Colón has been consistently hailed as one of the world's great opera houses. *See p130, 248.*

Officially called San Nicolás but known to all as the Centro (the financial district between Avenida Corrientes and Plaza de Mayo is the Microcentro or La City), downtown Buenos Aires is where you'll find many of the city's most celebrated sights and monuments and many of its most congested streets. To avoid the bankers, pickpockets, impatient drivers and tourist-hounding sales people, come at the weekend, when the neighborhood's pace slows to a crawl and sightseeing becomes a pleasure rather than a challenge. The one part of the Centro that livens up in the evening is Avenida Corrientes, the city's neon-soaked theater district.

5 Obelisco and Avenida 9 de Julio. Regarded by some as a blot on the cityscape, the Obelisk has nonetheless been Buenos Aires' most emblematic monument since completion in 1936. It soars 67.5m/221ft over 9 de Julio, one of the world's widest streets. *See p127.*

6 Newstand on Calle Florida. Lined with fast food restaurants, leather outlets and the occasional historic gem—like the former Harrods store—pedestrianized Florida links Avenida de Mayo with Plaza San Martín. *See p120.*

1 Edificio Kavanagh.
One of South America's landmark modernist structures, the Kavanagh building was the tallest building on the continent when it was completed in 1936. Unswervingly functional, it marked out a bold new direction for the city's architecture.
See p135.

2 Museo de Arte Hispanoamericano Isaac Fernández Blanco. Housed in the Peruvian Baroque-style Palacio Noel, this splendid museum exhibits artefacts from the Spanish Colonial era. It also has a beautiful garden.
See p142.

3 Palacio Paz/Palacio Retiro.
Built by newspaper magnate José Camilo Paz in 1914, this French-style mansion was the largest private residence in the country until it passed into the hands of the military in 1938.
See p137.

A small neighborhood north of the Centro, Retiro makes up in diversity what it lacks in size. The streets around gorgeous Plaza San Martín, lined with upscale art galleries and grand palaces built during the city's gilded age, represent Buenos Aires at its most affluent and patrician. Proceed down toward the river, however, and you will find yourself dodging the freight lorries that roar along Avenidas Madero and Alem, and the hordes of traders and commuters that mill around the railway station. On the other side of the tracks, in both senses of the phrase, is Villa 31, the city's largest shanty town.

4 Estación Retiro.
Completed in 1915, near the peak of Argentina's prosperity, this majestic railway terminal is a legacy of the country's once-great railway network. *See p134.*

5 Plaza San Martín and Torre Monumental.
Shaded by more than 37 species of trees, Plaza San Martín is arguably the city's loveliest square. Overlooking it from the east is the so-called English Tower, sometimes dubbed the "Big Ben of the South." *See p134, 140.*

SAN TELMO AND PUERTO MADERO

While both of these neighborhoods lie south of the Centro, they are as different as tango and techno. San Telmo is one of the city's oldest and most picturesque barrios, a maze of narrow, often cobblestoned streets overlooked by a hodgepodge of constructions ranging from British-style townhouses (the ones on Avenida Caseros are particularly fine) to grimly functionalist tower blocks. Puerto Madero, by contrast, has only been a barrio since 1991 and most of the buildings in this docklands regeneration zone are either new, good as new, or unfinished. The real estate on the eastern side of the docks—Puerto Madero Este—is said to be the most valuable in South America.

1 Plaza Dorrego. Located at the heart of San Telmo, this is the second-oldest square in the city after Plaza de Mayo and a great place to enjoy a coffee or beer. *See p147.*

2 El Zanjón de Granados. This painstakingly excavated and restored Colonial mansion, with features dating back to the early 18C, is one of the city's most interesting museums. *See p149.*

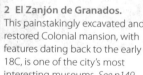

3 Reserva Ecológica. Reptiles, butterflies, burrowing mammals and sea birds are among the denizens of this belt of reclaimed land jutting out into the river. On fine weekends they're joined by hundreds of Argentinians. *See p157.*

4 Feria de San Pedro Telmo. Tango memorabilia, vintage postcards, brightly hued soda siphons and all manner of knickknacks fill the stalls at San Telmo's hugely popular Sunday market, held in and around Plaza Dorrego. *See p147.*

5 Museo de Arte Moderno de Buenos Aires. Known as MAMBA, Buenos Aires' Modern Art museum reopened in late 2010 after a lengthy hiatus. The permanent collection consists of over 7,000 works. *See p149.*

6 Puente de la Mujer. Inaugurated in 2001, Santiago Calatrava's "Bridge of the Woman" is a graceful suspension bridge connecting the west and east sides of the Puerto Madero docklands zone. *See p156.*

13

1 Soccer fans cheering on Boca Juniors. Boca Juniors football club, who play at La Bombonera, are the pride of the *barrio*. The passion exuded by their fans reaches maximum intensity when the team play their biggest rivals, River Plate. *See p167, 168.*

2 Puente Nicolás Avellaneda. Opened in 1940, this imposing bridge made from steel and cement was built to replace the old transporter bridge that still stands close by. *See p164.*

3 El Obrero. With its walls plastered with football pennants, daily specials scrawled on chalkboards, inexpensive wine and diverse clientele—U2's Bono is a notable devotee—El Obrero is a Buenos Aires classic. *See p243.*

Preposterously romanticized by some and unjustly maligned by others, La Boca is the city's most polarizing neighborhood. Once humming with ships and sailors and all the amenities ships and sailors require, La Boca's economic fortunes declined when the docks moved north. This bohemian and working class neighborhood is where tourists come to photograph the colorful houses that line calle Caminito and to buy tango memorabilia. Terrific cultural projects like Fundación PROA ensure that La Boca's future is bright.

4 Fundacíon PROA. Cutting-edge modern art spaces are not the first thing you'd associate with La Boca, but PROA has been drawing big crowds to its temporary shows since 1996. *See p165.*

5 El Caminito. Named for a famous tango, this "open-air museum" was the brainchild of painter Benito Quinquela Martín who organized the painting of these now famous walls in the mid-1950s. *See p163.*

RECOLETA

Famous for its five-star hotels, foreign embassies, immaculate parks and plazas and, above all, its cemetery, Recoleta is also regarded, fairly or otherwise, as an exclusive enclave for Argentina's monied classes. The **barrio's** restaurants and shops reflect the preferences of this demographic, and are more traditionally luxurious and less funky than their counterparts in (say) Palermo. Recoleta boasts excellent museums and cultural centers, as well as flamboyant mansions and palaces built by Argentina's elite in the early years of the last century.

1 Floralis Genérica. Known simply as "La Flor" or "The Flower", the late Eduardo Catalano's much-loved sculpture was inaugurated in 2002. The "petals" are made from aluminium and stainless steel. *See p181.*

2 Centro Cultural Recoleta. Housed in what was originally a Franciscan monastery from the early 18C, this high-profile cultural center was completely remodeled in 1980. *See p180.*

3 Cementerio de la Recoleta.
This world-famous necropolis, whose
current layout dates back to the 1880s, is
arguably the city's top tourist attraction.
Numerous important historical figures
are interred here, including Eva Perón.
See p179.

4 The French Embassy. Also known as
Palacio Ortíz Basualdo after its original
owner, this Beaux-Arts construction overlooking Plaza Carlos Pellegrini has been
the French Embassy since 1939. *See p174.*

**5 Basílica Nuestra
Señora del Pilar.**
Built in the early 18C
but tinkered with and
restored several times
since, this bright-white
Colonial-style chapel has
a stunning Baroque altar
that was fashioned in
Peru. *See p180.*

17

PALERMO

Comfortably the city's largest neighborhood, Palermo is also its hardest to pin down, comprising as it does both large tracts of parks and gardens and densely populated residential zones. Orientation is eased, however, by the existence of any number of unofficial "sub-barrios". Some of these, like Palermo Viejo and Las Cañitas, have been around for decades and have clearly defined boundaries; others, like Palermo "Brooklyn" and Palermo "Dead" (pushing towards Chacarita Cemetery) are non-places dreamed up by devious realtors. It's hard to blame them: Palermo has been the city's most fashionable *barrio* for some time now and doesn't look like ceding the crown any time soon.

1 **MALBA.** This is the city's best Modern Art museum, housed in a strikingly angular building opened in 2001. The permanent collection comprises important Latin American works from the whole 20C. *See p188.*

2 **Parque Tres de Febrero.** Also known as Bosques de Palermo (Palermo Woods), this sprawling green space was designed by landscaper Carlos Thays in the late 19C. Its centerpiece is the Rosedal, or rose garden. *See p191.*

3 Polo at the Campo Argentino de Polo de Palermo.

This wonderful polo facility can accommodate close to 45,000 spectators. It's at its busiest in late November, during the Argentinian Open. *See p254.*

4 Palermo Soho Boutique.

Lupe *(El Salvador 4657)* is just one of scores of fashionable clothing boutiques that have sprung up over the last decade in the southern half of Palermo. *See p197, 256.*

5 Museo Evita.

Formerly a women's shelter run by Eva Perón's state welfare agency, this compact museum exhibits all manner of Evita-related artefacts, from ball gowns to posters. *See p193.*

1 Barrancas de Belgrano. This sloping green space is popular with picnickers, groups sharing a gourd of yerba mate, and, most notably, professional dog walkers. *See p200.*

2 Museo de Arte Español Enrique Larreta. This is Belgrano's most interesting museum, housed in a Neocolonial mansion whose lush gardens can also be visited. Among the exhibits are Spanish paintings and intricate silverware. *See p200.*

3 A tango milonga at La Glorieta. This charming bandstand in Barrancas de Belgrano park is the setting for Buenos Aires' only open-air tango milonga. Classes, practise sessions and the milonga itself take place Friday through Sunday evenings. *See p252.*

1. © Chad Ehlers/age fotostock 2. © Museo de Buenos Aires 3. © Michael S. Lewis/Getty Images

Located just north of Palermo and resembling that *barrio* in some ways, Belgrano has the vibe of a transitional zone between city and suburbs. Avenida Cabildo, the busy commercial artery that is the continuation of Avenida Santa Fe, slices the neighborhood in two. Stretched out on either side are the leafy residential districts that have made Belgrano a bastion of the upper-middle classes. Perhaps this first worldliness is the reason foreign visitors have traditionally given the neighborhood a miss, but a growing number of good places to dine and hang out and an expanding Chinatown are putting Belgrano on the tourist map.

4 Barrio Chino. This compact Chinatown has grown in recent years, drawing both locals and tourists to its shops and restaurants. A big street party is thrown here to mark Chinese New Year. *See p82, 201.*

4 © Lonely Planet Images/Alamy. 5 © Norberto Mario Lauria/Dreamstime.com

5 Iglesia de la Inmaculada Concepción. Usually known simply as "La Redonda" ("The Dome") for its Renaissance-style cupola, this impressive church dates from the mid-19C. It over-looks Plaza Manuel Belgrano. *See p201.*

OUTER NEIGHBORHOODS

Beyond the five or six neighborhoods on the city's eastern fringe where the majority of tourists sleep, eat and see the sights are the forty or so *barrios* where the majority of *Porteños* sleep, eat and live. Not every backstreet conceals a hidden gem, of course—but some do, and for many travelers, getting off the tourist trail is reward in itself. Areas worth exploring include the streets surrounding the Mercado de Abasto shopping mall (known as Abasto but actually part of the Balvanera *barrio*); Chacarita, with its enormous cemetery and old-school pizzerias; and, for those who think Buenos Aires is just too urbane and European for its own good, the rambunctious and diverse Once district.

1 Tomb of Carlos Gardel at Cementerio de la Chacarita. Much larger than its more celebrated "competitor" in Recoleta, Chacarita Cemetery is best known for being the final resting place of tango legend Carlos Gardel. *See p208.*

2 Palacio de las Aguas Corrientes. Still a working facility, this water pumping station from 1894 is one of the city's architectural marvels. Its exterior is covered in 300,000 terra cotta tiles from Royal Doulton. *See p214.*

3 River Plate supporters at the Estadio Monumental. Associated with the northern *barrio* of Núñez, El Monumental is the home of River Plate, arch rivals to Boca Juniors. The national team also play here. *See p200, 206.*

4 Feria de Mataderos. A not-especially-attractive neighborhood in the far west of the city, Mataderos is worth visiting for its unique weekend fair, which is a celebration of Argentinian rural culture. *See p206.*

5 Façades in Abasto neighborhood. The blocks clustered around the Mercado de Abasto are closely associated with tango, this being the neighborhood where Carlos Gardel grew up. You'll also see houses decorated with fileteado, a design style unique to Buenos Aires. *See p214, 215.*

EXCURSIONS

1 Almacén de Ramos Generales Los Principios. This wonderfully preserved almacén or general store *(Moreno y Mitre)*, with its shelves lined with tinned goods, pickles and liquors, is one of San Antonio de Areco's gems. *See p221.*

Buenos Aires is a big, brash, boisterous metropolis, and you may find yourself wanting to take a break. There are several excellent options. Tigre, the gateway to the Paraná Delta, is a short train ride away. Spend a little longer on a bus and you can be in the pampas proper, exploring towns rich in gaucho lore, like San Antonio de Areco, polo centers, like Lobos, or even pilgrimage destinations, like Luján. An overnight stay at an *estancia* will allow you to roleplay a cowboy or an aristocrat—or a little bit of both. And if you want to duck out of the country entirely, Uruguay is just an hour away by fast boat.

2 Club de Regatas La Marina. Tigre has a number of important boat and rowing clubs of which this one, founded in 1876, is the grandest. Non-members who want to explore the river can take a river taxi or hop on a barge at the main port. *See p222.*

1. © Andrew Gibson/Alamy 2. © Harriet Cummings/Alamy

3 Estancia Villa María. This huge Tudor-style mansion in Máximo Paz dates from 1925. It was designed by noted architect Alejandro Bustillo, with the equally celebrated landscaper Carlos Thays taking charge of the grounds. *See p70.*

4 Basílica de Nuestra Señora de Luján. This monumental neo-Gothic cathedral dominates the flat pampas from which it rises. Dedicated to Argentina's patron saint, it was consecrated in 1910. *See p225.*

5 Basílica Matriz, Colonia del Sacramento, Uruguay. Dating from 1695, this is the oldest church in Uruguay and one of the key landmarks of this former Portuguese settlement, now a UNESCO World Heritage Site. *See p230.*

25

WELCOME TO
BUENOS
AIRES

Tango dancers
Photo: © Jose Antonio Sánchez Reyes/Dreamstime.com

Buenos Aires Today

The Autonomous City of Buenos Aires, to give it its full name, is the federal capital of the Argentine republic and its political, economic and cultural hub. Close to three million people live in the federal capital itself, while a further nine million or so inhabit the vast suburbs known as Greater Buenos Aires. Taken together, the total metropolitan area is the second largest in South America and one of the twenty largest in the world. Buenos Aires is, therefore, a bona fide megacity, with all the logistical and administrative problems that entails but also all of the vibrancy, diversity and yet-to-be-unlocked potential.

People and Population

Buenos Aires is a city of immigrants—or at least, the descendants of immigrants. Ninety percent of the population is of European descent, and on many a mantelpiece you'll find a sepia photograph of the great great-grandparent who crossed the Atlantic during one of the great waves of immigration between 1870 and 1930. Most of these pioneers were Italians, fleeing the poverty and political instability of their homeland; others were Spanish (mostly Galicians and Basques). Smaller (albeit influential) groups of immigrants came from areas such as Great Britain, Germany and the Scandinavian nations.

STREET BY STREET

Buenos Aires stretches some 20km/12mi along the length of the Río de la Plata, which marks a natural border on the east of the city. It is also bordered by the much smaller Río Riachuelo to the south and the orbital road Avenida General Paz, which runs around the city from north to west. The city comprises 48 neighborhoods, or *barrios*. San Nicolás, almost always known as the Centro or Microcentro, is the heart of the city. It is crossed by Avenida 9 de Julio, which runs some 4km/2.5mi north to south, from Plaza Carlos Pellegrini to Plaza Constitución. It is also divided east to west by Avenida Rivadavia, by far the longest road in the city and the point at which all north–south roads change their name (except for Avenida 9 de Julio). To the south of San Nicolás (Centro), are the historic districts of Monserrat and San Telmo, as well as the port districts of Puerto Madero and La Boca. To the north stretch the elegant residential districts of Retiro, Recoleta, Palermo and Belgrano.

Ethnographically speaking, the remaining ten percent comprise mestizos, Arabs, Chinese, Japanese, Armenians (a substantial community largely descended from refugees fleeing the Turkish genocide of 1915-23) and many others. There are also substantial Paraguayan, Bolivian and Peruvian communities. It is estimated that the city's Jewish community numbers 100,000, making it one of the largest in the world.

From these disparate roots the inhabitants of Buenos Aires have forged a common culture—you're as likely to see someone of Syrian descent dancing tango as someone with Italian blood—and acquired a common demonym: *porteños*. (Those from Greater Buenos Aires, which is administered by the province of Buenos Aires, are known as *bonaerense*.)

Language
Argentinian Spanish

When you ask the average Argentinian what language they speak, they will of course tell you that they speak Spanish, while recognizing that it is in fact a variation of Castilian (Castellano), of which there are others in Latin America. It is estimated that 91 percent of Argentinians consider Spanish as their first language and that 97 percent use it. (Other languages spoken include Quechua and Guaraní, but their use is mostly restricted to indigenous communities in the north of Argentina; you are very unlikely to hear these languages in Buenos Aires.) In fact, in the different provinces, the language has been enriched and changed over time with terms from local dialects and input from immigration. This can be seen in specific terms, turns of phrase and expressions. The strongest influence in Buenos Aires is that of Italian. The pronunciation, the accent, which is softer and more musical and, for example, the disappearance of diphthongs, can be disconcerting for those used to European Spanish. Certain aspects of the grammar are also slightly different, in particular the use of *vos* instead of *tú* for the second-person singular pronoun.

Lunfardo

If you overhear someone saying that they want to catch a *bondi* but can't because they don't have any *guita*, and work out that they are trying to catch a bus but lack the funds to do so, congratulations—you have learned your first words in *lunfardo*. This slang dialect originated among the lower and criminal classes in Buenos Aires toward the end of the 19C. It remained underground until the 1920s, when the copious use of words such as *gil* (idiot), *chorro* (thief) and *pibe* (kid) in tango lyrics, at a point when the dance itself was becoming more socially acceptable, led to an expansion in the use of *lunfardo* among classes that

had previously shunned it. While some *lunfardo* words and phrases have died out, others, such as *mango* for peso, are used on an everyday basis.

Religion and Beliefs

As is often the case in Latin America, religion holds an important place in Argentinian society. Until 1994, the president of the Republic was required to be Catholic, and even today the preamble to the Constitution calls on the "protection of God, source of reason and justice." Although Article 14 guarantees freedom of worship, the State recognizes the supremacy and special status of the Catholic Church, its affiliation being governed by a concordat with the Holy See.

Grafted onto the "official" religion is a host of rituals inherited from the syncretism of Catholicism with Andean and Inca tribal religions.

Catholic roots

Inherited from the Spanish conquest, the Catholic faith remains the country's main religion, but a study undertaken in 2008 by CONICET (Consejo Nacional de Investigaciones Científicas y Técnicas) shows a rapid change in the religious culture of Argentina. An estimated 88 percent of the population are baptised into the Catholic church, while 76.5 percent practice their faith or call themselves Catholics (a marked upturn, as in 2005, the same study put this figure at 70 percent). However, only 8 percent of Catholics attend Mass more than once a month and 25 percent admit to never going except for marriages, funerals and major festivals.

Christian minorities

Curiously, the surge in religious affiliation highlighted by the CONICET study *(see above)* has not affected all confessions. Evangelical churches, which, throughout Latin America, had experienced a significant resurgence, have lost ground, going from 12 percent in 2005 to 9 percent in 2008. Next to them, Jehovah's Witnesses represent 1.2 percent and the Mormons less than 1 percent. Orthodox churches have few followers outside the capital.

... and others

The Jewish community is well represented in Argentina and particularly in Buenos Aires. Rosh Hashana (Jewish New Yeat) and Yom Kippur (Day of Atonement) are recognized as public holidays. Now more numerous than Jews, but more recent immigrants, Muslims account for 1.5 percent of Argentina's population, mainly in the cities of Buenos Aires (a quarter of their number), Córdoba, Mendoza, Tucumán and Rosario.

Consistent with the general increase in religious affiliation, fewer Argentinians said that they had no religion in 2008 (11.3 percent) than in 2005 (16 percent).

Carnival

Unlike in the northern hemisphere, where Carnival comes at the end of winter, in Argentina it marks the harvest period. Carnival festivities are most colorful in the country's northwest, but recent years have seen an uptick in Carnival activities in the capital, with a new two-day public holiday added to the calendar to mark the event.

Government and Economy

According to the 1853 Constitution, revised five times before 1994, Argentina is a federal republic organized into 23 provinces (including the province of Buenos Aires), plus the Autonomous City of Buenos Aires, which is also the federal capital. Buenos Aires' autonomous status stems from the constitutional reform of 1994, which also created the post of the Buenos Aires Chief of Government, or mayor, who is directly elected by *porteños*. The mayor has substantial powers in terms of infrastructure, health, transport and education policy. Until recently, she or he had no control over the city's police force, which was administered by the federal government. In 2011, the Policia Metropolitana was established; administered by the city government it currently works alongside the federal police force in the capital.

The current mayor of Buenos Aires is **Mauricio Macri**, the former president of Boca Juniors soccer club and son of one of

COMPULSORY UNIONS

There are nearly 1,500 union associations in Argentina, all of which are affiliated with the Péronist Confederación General de Trabajadores (CGT). Membership is obligatory for employees and costs around 2 percent of their salary. These unions manage prevention schemes, which cost the employee an additional 3 percent. The union leaders, who handle these huge sums of money, are elected quite undemocratically because there is only one list. Some are therefore re-elected several times, in an organization that is very structured and often accused of corruption. In confrontations with politicians, the unions most often emerge as the winners.

TRAVEL ...LIKE A LOCAL

What's the difference between a tourist and a traveler? A tourist is someone who only eats at the hotel, takes the tour bus, and shops for souvenirs at the airport. Why would you do that when you can travel like a local? That means looking for more immersive, authentic experiences that not everyone knows about. Believe me, when you travel like a local, you're truly traveling. Here are my top five tips on how to really get the most out of your experience:

Tip One: Get off the computer

I've said it before and it's worth repeating. Don't do all your research online. You learn so much more by talking to a human being. Consider this: In Buenos Aires, the Teatro Colón opera house has a website listing its schedule. No surprise there. After all, just about anyone has a website. But guess what… not all performances or seats are listed on that site. When you go to the box office, and have a conversation, they'll tell you all of the shows that aren't available online.

Tip Two: Eat Like a local

Most hotels have their own restaurants, and many are quite good, but going local means going to the local food markets. Instead of stopping at a cafe in San Telmo, visit Mercado de San Telmo to check out the local food stalls.

Tip Three: Visit residential neighborhoods

Belgrano is Buenos Aires' most populated barrio as well as its main residential neighborhood. Far from just a sleepy suburb, you'll find a real diversity of people going about their day-to-day lives. You don't always have to eat another great steak in the Argentina capital. Instead, check out the busy Chinatown area and make time for a nearby soccer game.

Tip Four: Make your own excursions

You'll find tour operators eagerly waiting to put you on a bus or boat to Tigre or the Paraná Delta. But instead of following the tourists there on the weekend, head out during the week to beat the crowds, and get a regular ferry to hang with the locals.

Tip Five: Visit local hot spots

Many concierges will be the first to send you to a restaurant with a tango show, but that won't be the local experience. It will be a performance staged for tourists. For a local's weekend, head to La Glorieta (gazebo) in the Barrancas de Belgrano (park), where locals dance the night away. And if you show up early, around 7pm, you'll get tango tips from veteran dancers eager to share their moves.

Travel, Dine and Explore with Confidence

TRAVEL ADVICE

MICHELIN
COLOMBIA

MICHELIN
Rio de Janeiro

Experience the laidback Carioca lifestyle
Visit Christ the Redeemer at Corcovado's summit
Try the famous feijoada

762 NATIONAL   762
MICHELIN
Argentina

Michelin, experts in travel guides and maps for more than 100 years. Available wherever books are sold.

www.michelintravel.com

MICHELIN
A better way forward

Argentina's most successful businessmen. Under the banner of his PRO party, which is in opposition to the governing Frente de la Victoria party, Macri first came to power in 2007, comfortably beating the government candidate Daniel Filmus. He was reelected in 2011, again with great ease and again besting Filmus.

The Kirchner years

The "autonomy" of Buenos Aires only goes so far, of course, and it is the decisions of the national government that have the greatest impact on people's lives. Since 2007, **Cristina Kirchner** has held the Argentinian presidency. Like her late husband, **Néstor Kirchner**, who led the country from 2003 to 2007, and died of a heart attack in 2010, Cristina is a member of the Justicialist Party, founded by Juan Perón in 1945. She won re-election in October 2011, crushing a fractured opposition and winning 55 percent of the national vote.

Cristina's national policy is essentially a continuation of that formulated by her late husband, who came to power in 2003 in the wake of Argentina's worst-ever economic crisis (2001-02). By keeping the peso cheap (around four to the dollar, as opposed to the one-for-one convertibility of the 1990s), Argentina has become an export powerhouse (helped, it must be said, by the global hike in commodity prices in the mid-2000s). Argentina's economy has seen healthy growth since 2003, and the proceeds have been used to fund housing programs and other redistributive initiatives.

Media
Newspapers and magazines

The dominant player across the whole range of Argentinian media is the **Clarín Group**: aside from operating a number of television channels and radio stations, it publishes the country's leading print daily, *Clarín*. It is no exaggeration to say that the relationship between *Clarín* and the Kirchner government is one of mutual loathing, with the former accusing the latter of being authoritarian and the latter accusing the former of being a monopoly. *La Nación*, the country's leading conservative broadsheet, is also antagonistic to the government's agenda, though it carries less clout than *Clarín*.

Newspapers on the left, such as *Página/12*, tend to back the government. Politics aside, all of the above offer excellent coverage of sports, arts and culture.

ASK PETER...

Q: I like to keep up with the news when I travel. Can you recommend local English-language newspapers?

A: For a local take on current events in English, the *Buenos Aires Times* and news-driven *Buenos Aires Herald* are publications that will keep you in the loop. Both are available online, and the *Buenos Aires Herald* has a daily print version available.

The country's leading (in fact, only) English-language daily is the *Buenos Aires Herald*, which won renown in the late 1970s for its opposition to the military dictatorship but has since gone through several owners and is underfunded. A wide variety of weekly and monthly magazines are also available, ranging from quasi-pornographic "men's mags" like *H* to gossip and paparazzi-driven glossies like *Caras* and *Gente* to serious, agenda-setting political and current affairs publications like *Noticias*.

Television

Spend a couple of hours watching Argentinian television and you'll probably find yourself thinking, "This isn't as bad as I expected it to be." True, the daytime schedules are heavy on cartoons and Zorro re-runs, but the evening news broadcasts are generally strong and well produced—if a little heavy on lurid crime stories—while the *telenovelas* (soap operas) that follow hit all the right notes for those who like that kind of thing.

The main free-to-air channels are the state-run Canal 7 (which shows top-division Argentina soccer action as part of the subsidized "football for everyone" initiative), Telefe, and Canal Trece which is owned by the Clarín Group. América TV and Canal 9 are the other free-to-air channels. Local cable channels include the tabloid-style Crónica (lottery results, celebrity gossip, puppets reading the news, violent crime), Gourmet (food and drink), the regional ESPN and Fox Sports franchises and some excellent, fairly highbrow arts and culture channels like Encuentro.

The stars to look out for are the "divas" Mirtha Legrand and Susana Giménez, who have been around for decades and show no signs of slowing down, and current kingpin Marcelo Tinelli, whose late-night show Videomatch (essentially a repackaged version of Dancing with the Stars with added nudity and innuendo) is loved and loathed in more or less equal measure.

Food and Drink
Food

There is much to be said about Argentinian cuisine—it's regional diversity and it's international influences—but in the end, most lines of inquiry lead back to meat. The average Argentinian ate 54kg/119lb of beef in 2011. This sounds like a lot, but was actually the lowest figure recorded in over 50 years, leading some to speculate that Argentinians are turning away from their national cuisine and taking up exotica like vegetables instead.

Regardless of such trends, the first and last thing carnivorous visitors to Buenos Aires want to eat is a juicy chunk of steak in a bustling *parrilla* (steakhouse). The trimmings should include *chorizos* (sausages), *papas fritas* (french fries) and certainly a selection of *achuras* (offal). If you're lucky you'll be invited to a home *asado*, the sacred Sunday ritual in which men (it's always men) fire up the garden barbecue and grill assorted cuts for their friends and families. No garden or terrace in Buenos Aires is complete without a *parrilla* (in this sense, it simply means grill).

When they're not eating meat, *porteños* are channeling their Italian heritage. If it's too wet for a barbecue, grandma will make her famous raviolis. People drop in to pizza parlors for a slice at the counter on the way home from work, in much the same way as the Spanish snatch a plate of tapas. And every *porteño*, from the youngest to the oldest, is addicted to gelato-style *helado* ice-cream—particularly if it's flavored with *dulce de leche*, the adored local caramel.

Wine

Although the wines of Mendoza province are the most celebrated, particularly the outstanding Malbecs, those of San Juan and Cafayate are also terrific. Many different grape varietals are grown, imported by immigrant winemakers from Italy and France (Bordeaux and the southwest), but those that have made Argentinian wine famous are Malbec and Torrontés.

Maté

This infusion of *yerba maté*, a plant cultivated in the country's northeast, is the traditional drink of the gauchos, but everyone drinks it, everywhere and at any time of day. In the morning, Argentinians take their *maté* cup (often a hollow, decorated gourd), line it with leaves, fill it with boiling water and drink it slowly through a *bombilla*, a straw with holes in the end that prevents them sucking up the leaves. Each person carries a thermos flask of hot water to top up his or her cup. It is common to pass the drink around, with each person taking a sip in turn.

ARGENTINIAN BEEF

There are three ways to order beef in Argentina: *jugoso* (medium rare/juicy with a red center), *a punto* (medium, pink throughout) and *cocido* (well done, no pink). As the biggest beef-loving country in the world, it will only benefit you to learn the different cuts. The most expensive cut is *bife de lomo* (tenderloin), a thin cut of meat is *entrana* (skirt steak), the cheapest option is *asado de tira* (short ribs), one not usually served outside Argentina/Uruguay is *vacio* (flank steak) and the biggest, juiciest steak is *bife de chorizo* (sirloin).

History

How did a precarious Colonial backwater on the edge of the map become one of the world's great cities? Like most New World narratives, the story of Buenos Aires is a breathless one, with hope, peace and achievement frequently giving way to despair, war and catastrophe—before coming full circle.

One City, Two Beginnings

Anthropologists can't agree on when the first human beings arrived in the pampas region where Buenos Aires now stands, but one thing can be said for sure: it was many thousands of years before the Spanish arrived. The Querandí, who hunted dear, rhea and guanacos, were among the area's original inhabitants, and it was they who watched from the shore when the ships of Spanish navigator Pedro de Mendoza dropped anchor in the Río de la Plata, in February 1536.

Legend and some archaeological evidence suggest that Mendoza landed and set up camp in what is now Parque Lezama, in San Telmo. He christened his settlement "Nuestra Señora del Buen Ayre" (Our Lady of the Fair Winds). The indigenous population resisted the intruders, however, and their attacks forced the Spanish to abandon the settlement in 1541.

Another forty years passed before, on June 11 1580, Juan de Garay founded a permanent new colony. Evidently deciding that Mendoza's choice of name had been too pithy, he called the city "Santísima Trinidad y Puerto de Nuestra Señora de los Buenos Ayres" (Saint Trinity and Port of Our Lady of the Fair Winds). This mouthful of a title metamorphosed gradually and mercifully until it reached its definitive form: Buenos Aires.

The town was arranged around the present-day Plaza de Mayo, which is believed to have been the site of this new foundation. Roughly bordered by the present-day streets and avenues of 25 de Mayo and Balcarce to the east, Salta and Libertad to the west, Viamonte to the north and Independencia to the south, it contained 135 blocks and covered an area of about 2.5sq km/1sq mi. It changed relatively little during the 16C and 17C, but in the 18C, the town began to stretch out to the south, as far as the estuary of the Río Riachuelo, the natural port of Buenos Aires, where legal and illegal trading started up. In 1769 the six first parishes were created: Catedral, San Nicolás, El Socorro, Monserrat, La Piedad and La Concepción.

Buenos Aires' economic success was mainly linked to maritime trade, but the Spanish administration of the 17C and 18C required that all trade with Europe pass through Lima (Peru), the capital of the colonial empire. This policy, which led to the levying of taxes, was the source of true discontent on the part of the *porteños* (as the inhabitants of the port of Buenos Aires became known by the Spanish authorities). To defuse the troubles and limit the growing trade in smuggled goods, Charles III of Spain progressively abolished trade restrictions, eventually creating, in 1776, the viceroyalty of Río de la Plata, comprising modern-day Bolivia, Paraguay, Argentina and Uruguay, of which Buenos Aires was the capital.

Administratively, the town became the equal of Lima. Thanks to the free trade agreements that the new authorities set up with Chile, Peru and Spain, the port boomed during the last thirty years of the 18C, attracting the first of the many waves of immigrants that would arrive from Europe.

Removing the Reign from Spain

The growing prosperity of Buenos Aires' new middle classes only compounded their frustration at being ruled by what they increasingly perceived as an alien power. Variations on the battle cry that had rallied the North American revolutionaries—"No taxation without representation!"—were beginning to echo around the southern American continent. Second- and third-generation colonists, known as *criollos*, began to feel the stirrings of a new national consciousness—a sensation that was swelled in 1806 and 1807 when the British twice tried to conquer Buenos Aires. Both times, despite the inglorious flight of the viceroy and his troops, the *porteños* managed to drive out the invaders.

In repulsing the British, they became aware of their ability to defend themselves, and began to dream of independence. Political upheavals in Europe and Napoleon's conquest of Spain in 1808 gave them a window of opportunity. In 1810, they drove out the viceroy of Buenos Aires and formed a "revolutionary" junta: this was the famous May Revolution, after which the central square and many streets in Buenos Aires are named. Among the architects of Independence were Mariano Moreno, Manuel Belgrano, Bernardino Rivadavia, José de San Martín and Juan Martín de Pueyrredón.

At the time of independence, Buenos Aires had 46,000 inhabitants, a figure that was to more than double in half a century to reach 100,000 inhabitants by the middle of the 19C.

Centralism or Federalism

The 19C was marked by incessant struggles between Buenos Aires, which advocated a centralist vision of the country's administration, and other provinces, which wanted a federalist system.

THE MEMORY OF THE MISSING

During the so-called "Dirty War" conducted by the military dictatorship that ruled Argentina between 1976 and 1983, the authorities abducted many thousands of Argentinians, detained them without trial, tortured and often killed them. Varying between 10,000 and 40,000, depending on the source, the number of missing persons—known as *desaparecidos*—is officially given as 30,000, not including the children who were taken from their parents and given to military families. Since 1977, the Mothers of the Plaza de Mayo association has marched every Thursday, the women wearing white headscarves, demanding to be told the truth about what happened to their missing children. When he was elected president in 2003, Néstor Kirchner made bringing the perpetrators of these crimes to justice one of his top priorities. The various amnesty laws and pardons that had protected them since the mid-1980s were annulled, allowing for new trials. Former dictator Jorge Videla is now serving a life sentence, as is the notorious "Blonde Angel of Death" Alfredo Astíz. Inaugurated in 2006, the Parque de la Memoria de Buenos Aires *(www.parquedelamemoria.org.ar)* is a 14ha/35-acre site on the Costanera Norte dedicated to remembering and honoring the dead and missing. Eighteen sculptures are scattered around the site; but the dominant feature is the Monumento a la Victimas del Terrorismo de Estado, a dark wall resembling Washington's Vietnam memorial that is engraved with the names of the "disappeared."

These antagonisms led to a series of bloody confrontations. It was finally decided to federalize the country, and in 1880, Buenos Aires was definitively chosen as the federal capital.

Immigration

During this century, the country also saw its first great waves of immigration, which were encouraged by the Argentinian government to populate the country. From 1871 to 1940, around 55,000 immigrants—from Spain, Italy, Lebanon, Syria, Poland and Russia—disembarked each year at Buenos Aires in the hope of starting a new life there. The city, which covered an area of around 45sq km/17.4sq mi in 1880, had reached an area of 190sq km/73.4sq mi by 1888, with the annexation of the adjacent towns of Flores and Belgrano. In parallel, the first national census, taken in 1887, estimated the population of Buenos Aires to be in excess of 433,000 inhabitants. By 1914 the figure had exceeded 1.5 million.

The Golden Age

The end of the 19C and the beginning of the 20C was a *belle époque* for both Buenos Aires and Argentina. The city saw some tremendous transformations: the construction of modern means of transportation, mainly railroads, the opening of wide avenues and the appearance of South America's tallest skyscrapers. The opening of the first subway, in 1913, confirmed the capital's accession to modernity. Rich Buenos Aires families, many of whom had been driven from the city's southern *barrios* (San Telmo, La Boca) by a yellow fever outbreak in 1871, migrated farther north (Retiro, Recoleta, Palermo) and built for themselves sumptuous homes and luxury palaces, where French style, then very fashionable in the New World, mostly prevailed. Despite having an economy that relied exclusively on exports of agricultural produce and was not industrialized, Argentina was, at the beginning of the 20C, one of the richest countries in the world.

Demands for Reform

Several factors of dissatisfaction remained, however: the land (and therefore the wealth and power) remained in the hands of a few major colonists. Newcomers, employees, workers and small landowners, frustrated at their lack of political clout, became more radical and launched major strikes. The government finally implemented universal suffrage for men in 1916.

The Unión Cívica Radical (UCR) party, founded in 1890 to represent the aspirations of the middle classes, came to power, under the presidency of Hipólito Yrigoyen, son of a Basque immigrant, who was president from 1916 to 1922 and from 1928 to 1930). Despite his progressive politics in favor of small landowners, he alienated workers. An interventionist, he was hampered by the absence of a domestic industry and his dependence on foreign economies. Undermined by the collapse of the economy in the crisis of 1929, he was overthrown by the first of a long series of military coups.

Peronism

Inextricably linked to the history of modern Argentina, **Juan Domingo Perón** (1896-1974) was a true product of the reigning military class. Perón joined a secret military organization, the GOU (Grupo Obra de Unificación), which seized power in 1943. Appointed Secretary of State for Work and Health, he implemented important social reforms that made him hugely popular. In 1944, at a charity fundraising event for victims of the San Juan earthquake, he met his future wife Eva Duarte, a young actress from an impoverished rural family. The following year, when the military junta, jealous of his popularity, arrested him,

Eva mobilized the unions and organized large demonstrations to obtain his release. In 1946, Perón was elected President. The country was in good economic health, which gave the new head of state the scope to make some important reforms, in a curious mixture of populist Communism, un-inhibited capitalism and almost Fascist protectionism and authoritarianism. This blend, which came to be known as Peronism, enabled him to stay in power until 1955. For her part, Eva Perón (whom he married in 1945) was an ardent supporter of workers, women and the poor. Her premature death, in 1952, was felt as a huge shock in Argentina. Moreover, Perón's policies failed to stabilize the economy. The foreign trade deficit and the enormity of the debt led to brutal recession and inflation.

Military Rule

Taking advantage of the unpopularity of Perón among the young and the clergy, the military seized power again in 1955, under the pretext of Revolución Libertadora (Liberating Revolution). To finish with Perón, they simply prohibited Peronism. For eighteen years, the country led a predictable dance, alternating, every three or four years, between military coups and brief spells during which the Radical Party held power. With each new coup from the army, the dictatorship seemed more repressive, condemning the country to political chaos, fraud and protests that were quelled with violence. In the same vein, political assassinations, torture and imprisonments marked the transition to power of General Lanusse. But the worst was yet to come.

Perón Redux

Taking advantage of a momentary loss of power of the military, Perón returned from his exile in Spain and won the elections of 1973. He was accompanied by his new wife Isabel Perón, who was appointed Vice-President. But the old leader no longer had the wind in his sails and died suddenly in 1974. His wife succeeded him, but her ultra-conservatism led to her being deposed by the military in 1976.

The Dirty War

Thus began the most tragic episode of Argentina's history. From 1976 to 1983, the dictatorship of a trio of generals—Videla, Viola and Galtieri—banished the country from the civilized world. All power was in their hands. All freedoms disappeared. Under the name Operation Condor, it engaged in the massive and systematic repression of those it suspected of terrorism. In a climate of extreme paranoia, that could apply to anyone. The number of arrests increased. Meanwhile, the economy continued to deteriorate.

In 1982, desperate for some initiative that would win popular support, the junta launched a surprise invasion of the Islas Malvinas (or the Falkland Islands, as they are known in English), a British colony whose sovereignty Argentina had long contested. At first, all went well. The invasion was met without resistance, and large crowds gathered in Plaza de Mayo to express

With its cast of gauchos, rogues, statesmen and soldiers, you could be forgiven for thinking that Argentinian history is an all-male production (Eva Perón being the exception that proves the rule). In an attempt to redress this imbalance, in the 1990s the city decided to name the streets of Puerto Madero after women who had made important contributions to the country's development. Among those so honored are Olga Cossettini (1898-1987), a celebrated educator; Azucena Villaflor (1924-77), one of the founders of Mothers of the Plaza de Mayo; and Alicia Moreau de Justo (1885-1986), the English-born campaigner for women's suffrage.

support for the war. But the junta had both underestimated the resolve of British Prime Minister Margaret Thatcher and overestimated the fighting capacity of their own forces, many of whom were poor conscripts, inadequately trained and almost comically under-equipped. After a 74-day war, the British retook the islands. 649 Argentinians lost their lives (against 249 British). The junta merely lost their jobs.

Democracy, Crisis and Recovery

In 1983, amid national rejoicing, UCR leader Raúl Alfonsín was elected president. Before handing over the reins, the military signed a general amnesty. But the disastrous economic situation now occupied center stage. The failure of the UCR to get it back on an even keel opened the way, in 1989, for the neoliberal Carlos Menem, whose finance minister Domingo Cavallo introduced a policy of one-to-one parity between the peso and the US dollar. Attracted by this chimera of economic stability, foreign investors poured money into Argentina. Furthermore, owing to the new strength of their currency, ordinary Argentinians were able to take foreign holidays like never before, as well as purchase luxurious imported products.

The party didn't last. In 1999, the UCR returned to power with Fernando de la Rúa. In 2001, Argentina hit rock bottom. The government fell again, and in one fateful week, five presidents succeeded each other. The last of these, Eduardo Duhalde, ended the peso–dollar parity. Argentina defaulted on its massive foreign debt, the largest such default in history.

ASK PETER...

Q: I'm told that reminders of the Dirty War and the military dictatorship still exist today, how so?
A: "Mothers of the Plaza de Mayo" is the name for women whose sons and daughters disappeared during the Dirty War. Today these women have become activists, whom you can see at protests wearing white headscarves. You'll even see a white headscarf painted onto the ground of the Plaza de Mayo.

EVA PERÓN

It is astonishing to reflect that "Evita" Perón was only 33 when she died, so large does her figure loom over 20C Argentinian history. One of a trio of Argentinians (the others are Ernesto "Che" Guevara and Diego Maradona) whose life stories have resonated with people around the globe—many of whom would struggle to find Argentina on an atlas—Evita has inspired musicals and movies and shifted mountains of memorabilia. But it is the reverence in which she is still held by the poorer sectors of Argentinian society that is her true legacy.

The illegitimate daughter of a rich landowner from Junín, Evita had a disadvantaged childhood until, aged 15, she left home to try her luck as an actress in Buenos Aires. However, it was neither in cinema nor in radio that she really made her career. In fact, in 1945, she married Colonel Juan Perón, whom she had met at a charity auction. Becoming first lady of Argentina in 1946, this young girl from humble beginnings, who used to dream of being a star, became the icon of the working class, the "shirtless" *(descamisados)*. Nicknamed Evita, she became very influential at the heart of Perón's authoritarian regime, setting herself up as the people's benefactress: in 1948 she created the Fundación Eva Perón, with the goal of helping the poor, but also established hospitals, orphanages and social housing. She created the Female Peronist Party, which is credited as the first large female political party in the nation and influenced thousands of women to enter politics.

She died in 1952, aged 33, of a cancer of the uterus, and was buried in Italy under a false identity for sixteen years before her body was repatriated to Argentina in 1974. She now rests in Recoleta Cemetery, her plain tomb in stark contrast to the grandiloquent mausoleums that surround it. (It is said, however, that her grave was built to withstand the force of a nuclear blast—just one of the many urban myths that swirl around Evita.)

Evita was a controversial figure in her lifetime, and remains one today. For those households who keep a photograph of her above the mantelpiece, she was the tireless campaigner for social justice and women's suffrage—a saint in a century littered with sinners. To her detractors, she was an insufferable parvenu who adorned herself with expensive clothing and jewelry while preaching the rhetoric of class warfare. The truth, as usual, is probably somewhere between these two poles. But few would deny that Eva Perón was a courageous, charismatic figure, whose hold on the affections of the masses was a key factor in her husband's attempt to re-cast Argentinian society.

In a process known as "corralito," savings held in dollars were converted to pesos, thereby impoverishing large swaths of the middle classes. The short-lived Duhalde administration began the recovery, which continued under the presidency of Néstor Kirchner (2003-07). His wife, Cristina Fernández de Kirchner, was elected by a landslide in 2007, and re-elected by an even bigger margin in 2011.

Chronology

1516 - The Spanish navigator **Juan Díaz de Solís** discovers the **Río de la Plata**.

1536 - **Founding of a small colony** at Buenos Aires, abandoned then reestablished in 1580.

1776 - **Creation of the viceroyalty** of Río de la Plata. The population of Buenos Aires quadruples in 20 years.

1806-07 - The British make two attempts to take Buenos Aires. Their defeat, thanks to the courage of the inhabitants, sows the seeds of Independence.

1810 - Buenos Aires has nearly 100,000 inhabitants.

May 25 1810 - The **May Revolution** overthrows the viceroy of Río de la Plata and replaces him with a junta.

July 9 1816 - Official **Declaration of Independence** in Tucumán.

1817 - José de San Martín and his "Army of the Andes" go to Chile where they defeat the Spanish.

1820 - San Martín and his army set out to liberate Bolivia and Peru, then the whole of Latin America. He brings about a meeting with Simón Bolívar in 1822. Meanwhile, Argentina is ravaged by conflicts between the caudillos or local chiefs.

1829-52 - The dictatorship of General Juan Manuel de Rosas.

May 1 1853 - Adoption of the Constitution of a Federal Republic. Buenos Aires does not take part. The capital is Paraná.

1862 - **Buenos Aires joins the republic**. Bartolomé Mitre elected first president of the new Republic of Argentina.

1871 - An outbreak of **yellow fever** kills over 7,000 residents of Buenos Aires, most of them in the south of the city.

1880 - Buenos Aires is appointed the **federal capital**. Presidents succeed each other amid mass Spanish and Italian immigration and economic development.

1913 - The first South American underground railway— the **Subte**—is inaugurated in Buenos Aires.

1916 - Institution of universal suffrage. Election of the radical UCR Hipólito Yrigoyen, the son of an immigrant Basque laborer. He was president twice, from 1916 to 1922 and from 1928 to 1930.

1930 - The first of the many **military coups** that would disfigure Argentinian history throughout the 20C.

1937 - The official **inauguration of Avenida 9 de Julio**. At 140m/459ft, it remains the widest avenue in the world.

1943 - New **military coup** by secret organization, the GOU (Grupo Obra de Unificación). Colonel Juan Perón is involved and is appointed Secretary of Work and Health, then of War. His reforms make him very popular.

1945 - Fearing his popularity, the ruling junta arrests Perón. Mass demonstrations and the activism of his paramour Eva Duarte and union leaders leads to his liberation. **Perón marries Eva** on December 10. Nicknamed Evita, she becomes an icon of women and the so-called *descamisados* (shirtless ones).

1946 - **Perón is elected President** with a nationalist and populist manifesto. He nationalizes industries in foreign hands and instigates social measures in favor of the working classes.

1951 - Perón is re-elected.

1952 - **Death of Eva Perón**.

1955 - The military stage another coup under the guise of a Revolución Libertadora (Liberating Revolution). Perón flees to Spain. The **Peronist party is outlawed**.

1958-62 - In the face of imminent political chaos, UCRI leader Arturo Frondizi is elected President (UCR had formally split into two in 1956). He is elected largely due to the support of the Peronists, who no longer have a legal party.

1962-3 - **Military coup**.

1963-6 - The return of the UCR, this time the UCRP faction, with President Arturo Umberto Illia, a humanist who legalizes Peronism and the Communist Party again. He combats racial discrimination and establishes a minimum wage.

1966-73 - A new **military coup**. Brutal dictatorship and repression.

1973-4 - The Peronists win the elections. **Perón returns to Argentina** and becomes President. He appoints his wife Isabel Vice-President but dies the same year. Surrounded by ultra-conservatives, she is unable to govern effectively.

1976-83 - A **military coup** overthrows Isabel Perón and places General Videla in power. This is the beginning of the darkest period of Argentinian history, with mass arrests, tortures, summary executions and "disappearances."

1982 - To divert attention from internal unrest, the military enters into and loses the **Malvinas/Falklands War**.

1983-9 - Amid catastrophic hyperinflation, elections restore the reunited UCR to power with Raúl Alfonsín. Relations with other countries improve.

1989-99 - **Hyperinflation** returns, forcing Alfonsín to bring forward the election, which is won by the charismatic neoliberal Carlos Menem. He stabilizes the economy, but unemployment, the burden of foreign debt, the recession and corruption plague the country.

1994 - A bomb attack on the AMIA Jewish center kills 86 and wounds more than 250. The perpetrators have never been brought to justice.

1999-2001 - President Fernando de la Rúa takes over from Meném but is unable to prevent the country from descending into social and economic chaos in late 2001. **Argentina defaults on its foreign debt**. Eduardo Duhalde becomes caretaker president in 2002. One of his first actions is to devalue the peso, which plummets against the US dollar.

2003-7 - Presidency of Néstor Kirchner, during with the **Argentinian economy beings to recover**.

2007 - The **election of Cristina Fernández de Kirchner**, who succeeds her husband.

2010 - Death of former president Néstor Kirchner, at the age of 60.

2011 - **Re-election of Cristina Fernández de Kirchner** by a landslide.

Architecture

Other world cities might have taller, cleaner, more expensively assembled buildings, but few, if any, can match the architectural diversity of the Argentinian capital. Just a ten-minute stroll along Recoleta's Avenida Alvear will take you past Art Deco, neo-Gothic, Beaux-Arts and Neoclassical landmarks; and that's just one street among thousands.

Colonial and Colonial Revival

Don't judge a building by its façade; a lot of the constructions in Buenos Aires that get lazily described as "colonial" are, in fact, nothing of the sort. The Argentinian capital was a backwater of the Spanish Empire, and the kind of grandiose edifices that can still be seen in Lima and Mexico City are almost entirely absent here.

What's more, even those buildings that were important in the Colonial era, such as Plaza de Mayo's **Cabildo** *(see p109)* were torn down and rebuilt in the late 19C during the mad rush to replace anything that looked Hispanic with something that looked Parisian. It wasn't until 1940 that the architect Mario Buschiazzo was commissioned to restore the Cabildo to its original, bright white and unadorned form. The same is true of the **Basílica de Nuestra Señora del Pilar** *(see p176)*, whose foundations date from the early 18C but whose main structure suffered countless demolitions and remodeling before being restored to its former glory in 1932.

The city's surviving examples of Colonial architecture tend to be fragments rather than wholes. For example, the façade and the left tower of the **Iglesia de San Ignacio** *(see p114)*, the city's oldest church, date from the 18C, while other parts of the construction were tacked on later. To see an example of a Colonial dwelling, visit **Casa de Rivadavia** *(Defensa 350)*, the birthplace of Argentina's first president.

Perhaps the city's best example of the colonial-revival style is the **Museo de Arte Hispanoamericano** *(see p142)*, also known as Palacio Noel, after its architect. Its prominent balconies and whitewashed exterior evoke the 18C Peruvian Baroque; but it was actually constructed in the early 1920s, at a time when local architects were beginning to re-explore the Hispanic tradition.

The Belle Époque

Whereas Europe's gilded age ended abruptly and bloodily in 1914, Argentina's continued much longer. This is reflected in the fact that several of the city's most grandiloquent Neoclassical structures, such as Plaza de Mayo's **Banco de la Nación**, *(see p110)* weren't completed until after World War II.

The "renovation" of Buenos Aires began much earlier, however, with 1894, the year of Avenida de Mayo's inauguration, a useful historical marker. Work began on La Prensa building *(Avenida de Mayo 575)*, now the **Casa de la Cultura** *(see p111)*, in the same year. This Beaux-Arts masterpiece is crowned with a 50m/164ft-high bronze lighthouse, imported from France in 1898. More Gallic grandeur can be seen in buildings like **Palacio San Martín** *(Arenales 761)*, from 1909; **Edificio Estrugamou** *(Juncal 749)*, from 1929; and the **Palacio de Gobierno de Buenos Aires** which also draws on Italian and German influences.

After Avenida de Mayo, the street that best represents this age of opulence is Recoleta's Avenida Alvear. Among the emblematic buildings crammed into this short thoroughfare are the French-style **Alvear Palace Hotel** *(see p174)*, from 1932; the neoclassical **Palacio Duhau**, built in 1934 and now reopened as the Park Hyatt Hotel *(see p174)*; and the neo-Gothic **Residencia Maguire** at no 1683, which is satisfyingly creepy-looking, as if it might be inhabited by a family of upper-crust vampires.

Considering how much cash was flowing into Argentina's coffers during this era, it's not surprising that many of the most impressive buildings of the age were banks. Alongside the aforementioned Banco de la Nación, designed by Alejandro Bustillo and boasting one of the largest domes in the world *(50m/164ft across by 36m/118ft high)*, other great monuments to mammon included **Banco Francés** *(Rivadavia 409)*, with its imposing portal and **Banco Central** *(Reconquista 266)*, with its Corinthian columns and huge clock. **Banco de Boston** *(Florida 267)*, which blends Neocolonial and Renaissance elements, is remarkable for its 4-ton bronze door.

The early 20C was also the era of Art Nouveau and Eclecticism and both these movements are well represented in Buenos Aires. Take a stroll along Avenida de Mayo and you'll find **Palacio Vera** *(nos 769/777)*, from 1910, with its curved lines and bevelled windows, and the even more sinuous and richly detailed **Hotel Chile** *(no 1297)*. Just across the street from the latter is one of the city's most dramatic architectural statements, **Palacio Barolo** *(see p112)*, designed by Italian architect Mario Palanti and inaugurated in 1923. Its bumps and lumps blow a rebellious raspberry at the strict edicts of the French Academy.

Modernism

Two iconic buildings represent the new direction Argentinian architecture began to take in the early 1930s. The first is the **Mercado de Abasto** *(see p215)*, from 1934, a curvaceous and

massive Art Deco structure that blends concrete and iron. The second is the **Edificio Kavanagh**, inaugurated in 1936, whose rationalist design, free of any ornamentation, represents a triumph of function over form. Towering 120m/393ft over Plaza San Martín, it was the tallest skyscraper in South America at the time.

The Peronist years (1946-55) were barren ones for Modernist architects, whose style was anathema to Perón. But a new cadre of architects emerged in the 1960s, led by figures such as Clorindo Testa. Testa either designed or collaborated on two of the most important—and controversial—buildings of that era: the mushroom-shaped **Biblioteca Nacional** (designed in 1962 but, incredibly, not completed until 1992) and the **Banco Hipotecario Nacional** (originally Banco de Londres), built between 1960 and 1966.

Both buildings can be loosely described as Brutalist, with reinforced concrete exposed to the elements, and vast windows flooding the interiors with light.

Into the 21C

Connoisseurs of paradox will enjoy the fact that, as Argentina descended into its worst-ever economic crisis in 2001-02, several of the most ambitious and expensive architectural projects in Buenos Aires' history were unveiled.

One of these was the **Puente de la Mujer** (Bridge of the Woman), which was inaugurated on December 20, 2001, the day the De la Rúa government fell *(see p43)*, sparking violent clashes across the capital. Luckily, few people seem to remember this, and Santiago Calatrava's US$6m, 100m/238ft-long pedestrian suspension bridge, which links the two sides of the Puerto Madero docks, has become one of the city's most popular structures. Another soon-to-be-iconic structure opened in 2001 was the **Museo de Arte Latinoamericano de Buenos Aires**, or MALBA. Funded by property magnate Eduardo Costantini, whose stellar art collection it holds, this strikingly angular structure was designed by three Argentinian architects, and achieves the feat of being rigorously modern without being in the least bit severe.

Some of the best and worst contemporary architecture can be found in Puerto Madero Este, home to some of the most expensive real estate in Latin America.

Skyscrapers have sprung up like weeds here—one of the best is Cesar Pelli's 160m/525ft-high **Repsol-YPF** tower, which has 36 floors, five of which (26 to 31) are given over to an enclosed winter garden in which jacaranda trees bloom.

Art

There was a visual arts tradition in the region long before the Spanish arrived, but what most people think of as "Argentinian art" postdates the conquest. Unsurprisingly, artists were heavily influenced by European styles and movements, though native subjects, such as the gaucho, because increasingly important in the 19C.

Pre-Hispanic Art

Although the nomadic tribes left numerous petroglyphs and rock paintings (geometric designs, zoomorphic and anthropomorphic figures and hunting scenes), it was mainly after they settled that they began to apply art forms to ritual objects, everyday utensils and jewelry. The Condorhuasi, Ciénaga, Aguada and Santa María cultures were the most prolific. From 1000 BC until the arrival of the Spanish, pottery, statues, weaving and jewelry bear witness to the cultural exchanges and high level of trade that was carried out between the populations of the Noroeste and other Andean peoples.

The Peruvian Influence

With the arrival of the Spanish and Christianization, art took a new turn. The indigenous populations preserved their traditions, particularly their motifs (snakes, jaguars, feathers, the moon and the sun) and materials, but Christianization introduced new themes, which were revisited in a local way. The fashion was for religious art, encouraged by the clergy and commissions from rich colonists. Initially, works of art—sculptures and paintings—were imported from Spain (quite rarely because of the cost) or, more often, from Cuzco, in Peru, the seat of the viceroyalty. Then, gradually, anonymous local artists took inspiration from them to decorate chapels and monasteries.

The Cuzco School *(Escuela Cusqueña)* is used to designate this trend. Its style is Baroque and luxuriant, distinctly adapted to indigenous imagery, with rich colors and a profusion of gold leaf. There is often a lack of perspective, people are distorted and importance is given to clothing (as is also the case in clothed statues) and to local details, such as crowns made from feathers of exotic birds, the presence of the sun and moon, or even a leopard.

Landscapes and Genre Paintings

With Independence and the arrival of new colonists from Europe, came lots of traveling artists. Here, a visit to the **Museo Nacional de Bellas Artes de Buenos Aires** *(see p67)* reveals a romantic view of the country that is more travel journal than detailed study. The 19C, which saw the emergence of truly Argentinian artists, was mostly the period of landscapes, genre painting and folklore. As in North America, this art above all depicts an epic story, that of the conquest of a new world, as portrayed with realism by Erneste de la Cárcova, José Antonio Terry, Pío Collivadino and Angel della Valle. Argentinian artists were also very attracted by Europe, where most had their roots, and visited Paris, London and Rome to keep abreast of the great movements of the end of the century. They brought back Impressionism, in the style of Eduardi Sívori and Justo Lynch.

Toward Modernity

The tide began to turn during the first quarter of the 20C as Argentinian artists began to adapt Cubism, Surrealism and Abstraction in line with their perception of their own country. Although their work was at first very badly received, they owed their success to European markets, particularly in Paris—the French capital had become infatuated with Argentina, and many of these painters lived there and were part of the "Paris Group"—where they continued to draw on their own inspiration while recreating violent and clashing works. They broke radically with artists of the preceding generation to bring to their painting a social reality that was becoming increasingly disturbing to them.

Among them, it's worth noting the painters Emilio Pettoruti, Xul Solar and Juan Del Prete, and sculptors Pablo Curatella Manes and Alicia Penalba. Figurative, Symbolist, Expressionist and Realist painters dominated the scene from the 1930s. They included Alfredo Guttero, Aquiles Badi, Héctor Basaldúa, Horacio Butler, Raquel Forner, Alfredo Bigatti, Lino Enea Spilimbergo and the original and prolific Antonio Berni.

The last of these, a student of Othon Friesz, was one of the most remarkable. He moved on from his early Surrealism to adopt an increasingly dramatic Social Realism, evolving toward Expressionism then to Pop Art and even Art Brut, with his Ramona and Juanito Laguna series. He career was a sort of mirror of Argentinian art in the 20C.

The Birth of Contemporary Art

The second half of the 20C and the early 21C have seen the birth of a young avant-garde, detached from past schools. They

A BURIED TREASURE

Of all the buildings, monuments and relics that were given a facelift to mark Argentina's 2010 Bicentenary, none had a stranger back story than David Siqueiros's "Ejercicio Plástico."
The celebrated Mexican muralist painted this work, which depicts various ghostly figures in a submarine world, in 1933, in the basement of a house belonging to the Argentinian journalist Natalio Botana. It was a collaborative project, completed with the help of Argentinian artists Antonio Berni, Juan Carlos Castagnino and Lino Spilimbergo, and the Uruguayan Enrique Lázaro.
Fast forward to 1989. At this point, owing to a legal dispute over the property, the mural was taken apart and packed into boxes, where its various pieces would languish for 17 years, their condition gradually deteriorating. All seemed lost until, in 2006, the Kirchner administration announced that it would fund the restoration of the mural (the final cost was US$600,000) and make it one of the centerpieces of the planned Museo del Bicentenario.
On May 20 2010, President Cristina Kirchner unveiled the mural in the Casa Rosada, as part of the Bicentenary celebrations. She told the audience that the restoration of the work was "the repaying of a debt, both to our own history and to the Mexican people."

use materials and colors in an informal and powerful way, as seen in the styles of Kenneth Kemble, Alberto Greco, Pérez Celis, and Mario Pucciarelli.

In the 1960s and 1970s, there was a return to the Neo-figurative art, with painters such as Luis Felipe Noé, Rómulo Macció, Ernesto Deira, Jorge de la Vega and, briefly, Antonio Seguí, who in 1961 had formed the group Otra Figuración, inspired by the European CoBrA movement. Also noteworthy during this period were Carlos Alonso and Jorge Demirjian. The 1970s also saw the birth of a new optical and kinetic art, characterized by Hugo Demarco, Julio Le Parc and Manuel Espinosa.

During the dark years of dictatorship, art served as a way to escape censorship, taking Neorealist forms that were not immediately readable but carried social criticism in the form of parody or metaphor. El Mudo by Juan Carlos Distefano (a tortured man with his hands tied behind his back) is a painting in this vein.

Since the return to democracy, the art scene has revisited movements of the 20C and rejoined the mainstream. Internationally acclaimed Argentinian artists include León Ferrari, who was awarded the Golden Lion for best artist at the Venice Art Biennate in 2007. In 2009, MoMA in New York hosted a huge retrospective of his work.

Travel Tip:
If you're passionate
about one particular
branch of the
performing arts,
consider arranging
your trip around one
of the many annual
festivals and events
hosted by the city
(see p82–85).

Performing Arts

With one world-class venue (the Teatro Colón), a host of lesser but still excellent spaces and a population of culture vultures, Buenos Aires has all the ingredients needed for a vibrant performing arts scene. Whether you're looking for Shakespeare in Spanish, puppet shows in the park, top-flight opera or lowest-common-denominator revues, you'll find it here.

For English language listings, pick up a copy of the *Buenos Aires Herald*.

Classical Music

The Teatro Colón isn't the only place to hear classical music and opera in Buenos Aires, but inevitably, this world-class concert venue hogs the limelight. Its orchestra, the **Buenos Aires Philharmonic**, was founded in 1946, and is considered one of the most prestigious in Latin America. In terms of opera and ballet, it would be far easier to name the major figures over the last century or so who *haven't* danced, sung or conducted in the Colón. Its status is such that even the most tone-deaf *porteños* refer to it with pride.

Argentina has produced several composers of regional, rather than global, distinction. **Alberto Williams** (1862-1949) incorporated the melodies and rhythms of Argentinian folk music into his orchestral and piano compositions. The work of **Alberto Ginastera** (1916-83) is more avant-garde, though his work crossed over into the mainstream in a unusual way in 1973, when the British progressive rock group Emerson, Lake and Palmer recorded a version of the fourth movement of his first piano concerto for their album *Brain Salad Surgery*. (Stranger still, Ginastera is said to have approved of the result.)

Several Argentinian classical performers have achieved worldwide acclaim. One is **Martha Argerich** (1941-), who is considered one of the great pianists of the post-war era. She lives in Brussels but usually returns to Buenos Aires at least once a year to perform at the Colón. Argerich is notoriously publicity-shy, a personality trait not commonly associated with the Argentinian-Israeli pianist and conductor **Daniel Barenboim** (1942-). Barenboim has conducted a number of the world's top orchestras, and is regarded as one of the great musicians of the modern era. To many, however, he is best known as the former hus-

ASTOR PANALEON PIAZZOLLA

Music and tango go hand in hand. Case and point, Astor Panaleon Piazzolla (1921-92), the Argentinian tango composer and *bandoneón* (button accordion) player. Traveling around the world, with key stops in New York, Paris and Rome, Piazzolla revolutionized both music and tango with his *Tango Nuevo* style *(see p55)*. Beyond being a composer, Piazzolla was a renowned *bandoneónist* who regularly performed his own compositions. Known for both full orchestral pieces and solo guitar works, it's estimated that Piazzolla wrote around 3,000 pieces and recorded around 500. Some of his most famous works include "Concierto para bandoneón, orquesta, cuerdas y percusión," "Tres tangos sinfónicos," "Balada para un loco and Adiós Nonino."

band of late British cellist Jacqueline du Pré. Barenboim's occasional visits to Buenos Aires are huge homecoming events, drawing thousands of people to Avenida 9 de Julio, where the concerts are usually staged.

Rock and Pop

Porteños are voracious consumers of international popular music and you're far more likely to hear "Eleanor Rigby" busked on the subway than any given tango. Nonetheless, the homegrown rock and pop scene is extremely strong, and fans are almost as devoted to their favorite band as they are their soccer team.

The godfather of *rock nacional*, as it is known, is **Charly Garcia**, who has been making music since 1967, first as the lead singer and songwriter of bands like Sui Generis, La Máquina de Hacer Pájaros and Serú Girán, then as a solo artist. With an ability to match a catchy tune to witty, often witheringly caustic lyrics, Garcia's reputation as a songwriter is only exceeded by his reputation for wild behavior, which even in an industry famously forgiving of excess, has tended to push the boundaries. In recent times, however, Garcia appears to have conquered many of his addictions without losing his magnetic stage presence.

Other important figures in rock nacional are **Andrés Calamaro** and **Fito Páez** (both alive) and **Luca Prodan** and **Pappo** (both deceased). Prodan was the scion of a wealthy Italian family who was educated at a posh private school in Scotland before fleeing to Argentina in an attempt to kick a heroin habit. He took up drinking instead, formed the legendary band Sumo and died of cirrhosis at 34. Pappo, a blues guitar legend who once jammed with BB King, died in a motorcycle accident in February 2005.

Not all Argentinian rock singers live fast and die young. **Roberto Sánchez** (1945-2010), aka Sandro, lived fast and died at the relatively ripe old age of 64. Arguably the most popular singer in Argentinian history after Carlos Gardel, Sandro made up for what he lacked in obvious talent with good looks and boundless charisma, and became known as the "Argentinian Elvis Presley."

TANGO

On one level, tango is simply a musical style and a dance step that originated in Buenos Aires at the end of the 19C and thence spread around the globe. On another, it is the very essence of *porteños'* identity and sense of cultural worth. Buenos Aires may look and feel like a European capital—its inhabitants may speak a European language—but, thanks to tango, it *sounds* unique.

From the brothel to the ballroom

The first stirrings of tango, in around 1880, coincide with the beginning of Argentina's golden age, when the country went from post-Colonial backwater to global economic powerhouse in a matter of years. But there was nothing "golden" about tango. Its first exponents were semi-literate *compadritos* (small-time crooks) from the city's poorer southern neighborhoods, such as La Boca and Pompeya. Brothels and bars, not ballrooms, were the dance's original *milieux*, and no evening was complete without at least one knife fight.

It was the French, embracing the dance in the twilight years of their own Belle-Époque, who "gentrified" tango. Londoners and New Yorkers quickly followed suit. Taking note, the *porteño* middle and upper classes, like a parent reconciling with a prodigal son who has surprisingly made his fortune, set about "reclaiming" tango. In the 1920s, Buenos Aires moved to tango like New York moved to jazz.

The king of tango

Blessed with a gorgeous tenor voice and cherubic good looks that masked a jack-the-lad personality, **Carlos Gardel** (1890-1935) was one of the great popular singers of the 20C, responsible more than any other for bringing tango to the masses. His recording of "Mi Noche Triste" ("My Sad Night") in 1917 is regarded as the first true *tango canción*, or tango song. Its central theme, that of a man abandoned by a woman and trying to make sense of the fact, is one that would be repeated time and time again.

Gardel composed as well as crooned, collaborating with lyricist Alfredo Le Pera on such standards as "Volver", "Mi Buenos Aires Querido" and "El Día Que Mi Quieras". Like Elvis Presley after him, Gardel cemented his popularity by appearing in movies, starring in Paramount productions like *Mi Buenos Aires Querido* and *Tango on Broadway*. Both were released in 1934, a year before Gardel's death in a plane crash over Colombia. To borrow Don McLean's description of the death of Buddy Holly, it was "the day the music died."

The hall of fame

Though he shone the brightest, Gardel was far from the only star in the tango firmament. **Aníbal Troilo** (1914-75) was a charismatic bandleader and *bandoneón* (button accordion) virtuoso, whose *orquestra típica* (popular music orchestra) dominated the tango scene in the 1940s and 1950s. He also wrote many tangos—the best of them, like "Sur" and "Che, Bandoneón," in collaboration with the poet Homero Manzi. Pianist **Osvaldo Pugliese** (1905-95) was another great innovator, composing numbers such as "Recuerdo", "Negracha" and, most famously, "La yumba". Many regard **Roberto "El Polaco" Goyeneche** (1926-94), a singer who began by imitating Gardel but later developed his own, more raspy style, as second only to the master. Finally, there's **Astor Piazzolla** *(see p53)*, the creator of so-called "New tango". Doing for tango what Charlie Parker did for jazz, and angering traditionalists in much the same way, Piazzolla injected the dance with an avant-garde urgency. His complex, highly syncopated works, with their sudden changes of pace and tone, are among the most haunting and emotionally charged compositions in the repertoire.

If this pantheon of greats gives the impression that tango is a gentlemen-only club, it's misleading. Many of the most important tango singers and dancers have been women. The queen of tango was **Tita Merello** (1904-2002), who appeared in almost 45 films between 1930 and 1985. Modern singers such as Adriana Varela and Soledad Villamil (who starred alongside Ricardo Darín in the Oscar-winning *The Secret in Their Eyes*), and dancers like Mora Godoy, continue the tradition.

New directions

Like most kinds of popular music, tango must constantly reinvent itself to appeal to new generations of listeners. By most measures, tango's popularity has been on the wane since the 1960s, when fresher sounds emanating from Liverpool, London and San Francisco began to hit the airwaves, enabling younger Argentinians to dismiss tango as "music for parents."

In recent years the wheel has turned once again, as it usually does. Bands such as Gotan Project, who are based in Paris, and Bajofondo Tangoclub have developed a sound known as "electrotango," fusing the wheezy, mournful melodies of old standards with contemporary dance beats. What's more, younger people have begun returning to Buenos Aires' *milongas* (dance halls), lowering both the average age of participants and the amount of Brylcreem and fishnets on display. Now in its third century, tango is alive and kicking.

Tourists who would like to get involved at the city's *milongas* are advised to join a tour company *(see p75)* or take lessons *(see p253)*.

His popularity extended well beyond his home country. He was the first Latino singer to sell out New York's Madison Square Garden and, at the same venue, the first performer in history to broadcast an entire concert via satellite. Like his hero, he appeared several times on the Ed Sullivan Show and in a number of movies of extremely uneven quality. The nearest thing to a modern-day Sandro is **Diego Torres**, a clean-cut balladeer with a great voice and tons of stage presence.

Theater
The colonial theater

The Spanish Viceroy ordered the inauguration of Buenos Aires' first theater on November 30 1783, a date that continues to be marked in Argentina as National Theater Day. The theater was an improvised, makeshift structure, sited on the intersection of the modern streets Alsina and Perú, and was known as Teatro de la Ranchería. The repertoire was limited to classics from the Spanish golden age. The theater burned down in 1792.

Circo criollo

Argentinian theater continued to be dependent on European works—and, indeed, European casts and managers—until the tail-end of the 19C. In the 1880s, however, a new, entirely indigenous style of theater emerged, known as *circo criollo*. A typical performance had two acts; the first consisting of various displays of acrobatics and clowning, the second of straight acting.

Circo criollo's main instigators and protagonists were the Podestá Brothers, a company comprising the nine children of a Genoese immigrant couple. Their adaptation of Eduardo Gutiérez's novel *Juan Moreira*, about a gaucho on the run from the police, was a seminal moment in the development of an original Argentinian theater.

Development and repression

Theater in Buenos Aires began to flourish in the early 20C, with playwrights like Roberto J Payró, Florencio Sánchez and Roberto Arlt producing powerful works of Social Realism. Mirroring developments elsewhere in the world, a more avant-garde scene emerged in the 1960s. Some of the actors who emerged during this period, such as Alfredo Alcón, Norma Aleandro and the comedian Enrique Pinti, are regarded as the best of their generation and are all still active today.

The military dictatorship of the late 1970s was a dismal period for the theater, as it was for all of the arts. Many authors were forced to either emigrate or confine themselves to producing "light comedies" with no political content.

Others were blacklisted and unable to work at all. Actors and playwrights responded to this repression in 1981 by inaugurating what they called Teatro Abierto (Open Theater), at the Picadero Theater. Within a week it had been burned down by agents acting on behalf of the military government, an act that provoked a wave of outrage in the cultural community, with artists donating the proceeds from their works so that the theater might recoup its losses.

The return of democracy sparked a fresh explosion in theater. As one would expect following a period of repression, the theater of the 1980s delighted in transgressive and avant-garde themes, mocking the reactionary values of a discredited ruling class.

Avenida Corrientes and beyond

As there is Broadway and off-Broadway, so there is Corrientes and off-Corrientes. Most of the theaters on this legendary (and lengthy) avenue are concentrated on a handful of blocks either side of Avenida 9 de Julio, and are interspersed with pizza parlors for pre- or post-performance sustenance. Serious and sober works are staged at venues like Teatro San Martín and Belisario, but the real crowd-pullers are the so-called *revistas porteñas*. Basically, these are cabaret revue shows that blend slapstick, satire and smut.

The essential ingredients are a) a couple of middle-aged male comedians, whose role is to drop none-too-cryptic innuendos and poke fun at the government; b) a number of young women clad in feathers and not much else, who are known as *vedettes*; and c) either a man in drag or a genuine transsexual. The most successful shows run for a few months in Buenos Aires and then transfer to Mar del Plata or another of the Atlantic coastal resorts for the summer season.

The Off-Corrientes scene couldn't be more different. There are countless numbers of small, independent theaters in the city, many concentrated in the Abasto neighborhood. Some are cabaret-style venues where you can grab a beer and a *milanesa* while watching some skits and monologs; others are word-of-mouth non-venues where audiences get in for free and a hat is passed around at the end.

Some of the most exciting developments in Argentinian theater over the past decade have involved the fusion of high-wire acrobatics, dance and electronic music to create eclectic extravaganzas that could be described as the modern-day answer to *circo criollo*. Two influential troupes that emerged from this scene before going on to achieve worldwide success are De La Guarda and Fuerza Bruta.

Cinema

It was only a few months after the birth of cinema in Europe that the first film footage was screened in Buenos Aires, in 1896. The following year, one Eugène Py, a French cameraman born in Carcassonne and living in Buenos Aires since 1880, filmed the first documentaries. Thanks to his film *La Bandera Argentina*, made in 1897, he is considered the pioneer of Argentinian cinema.

But by the time Juan Perón came to power, the situation facing Argentinian cinema was dire. The censorship that accompanied the new regime and the exile of the best and most independent filmmakers dealt it an almost fatal blow. The long succession of coups and dictatorships, which came to an end only in 1983, brought the artistic and creative worlds to a low point that they would take years to recover from.

Post-dictatorship

The revival of national cinema was all the more beautiful when it came. The film *La historia oficial* (The Official Story, 1985) put the spotlight on Luis Puenzo (born in 1946), who won the Oscar for Best Foreign Film in 1986.

Héctor Babenco (born in 1946) had already been noticed with *Kiss of the Spider Woman* (1985), to the point that he was made a jury member of the Cannes Film Festival in 1989 and of Mostra (the Venice Film Festival) in 1998. Continuing the tradition for Argentinian filmmakers, Fabian Bielinski with his *Nueve Reinas* (Nine Queens, 2000), was awarded Grand Prix at the Cognac Police Film Festival in 2002, and Daniel Burman with *El Abrazo Partido* (Lost Embrace, 2003), picked up Silver Bear at Berlin in 2004.

The most recent award was presented to Juan José Campanella. Having already achieved great success with *El Hijo de la Novia* (Son of the Bride, 2004), he received the Oscar for Best Foreign Language Film in 2010, with *El Secreto de Sus Ojos* (The Secret in Their Eyes, 2009).

The Argentinian Style

What are the distinguishing features of Argentinian cinema? Firstly, the films are often low budget and made by filmmakers who may also be writers, or surrounded by writers, and who always use amateur actors. They are also distinguished by their preoccupation with social issues, but in a way that is never heavy; close to Neorealism, but without being didactic. Their filming is light and agile, skimming over its subjects in an improvisatory way, and interweaving documentary footage with the main storyline.

WHAT TO WATCH

La Historia Oficial *(1985)*
directed by Luis Puenzo
The Official Story won the Oscar for Best Foreign Language Film at the 58th Academy Awards, the first Latin American movie to achieve this distinction. Telling the story of an affluent mother who comes to suspect her adopted daughter may be the child of a "disappeared" activist, it's a movie that's both emotionally exhausting and utterly necessary.

Sur *(1988)* directed by Fernando "Pino" Solanas
Released from military prison just prior to the return of democracy in 1983, Floreal wanders through a phantasmagorical Buenos Aires learning what has happened during his imprisonment from the ghost of his friend El Negro, who was killed during the military coup. Worth watching if only for the musical cameos by tango legend Roberto Goyeneche.

Evita *(1996)*
directed by Alan Parker
If you want to find out about the life and times of Evita Perón, read a good book about her. But for a slick and entertaining adaptation of the Andrew Lloyd musical, shot on location in Buenos Aires, this does very nicely.

Nueva Reinas *(2000)*
directed by Fabián Bielinsky
A rare genre thriller in a market dominated by kitchen-sink dramas, *Nine Queens* stars the incomparable

Ricardo Darín as Marcos, a seen-it-all-before conman mentoring the younger Juan, played by Gastón Pauls, in the dark arts of deception.

El Abrazo Partido *(2004)*
directed by Daniel Berman
Lost Embrace tells the story of Ariel Makaroff, a university dropout who spends his time hanging around his mother's lingerie store, feeling sorry for himself. But everything changes when his father, who left the family when Ariel was a baby to fight in the Yom Kippur war, returns to Buenos Aires.

Whisky Romeo Zulu *(2004)*
directed by Enrique Piñeyro
Written, directed by and starring Enrique Piñeyro, a former pilot for the LAPA airline, this powerful docudrama tells the story of LAPA flight 3142 which caught fire on take-off in 1999, killing 65 people. The film exposes the inadequate pilot training and management incompetence which led to the worst aviation disaster in Argentinian history.

El Secreto de Sus Ojos *(2009)*
directed by Juan José Campanella
The second Argentinian film to take home an Oscar, *The Secret In Their Eyes* is both a twisty, sometimes lurid, psychological thriller and a moving love story. The five-minute-long, single-take chase scene filmed in Huracán soccer stadium is a directorial tour de force.

Literature

Borges and His Contemporaries

Buenos Aires in the early 20C was a cosmopolitan city with a thriving late-night cafe culture; a fertile ground in which a literary bohemia might flourish. Rival literary groups developed, including the Boedo group, with its proletarian flavor, and the Florida group, which was more middle class. It was in the latter that **Jorge Luis Borges** (1889-1986) spread his wings, shortly after his return from Madrid, where he had been introduced to Dadaism. Borges has never been as revered in Argentina as he has been internationally. Other, more ideologically committed writers were offended by his Oscar Wilde-like insistence that art and politics are poor bedfellows. Few would deny, however, that he is Argentina's, and probably Latin America's, greatest and most influential modern writer. Read his famous *Fictions* (1944), *The Aleph* (1949) and his later works *The Book of Sand* (1975) and *Atlas* (1984).

In the 20C, unloved and sometimes persecuted by the military class, writers were often forced into exile, though they kept in touch with their Argentinian identity and were often socially engaged in the life of their country. They include Eduardo Molea (1903-82); Ernest Sabato (1911-2011), author of, among others, *The Tunnel* (1948) and *The Angel of Darkness* (1974); and Julio Cortázar (1914-84), known for *Hopscotch* (1963) and the short story *Blow-Up* (1964), which was made into a movie in 1967.

Contemporary Writers

While a number of Argentinian writers have spent most of their careers in the US, Madrid or Paris (such as Héctor Bianciotti, born in Argentina, who became a French Academician, and Santiago Amigorena, a writer and film director based in France), others have stayed in the country or constantly travel back and forth.

Among these should be mentioned Juan José Saer (1937-2005), who lived between Buenos Aires, Santa Fe and Paris and whose posthumously published novel *La Grande*, confirms his standing; Ricardo Piglia (1941-), Professor of Literature at Princeton, author of, among others, *Artificial Respiration* (1980) and, more recently, *The Last Reader* (2005), and lastly Tomás Eloy Martínez (1934-2010), who taught in the US and to whom we owe, notably, *The Tango Singer* (2004).

Some have chosen to remain entirely in their country, such as Alan Pauls (1959-), known for his book *The Past* (2003), Marcelo Figueras (1962-), who became famous with *La Griffe du Passé* (2004), and Pedro Mairal (1970-) for *Hoy Temprano* (2004).

WHAT TO READ

GASTRONOMY
Seven Fires: Grilling the Argentine Way
Francis Mallmann (2009)
Francis Mallmann is a chef who writes almost as well as he cooks. In this sumptuously illustrated book you'll learn how to make Mallmann signature dishes like Ribeye with Crushed Potatoes and Chimichurri, and Salt-crusted Sea Bass.

The Parrillas of Buenos Aires
Pietro Sorba (2010)
Available in most Buenos Aires bookstores in a bilingual edition, this up-to-date guide to the city's steakhouses should be on every carnivore's reading list. If you're hungry for more, Sorba has written a similar guide to the city's pizzerias.

NON FICTION
A Brief History of Argentina
Jonathan C. Brown (2010)
This comprehensive yet highly readable history of Argentina takes the reader from the earliest occupation of the area by indigenous tribes to the election of Cristina Kirchner in 2007. The author is Professor of History at Texas University.

Kiss and Tango: Diary of a Dancehall Seductress
Marina Palmer (2006)
Suffering from a premature mid-life crisis, our heroine heads for Buenos Aires on a whim, learns to tango and meets a succession of unsuitable suitors before meeting Mr. Right. This funny, racy and occasionally touching memoir is a must for anyone who wants to know what the Buenos Aires tango scene is really like.

FICTION
The Aleph and Other Stories
Jorge Luis Borges (author), Andrew Hurley (translator) (2004)
First published in 1949, this collection contains many of the Argentinian master's best and most mind-bending short stories. The title story, which describes an artifact that may or may not be able to reveal the entire universe at once, is both philosophically intriguing and hilariously playful.

Blow-Up: and Other Stories
Julio Cortázar (author), Paul Blackburn (translator) (1985)
The short stories collected in this edition show why Cortázar is regarded as second only to Borges among modern Argentinian writers. Internationally he is best known for Blow-Up, which was adapted for the cinema by Michelangelo Antonioni in 1966.

Santa Evita
Tomás Eloy Martínez (1997)
An intoxicating brew of memoir and fiction, myth and fact, this brilliant novel by the late Martínez examines Evita's life and, in more detail, her death. Read this book and you'll learn more about the art of embalming than you ever thought you needed to know.

Nature and Environment

Few cities obliterate their environment as well as Buenos Aires does. Unlike, say, Rio de Janeiro, most of the "scenery" in the Argentinian capital is man-made. Even the Río de la Plata is invisible from most points in the city, and you can easily spend two enjoyable weeks in Buenos Aires without catching a glimpse of it. Look more closely, however, and you will see that Buenos Aires is more than just a vast slab of asphalt plonked atop the Pampas.

For one thing, the number and diversity of trees planted in the capital is astonishing *(see opposite)*. For nature lovers who don't want to leave the city limits, there's the Ecological Reserve on the eastern fringe of the city. And it only takes an hour to get into the Pampas proper: an essential day-trip for those who are here for a week or more.

Buenos Aires and the Pampas

The term "Pampas" refers to the vast spaces that occupy the center of the country, to the south of the capital, as well as to the west and northwest as far as Córdoba. This is the land of the famous gaucho.

The humid climate encourages the pervasive growth of prairie grasses, which become shorter and sparser the farther west you go. The closest thing to a native tree is the ombú, an herbaceous plant that attains the size of a tree and is typical of the Pampas. For the early gauchos, whose daily routine consisted of hours on horseback under a fierce sun, these shade-providing behemoths must have resembled oases.

Indigenous animal species such as the guanaco, the maned wolf and the rhea have become rare in the Pampas. The coastal marshes and rivers are home to many birds, including herons and egrets. But the most revered feathered denizen of the Pampas is the hornero (literally, "baker"), a kind of ovenbird. Even if you fail to spot the bird, you will almost certainly see one of the nests it constructs out of straw and mud to resemble a baker's oven. Revered by gauchos for its work ethic, the hornero is Argentina's national bird.

Visiting the Pampas

There are no national parks and very few nature reserves in Buenos Aires province, which makes it hard to explore the Pampas. Your best bet is to organize a stay (or a day-long *día de campo*) at one of the province's many *estancias*, some of which are no more than an hour's drive from the capital. This will enable you to strike out on horseback into the backcountry *(see p70)*.

BLOOM TOWN

Here are some brief sketches of some of the city's most emblematic trees. For more information, and some beautiful photographs, go to Beatrice Murch's excellent "Trees of Buenos Aires" blog at *losarbolesde-buenosaires.blogspot.com*.

Palm trees of Plaza de Mayo

It's apt that some of the most iconic trees in this city of immigrants are non-indigenous to the country. When French landscaper Carlos Thays, who also designed Parque Tres de Febrero and the Jardín Botanico, was commissioned to spruce up Plaza de Mayo in 1900, he imported these palm trees from Rio de Janeiro. They now tower over the square, their sub-tropical gaiety juxtaposed against the stern European architecture that surrounds them.

Ceibo

Native to Argentina, the ceibo (sometimes known as the cockspur coral in English) provides the country with its national flower whose sensual, vivid-red petals unfurl between October and April.

Jacaranda

The city is rightly famed for its jacarandas, which are planted in most parks and plazas and alongside many streets. When they flower in November, large swaths of Buenos Aires look like they've been painted lilac. Plaza San Martín is a particularly good spot for jacaranda watchers.

Tipa

True forces of nature, tipa trees can soar 30m/100ft, their buckled and end-lessly bifurcating branches resembling a particularly complex river delta mapped against the sky. The powerful roots needed to feed this biomass are so sturdy they often break through the sidewalk. Carlos Thays planted many of the city's tipas in the early 20C. Where they flank narrow *calles*, like Honduras in Palermo Viejo, their branches form a natural vault over the street. Don't be surprised if they "spit" at you; in spring the parasite *Cephisus siccifolius* absorbs the sap from the tree, and excretes it in the form of a viscous liquid. The yellow flowers give off a heady, herby scent.

Palo borracho

Argentinians have a much better name for the *Ceiba speciosa*, or silk floss tree; they call it the *palo borracho*, which literally translates as "drunken stick." And they *do* look inebriated, particularly the older specimens whose distended trunks resemble the swollen belly of some stereotypical me-dieval friar. Their cuddly appearance is deceptive, however, since their greenish trunks are covered in sharp thorns. In spring the branches bud with seed pods which, when burst, release a fluffy, cotton like material that drifts across the city on the breeze. As late summer turns into fall, the tree blooms with delicate pink flowers.

PLANNING YOUR TRIP TO

BUENOS AIRES

Travel, Dine and Explore with Confidence

Michelin, experts in travel guides and maps for more than 100 years. Available wherever books are sold.

www.michelintravel.com

A better way forward

Manuel Belgrano statue in front of Casa Rosada, Plaza de Mayo
Photo: © Yadid Levy/age fotostock

Travel Tip:
There are daily **weather forecasts** on the television and radio and in local newspapers. Many Argentinian cable TV channels have chyrons at the bottom of the screen detailing the current air temperature and the heat index (*sensación térmica*, abbreviated to "ST"). The national weather center is the Servicio Meteorológico Nacional (✆ *(011) 4514 4253; www. smn.gov.ar)*.

When to Go

Seasons

Buenos Aires is a year-round destination and there's no "wrong" time to visit the Argentinian capital. That said, the city has four distinct seasons, each with its own peculiar rhythms, social calendar and climatic conditions.

Summer

December to February is when most *porteños* take their annual two-week vacation. As a consequence the city feels less hectic and crowded then than at other times of the year (this is particularly true in January), making it easier to get, say, a table in a restaurant or a seat on a sub-way train.

Bear in mind, however, that some art galleries and museums close in January and that the high temperatures (frequently soaring above 35°C/95°F) and humidity can be energy-sapping. An air-conditioned hotel room is a must at this time of year.

Fall

The city, its population tanned and refreshed, roars back to life in the fall (March to May). Many important annual events and festivals take place in this period *(see Calendar of Events)*. Expect pleasant temperatures—ideal for sightseeing and outdoor activities—with the chance of heatwaves at the beginning of the season and chilly spells toward the end.

Winter

June to August is the low season, during which many hotels try to lure tourists with discount rates and special packages—which is one reason you might consider planning a visit at this time. The weather is often excellent, with bright, crisp days lending themselves to more vigorous modes of sightseeing, such as cycling tours. In July the average daytime temperature is 11°C/52°F, but it feels much colder when the wind blows from the south (bringing air from Antarctica), so pack warm clothes.

Spring

Most locals will tell you that Buenos Aires is at its best in spring (September to November), and it's hard to argue with this assessment. November, in particular, when the city's many jacaranda trees flower in an explosion of lilac and purple, is a great month to be in town. The weather is extremely variable at this time of year; come prepared for both glorious sunshine and violent electrical storms.

Where to Go

Weekend Break

On Friday evening have a steak supper at one of the city's many *parrillas* (steakhouses). The next morning explore the city's historic center—**Plaza de Mayo★★**, **Avenida de Mayo** (drop in for coffee at Café Tortoni), **Plaza San Martín★** and pedestrianized Florida Street.

On Saturday afternoon take a stroll around Recoleta's Paris-style avenues, of which **Avenida Alvear★** is the grandest. View Argentina's national art collection at **Museo Nacional de Bellas Artes★★★**, and see the tomb of Eva "Evita" Perón (as well as those of many other celebrated Argentinians) at **Cementerio de la Recoleta★★**.

Saturday night catch a tango dinner show, or an opera at the **Teatro Colón★★★**. On Sunday, head south to **La Boca★**, where you can visit Caminito Street, the **Fundación PROA★** contemporary art museum and **La Bombonera Museo de la Pasión Boquense★**, the world-renowned home stadium of the Boca Juniors soccer team. In the afternoon, explore **San Telmo★★**, one of the city's oldest and most picturesque neighborhoods and home to the popular **Feria de San Pedro Telmo★★** Sunday market.

One to Two Weeks

With this amount of time you'll be able to add a number of other places of interest to the core sights and neighborhoods listed in the weekend break above. Must-sees include: the rejuvenated and ultra-contemporary **Puerto Madero★** waterfront neighborhood, behind whose lavish high-rises you'll find the reeds and marshes of the **Reserva Ecológica Costanera Sur★**, where rare birds and reptiles can be spotted; the **MALBA★★★** contemporary art museum; **Museo Evita★**; the fashionable stores and restaurants of the **Palermo Viejo★★** neighborhood; and **Parque Tres de Febrero★★** (or Bosques de Palermo), a sprawling patchwork of parks, plazas and lakes whose highlights include the rose garden, the **planetarium**, the **city zoo** and the **Jardín Japonés** (the largest Japanese garden outside of Japan).

If you long to get off the beaten path, consider visiting a less touristy neighborhood such as Abasto. Its large immigrant communities, tango tradition (learn more about this at the **Museo Casa Carlos Gardel**) and spectacular Art Deco **Mercado de Abasto★** market-turned-shopping-

ASK PETER...

Q: When should I go?
A: Argentina's seasons are completely reversed from the Northern Hemisphere's. So here's a tip— if it's summer weather you're truly after, travel between the months of December through February. But my advice is to travel in what's called the "shoulder season," when the tourists haven't descended upon the country. That means early spring, around September, and in May, just before winter falls.

Travel Tip:
Eat late, never early.
If you book a table
for 8pm at a Buenos
Aires restaurant,
which seems like a
reasonable time, you'll
find yourself alone
at the restaurant,
or perhaps with
two or three other
tourists wondering
why the place is so
empty. Buenos Aires
lovingly embraces
the "siesta then
fiesta" culture. Dinner
starts at 10pm and
hardly anyone goes
out to a club until
midnight or 1am.
Advice: you need to
get into training for
this lifestyle: take a
nap between 3 and
6pm and don't be
surprised to finally hit
the sack around 3am.

mall, make this neighborhood particularly interesting.

A fortnight in Buenos Aires affords you the opportunity to escape the city entirely for a day or two. Options include a day trip to **Tigre**, an attractive town in itself but more importantly the jumping-off point for excursions on the watercourses of the **Paraná Delta★★**; a day trip or overnighter to Uruguay's **Colonia de Sacramento★★** (just an hour from Buenos Aires by fast catamaran), whose historic center is a UNESCO World Heritage Site; and a one- or two-night stay in one of the traditional *estancias* (country ranches) that dot the pampas of Buenos Aires province *(see p70)*.

Budget Travel

Buenos Aires offers good value for money for flexible travelers on a budget. If you intend to visit during the low season (June to August), shop around for accommodation. Many hotels slash their room rates or offer special deals at this time of year. Use the city's cheap and fairly efficient public transportation network rather than taxis. (Ask the staff at your hotel to help you with orientation.) The tourist information office organizes free walking tours *(see p71)*, and we've listed several in the Discovering section. Avoid touristy restaurants in neighborhoods like Puerto Madero, which charge a premium for niceties such as bilingual menus. Note also that Wednesday is discount day, when many cinemas and museums cut their entry prices. Look out for free events organized by the Buenos Aires government, these are trailed on the website www.bue.gov.ar and in the local press. In summer the schedule is packed with events, which can feature anything from local rock bands to full symphonic orchestras and most commonly take place in Palermo's parks.

Culinary Travel

Among South American cities, Buenos Aires is second only to São Paulo in terms of the quality and diversity of its cuisine. Foodies are in for a treat, and should pencil in the following as "must-eats" on their gastro-itinerary:

• Grilled steak sourced from Argentina's famed grass-fed cattle. It's available in most restaurants and constitutes pretty much the entire menu in *parrillas* (steakhouses).

♦ *Dulce de leche*, a sweet and gloopy caramel that finds its way into most cakes, pastries and desserts.

♦ The *milanesa*, a kind of deep-fried breaded veal cutlet often served topped with cheese, ham and even fried eggs.

♦ Gelato-style ice-cream, known here as *helado*, and available in countless flavors from the city's many *heladerías*.

ARGENTINIAN CHEESE

Argentinian cuisine isn't just about meat. The country has a long history of dairy production, and there's no better place to taste the results than the Cheese Room at the Park Hyatt. Located in Duhau Restaurant & Vinoteca, guests can make an appointment to try out cheeses chosen by the Maître Fromager served with breads, dips and fruits and paired with regional wines. Make this a lunch stop. Because after the wine and cheese pairings, you'll be perfectly prepared for your afternoon nap.

Travel Tip:
Porteños are, as a rule, gregarious and sociable, and many will go out of their way to make tourists feel welcome in their city. If a new friend invites you to join them at their home for the family barbecue, consider it a genuine, not a polite, invitation. Female solo travelers should, of course, take all commonsense precautions, particularly when moving around the city after dark.

♦ Strong, plummy red wine elaborated from Malbec, the country's unofficial national grape.

Slightly harder-to-find regional delicacies include Patagonian lamb, South Atlantic king crab, and exotic meats such as llama, ostrich and caiman. Vegetarians needn't despair. Empanadas are the national comfort food, and there are cheese, sweetcorn, mixed vegetable and tuna varieties as well as meaty ones. You'll also find meat-free pasta and pizza options on most menus: when Italians immigrated to Buenos Aires in the late 19C, they brought their recipes with them. In terms of international cuisine, Buenos Aires has improved tremendously over the past decade. The Palermo Viejo neighborhood has the greatest concentration of restaurants serving global food; high-end Japanese and Peruvian restaurants are particularly fashionable. For Chinese and Taiwanese cuisine, head for the city's tiny Chinatown. For more about the Buenos Aires *asado* (barbeque) tradition, and cooking courses, see p207.

Romantic Travel

With its unique blend of Parisian style and Latin passion, it's not hard to see why Buenos Aires draws both young honeymooners and couples marking (say) their fiftieth wedding anniversary. Here's an itinerary that should sweep anyone off their feet:

Morning—Breakfast or brunch at Oui Oui *(see p245)* and then a stroll among the roses at the **Parque Tres de Frebrero★★**.

Afternoon—Have lunch in Recoleta's Sirop Folies *(see p244)* and then treat your loved one to something special (and expensive) in one of the boutiques on **Avenida Alvear★**. Take the famous afternoon tea at the **Hotel Alvear★**.

Evening—Wait for the sun to start setting—and for the office workers to start commuting—and then go for a stroll along Puerto Madero's dockside promenade. Watch an opera at the **Teatro Colón★★★** (you'll score extra points if you book a private box) before rounding off the day with a candlelit supper at Tegui *(see p246)*.

ESTANCIA TRAVEL

Whether you feel the urge to don espadrilles and a wide beret, tuck a sharp knife into your belt and bring out your inner gaucho or simply fancy some R&R in the countryside, an *estancia* break could be just the ticket. *Estancia* tourism has grown in recent decades as many of Argentina's old landed families found they could no longer afford to maintain their country estates. Faced with the choice of selling their houses or opening them to visitors, many chose the latter—and a new tourism sector was born.

Estancias come in all shapes and sizes. Some are simple, unpretentious farmhouses built in the Spanish Colonial-revival style, with smooth stucco walls (often pink, a color scheme that harks back the time when "paint" meant ox blood mixed with lime), flat roofs and porticoed arcades. The better known tend to be no-expense-spared architectural *tours de force*. **La Candelaría** *(nr Lobos; ℘ (02227) 424 404; www.estanciacandelaria.com)*, for example, is styled like one of the more opulent French châteaux, and is set in 245ha/605 acres of gorgeous landscaped gardens. The similarly grand **Villa María** *(Máximo Paz; ℘ (011) 4832 8737; www.estanciavillamaria.com)* is a sprawling, ivy-clad mock-Tudor mansion from 1925, with rooms overlooking lawns and a lake. Other impressive properties, albeit perhaps somewhat lower key, include **Dos Talas** *(Dolores; ℘ (02245) 443 020, www.dostalas.com.ar)*, **El Ombú de Areco** *(San Antonio de Areco; ℘ (011) 4710 2795; www.estanciaelombu.com)* and **Santa Rita** *(nr Lobos; ℘ (011) 4813 9034; www.santa-rita.com)*.

While each *estancia* is unique in terms of its appearance, history and level of comfort—expect traditional furnishings (often family heirlooms) that are not always as easy on the back as they are on the eye—the activities they offer are fairly standard. The price includes as much eating and horse-riding as your belly and backside respectively can handle. Some of the larger *estancias* are more or less self-sufficient, and serve their guests meat and vegetables sourced exclusively from the property. Build up an appetite for the inevitable *asado* (barbecue) by going on a long horse ride led by the resident gaucho. Don't be surprised if you find yourself sitting next to the owner or one of their children at the dinner table: the sense of being a guest rather than a customer is one of the things that separates the *estancia* experience from the hotel one.

At the ritzier, more touristy *estancias*, meals are followed by shows featuring folk music and dancing. Some ranches also offer "premium" activities like balloon rides, parachute jumps and golf and fishing excursions, though all of these incur an extra charge. If you'd like to try your hand at polo, consider a specialist polo ranch such as **La Aguada** *(nr Open Door; ℘ (011) 5168 8853)* or **Puesto Viejo** *(nr Cañuelas, ℘ (011) 5279 6893, www.puestoviejopoloclub.com.ar)*.

What to See and Do

Sightseeing

Sightseeing services for visitors to Buenos Aires may have burgeoned in recent years, but it's still the case that all you really need to explore the city is a decent map and a pair of comfortable shoes.

Some neighborhoods, like San Telmo, Recoleta and Palermo Viejo, might have been designed for strollers and loiterers, and you may find that visiting them as part of a guided tour simply cramps your style. On the other hand, if you're interested in architecture, history and local culture, having an expert at your side can be invaluable.

Your experiences may vary, but in general the best sources of advice will be your hotel concierges or desk staff or the owner of your B&B. (Be aware, however, that they will often try to push you toward their own "preferred" tours and services, which are not always the best available.)

If you get lost, don't hesitate to ask a local for directions. (The people who work in newsstands are usually a good bet.) Most *porteños* are extremely well disposed toward tourists. Unless otherwise stated, all the tours recommended in this section are either English-language only or English and Spanish.

Self-guided Tours

The Buenos Aires tourist information office *(see p88)* offers a fairly comprehensive guide, *Buenos Aires Quick Guide*, as well as a map, which is very useful for finding your way around the city. A free tourist helpline is accessible from 9am to 8pm *((011) 0800 999 2838)*.

The tourist information office organizes guided walking tours around the districts of Buenos Aires all year round *(no charge)*, but you can also consult the website www. bue.gov.ar, which suggests twenty or so self-guided tours, including three thematic walks that allow you to discover the city through iconic figures of Buenos Aires: Eva Perón, Jorge Luis Borges and Carlos Gardel. It's also possible to visit a dozen of the districts with a *audio guía móvil*. The map of the tours is available from tourist information offices or printed from the website; you then just need to call *8283 from your cell phone (cost of a local call) or download the audioguides as MP3 files *(www.bue.gov.ar/audioguia)*, and then load them onto any MP3-compatible audio device (MP3 player, iPod, cell phone). The tour is interspersed with

ASK PETER...

Q: What if I don't have time for an overnight stay in an **estancia**?
A: Consider a *día de campo* (country day trip) instead. This involves being picked up in the city and going for a horseback ride, spending time by the pool and checking out the country grounds. Two *estancias* within easy reach of the city offering *días de campo* are Los Dos Hermanos *(nr Zarate, ✆ (011) 4723 2880, www.estancialos doshermanos.com)* and Las Artes *(nr Mercedes, ✆ (011) 4811 6024, www.las artesendurance.com)*.

recorded accounts such as political speeches, film dialog, songs, etc. At each stop you have to key in a code to hear the corresponding recording. (In Spanish and English.)

Walking Tours

Buenos Aires Walking Tour ✆ *(011) 5773 1001; www. ba-walking-tours.com.* This experienced outfit offers 2–4hr guided walking tours, taking in some of the city's most important neighborhoods, buildings and landmarks. Popular tours include the "Best of BA" Florida–Recoleta walk, which departs from the Florida Garden Café at 10am (rain or shine), and the "Historical & Picturesque BA," which also departs from Florida Garden at 10am, and passes through Plaza de Mayo, San Telmo and (optionally) La Boca. The walks are interspersed with historical and humorous anecdotes and cost between US$35 and US$70. Private tours are also available.

Buenos Aires Free Tour ✆ *(011) 6395 3000; http://www. bafreetour.com.* As the name suggests, this group offers free walking tours of the city—though tips are appreciated. Tours last approximately 2.5hrs. The Buenos Aires City Tour departs from the corner of Avenidas Rivadavia and Rodríguez Peña at 11am, Mon–Sat, and takes in downtown landmarks like the Obelisco, the cathedral and the Teatro Colón. The Aristocratic Buenos Aires tour departs from Plaza San Martín (by the equestrian statue of General San Martín) at 5pm, Mon–Sat, and explores the upscale neighborhoods of Retiro and Recoleta, stopping at key sites like Plaza Francia, Iglesia del Pilar and Cementerio de la Recoleta.

Buenos Aires Local Tours *www.buenosaireslocaltours. com.* This tour, run by a highly knowledgeable and charismatic British expat, comes with the tagline "Showing you the Buenos Aires most tourists miss". True to its word the tour explores both the city's "postcard" neighborhoods and landmarks and more off-the-beaten-track destinations like Abasto. What's more, the group is taken from A to B not only on foot but on public transportation too, including stints on the historic Linea A subway line (the oldest in Buenos Aires) and several *colectivos* (city buses). The tour is free, but you should bring coins for the buses and tips are appreciated. Departs 11am, Mon–Sat, from Plaza Italia (by the central equestrian statue of Garibaldi).

Cicerones *www.cicerones.org.ar.* Multilingual volunteers lead free tours around the city. It's a great way of both getting to know Buenos Aires and meeting friendly locals.

Bus Tours

Buenos Aires Bus *(011) 5239 5160; www.buenosaires-bus.com*. This excellent, local government-subsidized "hop-on, hop-off" service has 20 stops across the city (details on the website). For the full, 2hr 45min experience begin at Stop 0, at the corner of Florida and Roque Sáenz Peña (usually known as Diagonal Norte). Buses depart from here every 30mins from 8.40am to 7pm. Each seat is equipped with headphones, enabling passengers to hear a running commentary (available in ten different languages) related to points of interest along the way. One-day passes *(70 A$, 4–12s 35 A$, under 4s no charge)* or passes lasting two consecutive days *(90 A$, 4–12s 45 A$, under 4s no charge)* allow you to get on and off the bus as often as you wish at any of the 20 stops on the tour. Buy the tickets on the bus, at the Buenos Aires Bus ticket agency, at tourist information offices, at the Ómnibus terminal *(Flechabus ticket office)* or on line *(5 percent discount)*.

Eternautas *(011) 5031 9916; www.eternautas.com*. In business since 1999, this outfit is run by historians from the University of Buenos Aires and has gained a reputation for being the "thinking person's" tour company. Comfortable and air-conditioned vehicles are used to take groups on meticulously researched tours, with themes such as Jewish Buenos Aires and Art and Architecture in Buenos Aires.

Opción Sur *(011) 4777 9029; www.opcionsur.com.ar*. Running several distinct itineraries—including day-long tours out of town to Tigre *(see p218)* and San Antonio de Areco *(see p221)*, as well as the standard 4hr Buenos Aires city tour—Opción Sur has taken the innovative step of using video as well as audio to accompany their tours. Each bus is fitted with two large television screens, and every five minutes or so archive footage is shown of historical events related to whatever area the bus is passing through or parked in at the time. So, for example, when in Plaza de Mayo you'll get to hear one of Eva Perón's famous orations. Tours cost around 200 A$ per person.

Cycling Tours

La Bicicleta Naranja *(011) 4362 1104; www.labicicle-tanaranja.com.ar*. The name means "the Orange Bicycle," which tells you most of what you need to know about the bikes used by this excellent tour outfit. Tours last 3–4hrs and leave from one of two locations: Pasaje Giuffra 308, in San Telmo, or Nicaragua 4824, in Palermo. From San Telmo you can take a guided tour of either "South" or "North" Buenos

Travel Tip:
Stop signals don't exist in the city and pedestrian crossings are definitely not respected by drivers, so don't expect them to stop for anybody. Keep this in mind when considering a bike tour. It may seem like the perfect way to spend a sunny day in Buenos Aires, but rider beware. If you're heading out on two wheels, it's best to go with a guide and don't forget a helmet.

A DAY IN THE LIFE OF
PETER GREENBERG

Morning

I like to begin my days early in "siesta then fiesta" cultures. The locals may already be up and at work, but most tourists are sleeping off the previous night's activities. I start the day with breakfast on the Avenida de Mayo at the Café Tortoni *(see p111)*. It's one of the oldest cafes in the city, and can get quite a tourist crowd at night, but you're more likely to spot the locals if you go when it opens at 8:30am. It's not a Buenos Aires morning unless I begin the day with a rich hot chocolate and a side of churros for dipping.

Starting here means I am in the thick of the city's historic center. I walk through the Plaza de Maya *(see p108)* and check out the historic Casa Rosada; sights I like to see on the go. My first real stop of the morning is Libería del Ávila *(see p114)*, the oldest bookstore in the city. I'm a huge history buff and the selection here is amazing.

Afternoon

The bookstore is my warm-up for my museum visit of the day. I don't like to run from one place to the next; instead, I like to take my time and really get to know one or two museums. It's all about managing my time and getting the most immersive experience. I prefer curated collections like MAMBA, Buenos Aires' brand new Museum of Modern Art *(see p149)*.

Argentinians are late-night eaters, and if you show up for dinner at 8pm, you're about two hours early. I accommodate that schedule by eating two small meals in the afternoon, starting with a very light lunch in San Telmo. Then I go for a long walk or hop onto the subte to the Palermo and Recoleta area. I work up an appetite with some window shopping on Avenida Alvear and then head straight to the Park Hyatt Hotel in Retiro *(Alvear 1661)*. Some people might want to enjoy high tea at the Alvear Palace Hotel *(Alvear 1891)*, and while that's an unforgettable and elegant experience, I prefer some serious wine and some equally serious cheese. I've made an appointment ahead of time to visit the cheese room in the Duhau Restaurant at the Park Hyatt, so the Maître Fromager is waiting for me with cheese, wine and assorted breads.

Evening

I grab a quick siesta to prepare for the night ahead. If I'm lucky and it's football season, my friends might have scored tickets to see Boca Juniors in which case I'm dining in La Boca. Otherwise, I'm heading to Palermo and Osaka—no, it's not typical Argentinian food, it's Peruvian/Japanese fusion. Buenos Aires is a late-night city so my night is far from over. It's off for a drink—most likely a glass of Malbec—at the Hotel Faena in one of the lounges and hopefully I'll catch one of the best tango shows in town.

Aires; from Palermo you can do "Lakes and Woods of Buenos Aires" or "Aristocratic Buenos Aires." Alternatively you can just rent one of the bikes and strike out on your own. Check the website for times and prices.

Urban Biking *(011) 4568 4321; www.urbanbiking.com.* Urban Biking offers a choice of four routes (3.5–8hrs), including one around the city's southern districts (Puerto Madero, Ecological Reserve, La Boca, San Telmo and Plaza de Mayo) and another around its northern districts (Retiro, Barrio Parque, Palermo Soho and Recoleta). There is also a tour of "Buenos Aires at night" (Plaza San Martín, Puerto Madero, Costanera Sur, San Telmo and Recoleta) and an excursion to Tigre and the Paraná Delta (train journey, cycle and kayak tour).

Art Tours

Artists Atelier Tours *(011) 4049 6109; www.arttour.com.ar.*
This tour gives you the chance to meet artists in their own workspaces, where you can see and discuss their work. You will be picked up at your hotel or apartment and taken to four different ateliers. The cost is US$100, which includes lunch and a cocktail and is refundable if you spend US$500 or more on a piece of art.

BA Local Art Tours *www.balocal.com.* As well as offering standard city tours, this well-established company takes small groups to both traditional and contemporary art galleries. Tell them what kind of art interests you and they'll tailor a four-hour tour to your tastes.

Graffitimundo *(011)36833219;www.graffitimundo.com.* Buenos Aires has become celebrated for the quality of its street-art in recent years. Trouble is, many of the motifs and political references used by street artists are unintelligible to foreigners—which is where this tour comes in. Bilingual guides take groups on a three-hour tour around the Palermo neighborhood, pointing out some of the best examples of street art and decoding their cultural references.

Tango Tours

Whether you're a complete beginner or someone who has learned the dance abroad but has yet to try it out in Buenos Aires, the city's tango scene can be extremely daunting. There are rules to be learned, codes to be followed and appropriate footwear to be purchased. Visitors who assume that tango is a bit like samba or salsa, where pretty much anyone is welcome on the dance floor so long as they're prepared to smile and strut their stuff, are in for a rude surprise. *Milongas*, as tango dance events are known, are governed by a strict set of unspoken codes, and those who ignore or flout these codes are likely to find themselves (politely) ostracized.

Travel Tip:
When you're exploring the tango scene, one term that will pop up frequently is *milonga*. Put most simply, *milonga* refers to a place or event where the tango is danced. *Milonga* is also a genre of music closely associated with the tango, though it has a slightly faster tempo than tango music. There are usually a half-dozen *milongas* occurring every night in Buenos Aires, with more on weekends. Go often enough, and you'll be considered a *milonguero*.

75

If this sounds rather intimidating and off-putting, that's because it's supposed to be. To address this, a number of tango tour companies have sprung up to help tourists acclimate to the idiosyncrasies of the scene. They will help you find teachers and dancing partners, and take you to *milongas* that are appropriate for your level. Two recommended outfits are **Tango Focus** (*www.tangofocus.com*) and **Tango Taxi Dancers** (*www.tangotaxidancers.com*). For more about the history of tango see p54–55 and for *milongas* and lessons see p251–253.

Soccer Tours

Visceral and memorable, an Argentinian soccer game can also be an intimidating experience. Just finding out the dates of the fixtures (they have a habit of changing at the last moment) and getting hold of a ticket is tricky enough. Then you have to get to the stadium, which may well involve a trip to one of the less salubrious parts of town. Finally, if it's a big game, such as the *superclásico* derby between Boca Juniors and River Plate, you'll be forced to run the gauntlet of mounted police officers and adrenalin-charged fans. Alternatively you could make a booking with a soccer tour agency and let them take the strain. The standard service includes a transfer from your hotel to the stadium, a bilingual guide to get you to your seat and answer any questions you may have, and return transfer once the final whistle has blown. Three good tour agencies that organize soccer tours are **Tangol** (*www.tangol.com*), **BA Free Tour** (*www.bafreetour.com*) and **Buenos Aires Local Tours** (*www.buenosaireslocaltours.com*). See also Spectator Sports, p254.

Sports and Recreation
Cycling

Getting around Buenos Aires by push bike can still be a heart-in-mouth experience, but the ongoing expansion of the cycle-path network, which will eventually link the northernmost and southernmost parts of the city, has improved matters enormously. For a map of the cycle lanes, known as *bicisendas*, go to www.buenosaires.gov.ar/areas/com_social/moverse/bicisendas.

Inaugurated in 2010, the *Mejor en Bici* (Better by Bike) program is a free bicycle leasing service. Show your ID at one of the 21 stations—Plaza Italia, Retiro and Parque Lezama are good starting points—and you will be given a yellow

bicycle that is yours to ride for up to one hour. For maps and more information, go to www.mejorenbici.gob.ar.

Golf
To play, take private lessons or practice your driving.
Campo de Golf de la Ciudad de Buenos Aires *Avenida Tornquist 6397, Palermo;* ✆ *(011) 4772 7261.*
Club Ciudad de Buenos Aires *Libertador 7501, Núñez;* ✆ *(011) 4703 0222; www.clubciudad.org.ar.*

Gyms
Just *joining* a gym in Buenos Aires can be an exhausting experience, with forms to fill in and doctors' certificates to provide. So if your hotel has a passable cardio and weights room, and you're not planning to be in town for very long, you should probably stick with that. All of the below offer a range of classes in such things as Pilates, step, aerobics, Fight-Do, etc., as well as machines and weights for personal use.
Always Club *Paraguay 4439, Palermo;* ✆ *(011) 4831 4164; www.alwaysclub.com.ar.*
Buenos Aires Fitness Center *2nd floor, Lavalle 655, Microcentro;* ✆ *(011) 4394 3126; www.gymfitnesscenter.com.ar.*
Fitness One *Bonpland 2168, Palermo;* ✆ *(011) 4899 2255; www.fitnessonegym.com.ar.*
Megatlón *Arenales 1930, Recoleta (and various other locations around the city);* ✆ *(011) 4811 2565; www.megatlon.com.*
Le Parc Gym & Spa *San Martín 645, Microcentro;* ✆ *(011) 4311 9191; www.leparc.com.*
Sport Club *Cabrera 4848, Palermo Viejo;* ✆ *(011) 4776 6236; www.sportclub.com.ar.*

Horseback riding
Whether you're a complete beginner or an accomplished equestrian, the best place to go horseback riding is at one of the many *estancias* in Buenos Aires province *(see p70)*. If you go for the day-trip option, known as a *día de campo*, you'll get a ride in the morning, a slap-up barbecue lunch and then, if you're not too sore or tipsy, another ride in the afternoon. Not all *estancias* are as health and safety conscious as they might be, so insist on a helmet if you are not offered one.
The following are riding clubs within the city:
Club Alemán de Equitación *Avenida Dorrego 4045, Palermo;* ✆ *(011) 4772 6289; www.hipico-cae.com.ar.* Individual and group lessons are offered here for riders of all levels.

Travel Tip:
If you're looking to get in a gym workout, you do have a few options beyond just buying a day pass at your local hotel gym. For a better-equipped option, you can purchase a week-long pass at Megatlón, or just go online where you can find a free pass.

Club Hípico Argentino *Avenida Figueroa Alcorta 7285, Palermo;* ℘ *(011) 4780 5349; www.clubhipicoargentino.org.ar.* Various classes are offered, with show jumping a particular specialty.

Ice skating
For freestyle skating and classes.
Winter *Herbal 1617, Caballito;* ℘ *(011) 4631 7883; http://www.winterweb.com.ar/.*

Karting
At Circuito 9, the biggest and best facility of its kind in the city, up to ten drivers can compete in races of around 20 laps.
Circuito 9 *Centro Costa Salguero, Costanera Norte;* ℘ *(011) 5093 8210; www.circuito9.com.ar.*

Pilates
While most gyms host Pilates sessions two or three times a week, the equipment and the instructors are not always up to scratch. The following are specialized Pilates studios:
Kali *Gallo 1486, Barrio Norte;* ℘ *(011) 4824 0488; www.kalipilates.com.ar.*
El Loft *Loft 5, Perú 715, San Telmo;* ℘ *(011) 4300 8021; www.loft-santelmo.com.ar.*

Running
If the growing number of races—usually 5 or 10k runs—staged per year is anything to go by, running in Buenos Aires is booming. Few spaces are un-clogged by traffic, however, so the ones that are—Palermo's **Parque Tres de Febrero★★**, the flat promenades of **Puerto Madero★** and the **Reserva Ecológica★★**, to name the most popular—tend to fill up with joggers at "peak" hours. The Buenos Aires marathon is held in October.

Swimming
The more upscale gym chains offer decent pools for their customers: those at Megatlón *(see Gyms)* are probably the best. If your daily swim is important to you, and your budget will stretch to it, consider booking a hotel with a good pool. The Hilton *(www1.hilton.com)*, the Inter Continental *(www.ichotelsgroup.com)*, the Sheraton *(www.starwoodhotels.com)* and the Four Seasons *(www.fourseasons.com)* all have good facilities, and non-guests can usually drop in for a swim provided they stump up for the day-rate.

Tennis
Unsurprisingly, most of the best tennis courts are located in private clubs, but any of the following are good enough for casual players and also offer squash and paddle courts.

Salguero Tenis *Salguero 3350, Palermo;* ☎ *(011) 4805 5144.*
Costa Rica Gym & Tenis *Costa Rica 4863, Palermo* ☎ *(011) 4832 3737.*
Pasco Tenis *Cochabamba 2258, Barracas;* ☎ *(011) 4941 0333;*
www.pascotenis.com.ar.

Workouts

If you want to work on your general fitness while exploring some of the city's
most attractive parks and open spaces, sign up for a session or two with **Boot
Camp Buenos Aires** *(www.bootcampbuenosaires.com)*. Friendly English-
speaking instructors put groups (individual sessions also available) through
some pretty demanding paces. Participants include locals, expats and tourists, so this is also a good way of meeting people if you're traveling alone.

Yoga

Most gyms run yoga sessions, but, as is the case with Pilates, they tend to be
tailored to casual practitioners rather than experienced devotees. **Buena
Onda Yoga** *(www.buenaondayoga.com)* is a studio run by North American
expats that offers group and individual classes across the city. The instructors speak both English and Spanish. **Maas Yoga** *(*☎ *156 285 0239 (cell);
www.maasyoga.com)* is another peripatetic service – usually covering Balvanera, Almagro and Recoleta – that also offers private sessions at home.
For Bikram yoga, try **Bikram Yoga Buenos Aires** *(Avenida Las Heras 3541;*
☎ *4800 1985; www.byba.com.ar).*

Activities for Kids

Porteños love kids of all ages, so don't be surprised if your children get
fussed over and generally spoiled rotten during your stay in Buenos Aires.
The line between kids' and adults' activities is finer here then in many cultures; children eat out at restaurants with their parents (sometimes at a very
late hour) and often go to bed at the same time too.
That said, there are numerous programs and activities laid on exclusively for
children. Most of them will be more then happy to incorporate your brood
who will almost certainly be less conscious of the language barrier than you
are. If you are in the city during the main school holidays (Jan, Feb and two
weeks in July), check the local press and the city government's tourism site
(www.bue.gov.ar) for information on special events such as outdoor puppet
shows, kids' theatre, circuses and so on.
Prominent cultural institutions like **MALBA**★★★ *(see p188)* and the **Teatro
Colón**★★★ *(see p248)* also run special holiday programs for young travelers.

Museums

Younger children (under 10s) will have a blast at the **Museo de los Niños**★
(www.museoabasto.org.ar) which is located on the second floor of the Abasto shopping mall *(see p257)*. This colorful space contains lots of tactile games
and exhibits, enabling kids to "role-play" various professions including jour-

nalism, nursing, construction work and even parenting. (There is also a small indoor fairground in Abasto, located alongside the food court on the top floor.) A similarly interactive experience can be had at the Museo Participativo de Ciencias *(www.mpc.org.ar)*, whose slogan is "Not touching is prohibited." Part of the **Centro Cultural Recoleta** *(see p177)*, the museum comprises several spaces devoted to themes such as visual perception and optical illusions, natural forces, technology and electricity.

Another excellent destination for kids with an interest in science is the city's **planetarium** *(see p194)*.

In addition to its regular shows and exhibitions (see the website for the schedule), the Planetarium organizes special events for children during the holidays. Museums that are not specifically aimed at children but that will engage their interest nonetheless include the **Museo Argentino de Ciencias Naturales** *(see p210)*, the **Museo de Armas de la Nación** *(see p139)* and Puerto Madero's **Buque Museo Fragata Presidente Sarmiento★★** *(see p156)*.

Theme Parks

The nearest amusement park proper to Buenos Aires is Parque de la Costa *(www.parquedelacosta.com.ar)*, in Tigre. Disneyland it ain't, but its roller coaster, pirate ship and other rides generate plenty of squeals and scares, and it has a good safety record. Tierra Santa *(www.tierrasanta-bsas.com.ar)*, located on the northernmost stretch of the city's coastline, claims to be the world's most important religious theme park. Reconstructions of the Resurrection and Last Supper take place at regular intervals, and puppet shows are laid on to entertain younger children.

ASK PETER...

Q: How can I squeeze in some shopping with my kids in tow?
A: Kids and shopping rarely go hand in hand, but the largest mall in Buenos Aires has you covered. You're sure to find something at Abasto Shopping, which has more than 230 stores. Plus, there are movie theaters, a large food court, an arcade and an educational museum for kids.

Zoos and Bioparks

While it's not quite up to the standard of zoos in the developed world, the **Jardín Zoológico** *(see p191)* has an intelligent pricing policy (under 12s don't pay) which ensures a steady flow of families through its gates. To give your kids a memorable treat, take them on one of the zoo's nocturnal tours that take place two or three nights a week *(see the website for details)*.

If you're in Buenos Aires with your family for ten days or more, add Temaikèn *(www.temaiken.com.ar)* to your must-do list. Located near the town of Escobar, about an hour's drive from central Buenos Aires, this wonderful privately-funded biopark is comfortably the best attraction of its kind in Argentina, and one of the best on the continent. Focused on indigenous rather than exotic fauna, this is the best place to see Argentina's most iconic beasts and birds, including pumas, condors and toucans, outside of their natural habitat. There are a number of excellent restaurants and ice-cream parlors on site, so it's easy to make a full day of it.

Outdoor Spaces

The city's many parks and plazas are great places to take your kids, though not all dog owners are as conscientious as they should be about clearing up after their pets, so keep an eye out.

Palermo's **Parque Tres de Febrero★★** *(see p191)* is packed with families at weekends. They come to rollerblade or cycle around the artificial lake, take out a pedalo or rowing boat on it, or picnic on the grass beside it. You can walk from here to the **Jardín Japonés** *(see p193)*, an oasis of peace within the urban chaos, whose main attractions for kids are the huge, multi-hued koi carp that leap from their ponds to snap at flies and scraps of food.

Other child-friendly parks and plazas include San Telmo's **Parque Lezama** *(see p152)* and Retiro's **Plaza San Martín★** *(see p134)*. Older kids with energy to burn will enjoy tramping around the **Reserva Ecológica★** *(see p157)*, where the views of both the Río de la Plata and the city skyline are unrivaled.

Eating Out

Virtually all of the traditional restaurants in Buenos Aires are family-friendly places where normally taciturn waiters will go out of their way to ensure your kids are comfortable and well fed. Don't be surprised if the owner comes to your table to compliment you on your offspring. While some restaurants have a separate kids' menu, most simply offer downsized portions of what the grownups get.

A number of establishments offer supervised play areas for younger children, enabling parents to eat their steak and fries in relative peace. We recommend the following: **La Escondida** (a *parrilla*), Arcos 3200, Núñez, ☏ (011) 4701 1648; **Restaurante El Mosquito** (also a *parrilla*), José María Moreno 907, Caballito, ☏ (011) 4925 3340; and **Down Town Matías** (a pub-restaurant hybrid), Echeverría 3195, Belgrano, ☏ (011) 4545 1050.

Festivals and Events

Children of all ages will love San Telmo's famous Sunday fair, located in and around **Plaza Dorrego★** *(see p147)*. If the antiques don't interest them, the human statues, street performers, tango dancers and general hustle and bustle surely will. If you don't mind the trek to the western edge of the city, another great weekend jamboree that your kids will enjoy is the **Feria de Mataderos★★** *(see p206)*.

For comprehensive listings on forthcoming children's events, pick up a copy of Planetario, an excellent free magazine that you'll find in many stores and hotels. You can also visit the website at www.revistaplanetario.com. It's in Spanish, but fairly easy to navigate.

Travel Tip:

Most hotels, restaurants and other venues are extremely family-friendly; however you may have to become extremely flexible about your kids' routines—in particular their bedtimes. Most restaurants don't start serving until 8pm, and it's not unusual to see families with young kids trooping in after 10.30pm. If you value your "down time," ensure your hotel has a babysitting service before booking.

Calendar of Events

January–February
Chinese New Year
Av. Arribeños Belgrano. Buenos Aires' sizable Chinese
community marks the Lunar New Year with a day-long party
on and around Av. Arribeños, the epicenter of the city's tiny
Barrio Chino, or Chinatown. Stalls sell a wide variety of tasty
street food, and everyone tries to "touch the dragon" to ensure
good luck for the forthcoming year.

Carnaval
www.buenosaires.gov.ar. Though not a patch on events in Rio
de Janeiro and Salvador, Buenos Aires celebrates Carnaval in its
own way, with numerous concerts throughout the city and a
parade along Av. de Mayo.

Abierto de Tenis de Buenos Aires
Buenos Aires Lawn Tennis Club; Olleros 1510, Palermo;
www.copaclaro.com. This is Argentina's most important annual
tennis tournament, drawing all of the country's top talent as
well as a significant contingent of international stars.

March
Buenos Aires Fashion Week (BAF)
(Fall/Winter collections)
Centro Costa Salguero; Av. Costanera Rafael Obligado and
Salguero, Recoleta; www.buenosairesmoda.com. Charmingly
shambolic and accessible compared to its brethren in New
York and Paris, this twice-yearly *(see August–September)* event
acts as a shop-window for Argentina's established
and upcoming fashion designers.

April–November
**Buenos Aires Festival Internacional
de Cine Independiente**
10 days in April; various of the city's cinemas; www.bafici.gov.ar.
A genuine success story, this film festival has grown rapidly in
recent years. Tickets for the most-hyped movies go quickly, so
check the website for advice on how to get hold of them.

Feria Internacional del Libro
3 weeks from mid-Apr to May; La Rural (on the corner of Santa Fe
and Sarmiento, Palermo); www.el-libro.org.ar. The Buenos Aires
International Book Fair is one of the most anticipated events on
the calendar and always draws huge crowds. You can browse
the stalls set up by local bookstores and publishers or attend a
talk by one of the many famous authors the event attracts.

Gallery Nights

www.artealdiaonline.com. Starting in April and running till November, various galleries around the city open their doors on the last Friday night of each month. Check the website to find out what galleries are opening on what night. The complimentary champagne is as big a draw as the art.

May
Feria Puro Diseño

La Rural (on the corner of Santa Fe and Sarmiento, Palermo); www.feriapurodiseño.com.ar. Designers and brands exhibit their latest creations at this well-attended annual fair.

arteBA

5 days in mid-May; La Rural (on the corner of Santa Fe and Sarmiento), Palermo; www.arteba.com. The largest cultural event of its kind in South America, this fair brings together many of the continent's leading contemporary artists and dealers. If you're an art buyer, arrange your trip to the city around this event.

Aniversario de la Revolución de Mayo

May 25; Plaza de Mayo. Commemoration of the 1810 revolution and the founding of the first Argentinian government, with military and popular parades and religious processions.

July–August
Día de la Independencia

Jul 9. To commemorate Argentina's declaration of Independence from Spanish rule, a celebratory mass is read in the cathedral and members of the armed forces hand out free hot chocolate to the public in Plaza de Mayo.

Exposición de Ganadería, Agricultura e Industria Internacional

2 weeks late Jul/early Aug; La Rural (on the corner of Santa Fe and Sarmiento), Palermo; www.exposicionrural.com.ar. Known simply as "La Rural," Argentina's annual agricultural fair is a huge event, where the country's rural elite rub shoulders with politicians, gauchos, local families and curious tourists. The various "best in show" prizes are highly coveted. If you own a waxed jacket, this is the time to wear it.

Buenos Aires Tango Festival

9 days in mid-Aug; in the city's cultural centers; www.festival detango.gob.ar. The country's, and thus the world's, most important tango festival: concerts, free shows and lessons, seminars and *milongas* are organized throughout the city.

Mundial de Tango
Last 2 weeks of Aug; in theaters and cultural centers around the city; www.mundialdetango.gob.ar, www.tangobuenosaires.gov.ar. Tango, too, has its world championship, and the competition to be crowned king and queen of the dance floor is always fierce. The fact that couples from countries such as Japan regularly take home prizes is testament to tango's global appeal.

August–September
Buenos Aires Fashion Week (BAF)
(Spring/Summer collections) *(see March, above)*
Feria de Vinos y Bodegas
La Rural (on the corner of Santa Fe and Sarmiento), Palermo; www.expovinosybodegas.com.ar. The country's biggest wine fair gathers winemakers from the grape-growing regions in Argentina's west and northwest. As Argentinian wine (particularly Malbec) has grown in popularity, so has this festival.

October–November
Festival Internacional de Teatro Buenos Aires
Biennially; in various theaters in the city; www.festivaldeteatroba. gov.ar. Festival of theater and dance.
Festival Buenos Aires Danza Contemporánea
Biennially; www.buenosairesdanza.gob.ar. Contemporary dance performances in various theaters around the city.
Maratón de Buenos Aires
www.maratondebuenosaires.com.
Casa FOA
Various venues in the city; www.casafoa.com. This sophisticated event presents the latest trends in architecture and interior design. The venue changes from year to year, and is usually a space that has been specially renovated to accommodate the fair.
Alvear Fashion & Arts
Along the Alvear (Recoleta). Exhibitions by local artists in the galleries and shops of the chic district of Recoleta.
La Noche de los Museos
A Sat in Nov; lanochedelosmuseos.gob.ar. Museum night gives free access to more than a hundred museums from 7pm to 2am. Huge queues form outside the most popular venues, such as MALBA and Museo de Bellas Artes.

Día de la Tradición
Nov 10 (events & parade held on the nearest weekend); San Antonio de Areco. This annual celebration of all things gaucho draws big crowds to San Antonio de Areco, the spiritual home of Argentinian cowboy culture. As well as the main parade there are traditional song and dance performances and jaw-dropping displays of horsemanship.

Código País
Various venues in the city; www.codigopais.com. This celebration of the city's counterculture brings together young artists from eclectic fields, including music, cinema, theater, design and street art.

Marcha del Orgullo Gay
First Sat in Nov; Plaza de Mayo; www.marchadelorgullo.org.ar. Argentina's main Gay Pride parade.

Creamfields
Autodrómo de Buenos Aires; www.creamfieldsba.com. Fifteen hours of non-stop electronic music in an event that attracts more than 60,000 ravers.

Gran Premio Nacional
Hipódromo Argentino de Palermo; www.palermo.com.ar. A big day on the sporting and social calendar since 1884, this is Argentina's most prestigious horse racing event.

November–December
Abierto Argentino de Polo
Campo Argentino de Polo (Libertador and Dorrego), Palermo; www.aapolo.com. This is the world's most important polo championship, pitting top players against one another. Just as importantly, it provides a stage on which Buenos Aires' upper classes can strut, mingle and exchange gossip.

Festival Buen Día
www.festivalbuendia.net. Concerts, exhibitions, markets and fashion shows in Palermo.

Festival Buenos Aires Jazz
℘ 0800 333 7848; www.buenosairesjazz.gov.ar. Two festivals in one: the first, of international scale, in Oct; the second, gathering Argentinian artists, in Dec. In theaters and jazz clubs around the city.

Travel Tip:
"La Noche de los Museos" (Night of the Museums) is when the city's museums and cultural institutions not only throw open their doors to the public, but also host a dazzling variety of live performances, shows and special exhibits. Far from being a stuffy affair, about 600,000 take to the streets each year, creating a citywide festival atmosphere. To find out about this year's event, check out the website *(see opposite).*

JEWISH BUENOS AIRES

Argentina boasts the largest Jewish population in Latin America. That population grew tremendously in the late 1800s, and as a result, there is a rich Jewish history throughout the city. Many Jews fled to Argentina during the days of the Spanish and Portuguese inquisitions and ended up staying in the district. Although many Jews were in Buenos Aires before 1800, it wasn't until Argentina gained independence from Spain in 1810 that many of the Jewish communities, some still present today, formed. During this time, Jews from Western Europe also started to settle into the area.

Today, the neighborhood of Once (pronounced OWN-say), which is located near the Abasto shopping center, boasts several synagogues, kosher restaurants and a large population of Orthodox Jews. Villa Crespo, another neighborhood near Palermo, isn't as packed with tourists, and has plenty of authentic Jewish restaurants, cafes, synagogues and temples.

If you want to get more information on Argentina's Jewish history, be aware that you might have to do some advance planning. In 1994, the Argentine-Israeli Mutual Association (AMIA) was bombed, killing 85 people and injuring hundreds more. Since that bombing, security has been very tight and as a result, people cannot easily visit many Jewish historical centers. The new center stands on the sight of the old *(Calle Pasteur 633)*, but today is surrounded by a reinforced concrete wall. In order to get into this, and other Jewish sites, you will be required to give advance notice of names, passport information and the date of birth of anyone who is entering the premises. If you are attending a service at a synagogue, or any other historical buildings, make sure you bring a copy of your passport in case there is a security check—which happens periodically.

Given the security situation it might be easier to take a tour. Here are companies to consider: Eternautas *(http://www.eternautas.com)*, a historian-led tour company, will tailor the itinerary based on your interests, including a Jewish heritage tour. 1stClassArgentina *(www.1stclassargentina.com)* has offices in the US and Buenos Aires and offers both half-day and full-day tours. They ask that you book early to ensure that one of their Jewish heritage specialists is available to lead the tour. Another option is to contact Cicerones *(www.cicerones. org.ar)*, a free service that matches guides to visitors, but this can be hit-or-miss in terms of how in-depth the guide's knowledge is.

Know Before You Go

Useful Websites

www.bue.gov.ar
This is the Government of Buenos Aires' excellent tourist information portal, containing stacks of useful tips, maps, tour itineraries, event calendars and downloads.

www.guiaoleo.com.ar
The *porteño* answer to yelp.com, this invaluable site gives you access to a huge database of the city's restaurants and bars, complete with photos, contact details, price guides and user reviews. It's Spanish only but easy to use.

www.buenosairesherald.com
For breaking news, national and international politics, entertainment listings, sport, weather and so on, visit the website of Argentina's only English-language daily.

www.landingpadba.com
If you can get past the ugly design, this is a terrific English-language resource for visitors, put together by young expats. Everything from public transport advice to useful Spanish slang.

www.argentinaindependent.com
This online magazine offers in-depth and well written articles on local culture, politics and the arts. Click on the Directory for information on hotels, restaurants, tango venues and more.

www.recoletacemetery.com
Written by long-time American expat and guidebook author Robert Wright, this labor of love is arguably the best guide to Recoleta Cemetery in any language.

www.saltshaker.net
One of a growing number of English-language restaurant and food blogs, but comfortably the best of the bunch. American chef Dan Perlman, who also runs supper club Casa Saltshaker, has built up an unrivaled database of restaurant reviews. A must-bookmark for foodies.

www.juanelear.com
The city's best English-language blog on the visual arts, with daily updates on new and upcoming exhibitions as well as information on galleries and local artists.

Tourism Offices
Argentinian tourist offices abroad
For information and assistance in planning a trip to Argentina, contact the official Argentinian tourist office in your country:

Canada (Ottawa), 7th floor, 81 Metcalfe, Ottawa; ✆ (613) 236 2351; www.argentina.canada.net.

UK (London), 65 Brook Street, London W1K 4AH; ✆ (0207) 318 1300; www.argentine-embassy-uk.org.

USA (Washington), 1600 New Hampshire Avenue, Washington, 20009; ✆ (202) 238 6400; www.embassyofargentina.us.

Tourist offices in Buenos Aires
The National Tourist Office is located at Avenida Santa Fe 883 (✆ (011) 4312 2232). Other branches are at the following locations: Aeroparque Internacional de Ezeiza (the international airport) and Aeroparque Jorge Newbury (Buenos Aires airport); Avenida Pte Quintana 596, Recoleta; Terminal de Omnibus de Retiro (Retiro bus terminal), Unit 83; Avenida Alicia Moreau de Justo 200, Puerto Madero. All are open 9am–5pm, Mon–Fri, and a freephone helpline (✆ 0800 555 0016) operates during the same hours. To report a crime or other complaint visit the Comisaría del Turista at Avenida Corrientes 436, ✆ 0800 999 5000. You should also, of course, inform your embassy or consulate.

International Visitors
Embassies and Consulates
British Embassy - Luis Agote 2412, Buenos Aires; ✆ (011) 4808 2200;www.ukinargentina.fco.gov.uk.

Canadian Embassy - Tagle 2828, Buenos Aires; ✆ (011) 4808 1000; www.argentina.gc.ca.

US Embassy - Avenida Colombia 4300; ✆ (011) 5777 4533; www.argentina.usembassy.gov.

Entry Requirements
All foreign nationals wishing to enter Argentina must show a valid passport. Foreign nationals from the US, the UK, Canada or Australia do not require a visa. However, those from the US, Canada or Australia must pay a reciprocity fee ("Buenos Aires Entre Fee") when landing at Ezeiza or Aeroparque Newbery Airport. At time of writing this fee is US$140 for US and Australian citizens and US$75 for Canadians. For US citizens, the fee is valid for 10 years and allows unlimited entries. For Australians, the fee is valid for 90 days. Canadians must pay the fee each time they enter the country.

In general tourists are permitted to remain in Argentina for 90 days, after which time they must either apply for an extension to the standard tourist visa or leave and re-enter the country. The latter practice is common but increasingly frowned upon.

Customs

Customs offices are open 24hrs. Travelers from most countries are exempt from customs duties on luggage and personal effects (clothing, toiletries, cameras, camcorders, MP3 players, laptops, prescription medicines for personal use, etc.), as well as new items with a value under US$300. They are also exempt from customs duties on items under US$300 purchased from Argentinian duty-free stores. An import tax of 50 percent will be levied on items exceeding this amount. The baggage check at customs is generally electronic. Travelers must also declare whether they are carrying more than US$10,000 (or the equivalent in foreign currencies).

Health

All travelers should take out comprehensive travel insurance before entering Argentina. While no vaccinations are required to enter the country, you should ensure that yours are up to date before traveling. For more information on recommended vaccinations and diseases that may be encountered in Argentina, check the Argentina page on the website of the Center for Disease Control *(www.cdc.gov)*. All prescription drugs should be clearly labeled; it is recommended that you carry a copy of the prescription and always pack urgent medications in your carry-on baggage. In addition don't assume that medications available in the United States will be as easy to obtain in Argentina. If you do need buy medications in Buenos Aires, get them from one of the many branches of Farmacity, the city's biggest and most reputable pharmacy chain.

Accessibility

Buenos Aires is improving as a destination for disabled visitors, but from an extremely low baseline. The local government has made progress repaving sidewalks in previously neglected areas like Palermo Viejo, but those in other tourist hotspots, such as San Telmo, still resemble an obstacle course. All of the newer Subte stations (those built in the last decade or so) have elevator access from the street; the vast majority of the older ones do not. The same holds true of buses: newer vehicles are low-floor for (comparatively) easy access, but you may have to wait a long time for one of these to arrive at your stop. As for accommodation, do not assume that a hotel has good access just because it says it does. Talk to the management before making a reservation to ensure they understand your needs and are able to meet them.

Travel Tip:
Citizens of the United States, Canada and Australia must pay a reciprocity fee, similar to the amount that Argentina citizens pay for visa applications to visit the United States. In order to be allowed entry when visiting Buenos Aires for the first time, be sure to have extra cash handy. The process for payment may take 20 minutes at the airport immigration entries. And yes, they take credit cards.

Getting There and Getting Around

Getting There
By Plane
International airport – Aeropuerto Internacional de Ezeiza Ministro Pistarini; ℘(011) 5480 2500; www.aa2000.com.ar. Known simply as "Ezeiza," this is Argentina's main international airport. Unless you are arriving from a neighboring country, your plane will land here.

The best option for getting from the airport to downtown Buenos Aires is to take the shuttle run by Manuel Tienda León. Shuttles leave the airport every 30mins from 4am to midnight, and take around 45mins to reach the city. A single ticket costs 55 A$. In town, shuttles leave the Terminal Madero (Madero 1299) every 30mins 24hrs. Info: ℘(011) 4314 3636 or 0810 888 5366 (24h/24); www.tiendaleon.com.ar.

If you'd rather take a taxi (40 minutes), use one of the official taxi stands outside the arrivals exit (approx 75 A$). For an air-conditioned, chaffeur-driven car *(remise)*, ask your hotel to arrange a transfer, or book at one of the counters in the arrivals hall. Expect to pay around 150 A$ for a journey to the city center.

Domestic airport – Aeroparque Metropolitano Jorge Newbery; Rafael Obligado s/n (facing the river, between Sarmiento and La Pampa), 2km/1.25mi north of the city center; ℘(011) 5480 3000; www.aa2000.com.ar. Much smaller than Ezeiza, this airport mainly serves domestic flights.

City buses (lines 33 and 45 for Palermo; lines 37 and 160 for San Telmo) connect the Aeroparque Newbery with the center of Buenos Aires. The shuttle run by Manuel Tienda León provides a direct connection between the city center and the Aeroparque (30mins). Departs from Terminal Madero (Madero 1299) every 30mins or 1hr, 24hrs; 10 buses per day leave from the Aeroparque, between 9am and 11.30pm (22 A$).

By Train
There are three stations in Buenos Aires, from where various private operators serve the suburbs. The one that you will find most useful is the Estacion Terminal Retiro, from where TBA and Ferrovías run trains to the north:

Travel Tip:
When packing for your trip, be sure to pack your valuables, including electronics, in your carry-on. A few years ago, Argentina's TV network, Cana 13, conducted an investigation at Ezeiza Airport revealing that a group of security operators were stealing valuables at airports (iPods, cell phones, jewelry, laptops etc.) while scanning the checked luggage. They didn't just steal the entire bag, so you wouldn't notice until long after you've left the airport. To avoid being part of the scam, pack your expensive valuables in your carry-on luggage and have it with you at all times.

Trenes de Buenos Aires (TBA) – Dr Ramos Mejía 1302; ✆ (011) 0800 3333 822; www.tbanet.com.ar. TBA provides connections with, among others, San Isidro (35mins) and Tigre (50mins).
Ferrovías – Dr Ramos Mejía 1430; ✆ 0800 777 3377; www.ferrovias.com.ar.

By Bus
Terminal de Ómnibus (bus station) – Antártida Argentina, Retiro (subway Retiro); ✆ (011) 4310 0700; www.tebasa.com.ar.
The huge bus station at Retiro accommodates nearly 120 private companies offering regular routes to destinations throughout the country. Their ticket offices, grouped by geographic areas, are located on level 3. There are regular departures to all of the destinations covered in the Excursions chapter *(see p216)*. We recommend you use buses rather than trains to reach these places, as the former are both safer (purse snatchers are all too common on local trains) and more comfortable.

Getting Around
By Public Transportation
The public transportation network—subway and bus—is sufficiently concentrated to enable you to reach any district in the city. Subway maps are available free of charge at all stations; to find your way around the numerous bus routes, get hold of the indispensable Guia "T," sold at all newsstands (in a choice of two formats) as soon as you arrive.
Subte – The easiest and quickest way to get around in Buenos Aires, however, remains the subway, which is here called the *subte (see map inside back cover)*. Six lines serve 90 stations and nearly all them converge on Microcentro and lead to the main avenues and stops. They run from Mon to Sat from 5am until 10.30 or 11pm, Sun and public holidays from 8am to 10–10.30pm. Tickets can be bought from ticket offices located in each station and you will often be asked to provide the correct change. Single tariff at time of writing: 2.50 A$.
By Bus/Coach – More than 180 bus, or *colectivo*, routes provide services around the city center and link it to peripheral districts. Bus stops are marked by small signs showing the direction of the line, but the routes are not always easy to identify. Most of the buses operate 24/24, but they run less frequently after midnight. Tickets are bought

ASK PETER…
Q: I've just landed at Ezeiza Airport and need to know the cheapest way into the city.
A: Trying to make your way into the city can be expensive. One good option is the shuttle run by Manuel Tienda León *(see opposite)*. Otherwise, the *colectivo* (bus) is the cheapest way; costing 1.25 A$ at the time of writing, the *colectivo* will save you money but be sure you have the time, as it takes up to two hours to get to the city.

Travel Tip:
To help you find your way around on the *subte*, each line is identified by a letter and a color:
Línea A (pale blue): Carabobo/Plaza de Mayo.
Línea B (red): Los Incas/L. N. Alem.
Línea C (dark blue): Constitución/Retiro.
Línea D (green): Congreso de Tucumán/Catedral.
Línea E (purple): Plaza de los Virreyes/Bolívar.
Línea H (yellow): Caseros/Once.

CAR RENTAL

You must be aged over 21 and have a bank card with sufficient credit to pay for the car hire and security deposit. Make sure that the vehicle is well insured. Reckon on paying 170–220 A\$ per day (for a package that includes 200km/124mi) for a category A vehicle, significantly more for unlimited mileage.

Avis: ☏ 0810 9991 2847. www.avis.com.ar
Budget: ☏ 0810 999 2834. www.budget.com.ar
Europcar: ☏ 011 4136 6570. www.europcar.com.ar
Hertz: ☏ 0810 222 43789. www.milletrentacar.com.ar

on the bus. You will need to tell the driver where you are going and pay at the machine behind him or her. The machine doesn't accept notes, so it is essential that you have coins on you. The ticket price depends on the journey, at the time of writing varying from 1.10 to 1.25 A\$.

By Taxi or Remise – An innumerable number of taxis, recognizable by their black and yellow colors, operate in Buenos Aires, and you'll generally have no trouble finding one, whatever the hour of day or night. At time of writing, the pickup charge is 7.30 A\$; thereafter the price is based on the distance traveled *(0.73 A\$ every 200m/220yd)*.

There are also *remises* (private taxis) that have to be booked by telephone or in person at their offices. *Remises* are not metered—you agree the price with the driver before setting out—and almost always work out cheaper than radio taxis.

By Car – Despite the vastness of the city, exploring it by car is not recommended. The combination of bottlenecks blocking the center, the lack of respect for the rules of the road, the difficulty of finding your bearings and the problems of finding somewhere to park could ruin your stay.

It is possible, in certain conditions, to park on public roads. However, you will find lots of private car parks *(estacionamento)*, some open 24/24, all over the city. Charges vary depending on the district; allow from 7–15 A\$ an hour.

Basic Information

Business Hours

The majority of museums and historic buildings are open from 9–10am until 5–6pm, but close one day a week (usually Mon or Tue) and on some public holidays. Larger stores and supermarkets are generally open daily from 9–10am until 8–10pm. Smaller stores and boutiques sometimes close earlier on Sun. Banks generally open Mon–Fri from 10am–3pm. Avoid the lunch rush, which begins at 1pm. You can withdraw money 24hrs from ATMs, but for safety reasons you should avoid doing this after dark.

Communications

You'll find call centers *(locutorios)*, where payment is made at the counter at the end of your call, everywhere. Buenos Aires' area code is 011. In this guide, we have given the area code (in brackets), followed by the 6–8 digit number.

Making international calls from Argentina

Dial 00 + country code + the number of the person you're phoning.

Cell Phones

Argentina is covered by several cell phone networks, notably Claro *(www.claro.com.ar)*, Nextel Argentina *(www.nextel.com.ar)*, Personal *(www.personal.com.ar)* and Telefonica *(www.movistar.com.ar)*, all of which have agreements with certain foreign operators. To function in Argentina, your phone must be tri-band. Cell phone numbers in Argentina start with 15.

Electricity

Electric current is 220 volts. Plugs, which previously conformed to European standard, are progressively changing to the Argentinian standard, which have three flat pins.

Emergencies
Emergency Numbers

Ambulance: 107.
Police: 911 or 101
Tourist Police: 0800 999 5000
(multilingual service available 24/7).
Fire Brigade: 100.
Report stolen credit cards to the police immediately and

Travel Tip:
Nowadays, having a cell phone with you at all times is second nature. Given high roaming charges, it's in your best interest to purchase a *prepago* or prepaid cell phone plan to stay connected. First things first, before taking off on your trip, contact your cell phone provider to get the unlock code to enable your phone to function with any country's cell phone carrier; second, while in Buenos Aires, look for local carriers like Claro, Personal or Movistar. With Movistar for example, you can purchase a US$15 calling card that gives you a rate of US$0.51 per minute and US$0.11 per text message.

block the cards by phoning one of the following numbers:
American Express: ℘0810 555 2639
Diners Club: ℘0810 444 2484
MasterCard: ℘0800 555 0507
Visa International: ℘410 581 60 40

If your passport is stolen, get a theft report from the police and take it to your embassy or consulate.

Health

You will find numerous **Farmacity** *(www.farmacity.com. ar)* pharmacies everywhere in the city, some of which are open 24hrs. They also sell a wide selection of imported products.

Hospital General B. Rivadavia – *General Las Heras 2670, Recoleta.*
Hospital Británico – *Perdriel 74, Barracas.*
Hospital General Dr J. A. Fernandez – *Cerviño 3356, Palermo.*
Hospital Alemán – *Map V, D2 - Pueyrredón 1640, Recoleta.*

Mail/Post

Correo Central (central post office) – *Sarmiento 151, Microcentro; open Mon–Fri 8am–8pm, Sat 10am–1pm.*
DHL – A dozen addresses in the center; ℘*0810 2222 345; www.dhl.com.ar.*

Stamps *(sellos)* are sold in post offices *(correos)* and at news kiosks *(kioscos)*. The national postal agency is Correo Argentino, and you'll find branches in all neighborhoods. It currently costs 10 A$ to send a standard postcard from Argentina to the US.

Private companies (DHL, Oca, Correo Andreani...) also operate postal services within Argentina and internationally and can work out less expensive. An express service is available via FedEx *(www.fedex.com).*

Money
Currency

The official currency is the Argentinian peso (A$), which is divided into 100 centavos. There are notes of 2, 5, 10, 20, 50 and 100 A$, and coins of 5, 10, 25, 50 cents and 1 A$. (As the $ sign applies to two currencies, we have used US$ for the dollar and A$ for the Argentinian peso.) Many traders and taxi drivers refuse to take 50 and 100 A$ notes, and it is often difficult to get change. You can change high-denomination notes in a bank.

Travel Tip:
Avoid changing money on your arrival at the airport as the exchange rate will be very poor.

Change

You can change money in airports, banks, bureaux de change *(casas de cambio)* and large hotels. The exchange rate isn't the same everywhere, so it's worth shopping around. You will need to show your passport, and the banknotes must be in perfect condition. At the time of publication, the A$ is worth approximately US$0.25.

Although there are plenty of banks and bureaux de change in the city, most of them are in Microcentro. Certain districts, such as San Telmo, La Boca and Palermo, are less well equipped than others. You will also receive the best exchange rate in banks, notably in **Citibank** (Santa Fe 1634, 2570 and 3168, Corrientes 1780 and 886, Florida 199 and 746), and you will find numerous *casas de cambio* on the Calle Sarmiento (between nos. 300 and 500). Here are some addresses to help you out at weekends or outside bank opening hours:

Euroamerican Cambio – *Anasagasti 2078, Palermo; ✆ (011) 4825 1999; open Mon–Fri 9.30am–5pm, Sat 10am–3pm.*
Metropolis – *Corrientes 2557, Florida 490 and 814, San Nicolás.*

Be aware, though, that all banks and most bureaux de change are closed at weekends: remember to change your money on Friday before 3pm. Never change your money illegally on the street, where there are a lot of counterfeit banknotes in circulation.

ATMs and Credit Cards

Before you leave home, check the amount of money you are authorized to withdraw per day or week, because, with the exception of smart hotels, restaurants and stores, many establishments don't accept credit cards, or, if they do, might charge a commission. Do as the Argentinians do, and get used to paying in cash.

Most ATMs impose a limit of 320 A$ (less than US$400)—or at the most 600 A$, depending on the bank—on each withdrawal. Most of the time (though this is not always the case), you can withdraw cash two or three times at the same ATM or on the same day, but this will result in significant bank charges (a fixed commission of US$7 to $8 is levied on each withdrawal).

Travelers' Checks

Travelers' checks are not really very useful. They are accepted by some banks and bureaux de change, but the exchange rate offered is usually not good. Be warned that

Travel Tip:
Many travelers like to hold on to their leftover foreign currency from foreign countries to use if they ever go back. While it's a good way to avoid multiple currency exchange fees in some countries, it's probably not a good idea when it comes to Argentinian pesos. The inflation rate in the country, while at 10 percent annually according to the national statistics office, runs closer to 20–25 percent per year according to independent economists.

this method of payment is secure only if you keep your checks and the receipts on which their numbers are marked in two separate places: in fact, you will be asked for the latter should your checks be stolen.

Newspapers and Magazines

The press has many newspapers and magazines, including the national dailies **La Nación** *(www.lanacion.com.ar)*, **Clarín** *(www.clarin. com)*, **Página/12** *(www.pagina12.com.ar)*, **La Razón** *(www.larazon. com)* and **Perfíl** *(www.perfil.com)*. The **Buenos Aires Herald** *(www. buenosairesherald.com)* is an excellent English-language daily.

Safety

Buenos Aires is safer than most other South American mega-cities, but you should still keep your wits about you at all times and take commonsense precautions. When in tourist areas (Calle Florida, San Telmo, La Boca and so on), on public transportation, at airports and around stations, keep an eye on your personal belongings, which can be a target for thieves and pickpockets. Avoid walking alone at night in remote or rough areas, such as La Boca, Retiro, Constitución and Once. Don't venture into Buenos Aires' slums or shantytowns without being accompanied by someone you can trust. Never leave your bag on an overhead rack on public transportation or slung across the back of your chair in a pavement café.

Take all the usual safety precautions: avoid conspicuous signs of wealth (jewelry, designer-label clothing, expensive cameras or smartphones, etc.) that will attract attention, be vigilant when withdrawing money from ATMs (don't do it after dark), never change money illegally in the street and don't carry large sums of money with you. Don't leave valuables in your car and, if you can, use supervised parking lots. Leave official documents and valuables in your hotel room safe, but keep a copy of your passport with you.

An emergency hotline directing calls to one of the federal police's tourism commissions has been opened for tourists who have been the victims of robberies or assaults: ☎0800 999 5000 (toll-free). A multilingual service available 24hrs. *(See also Emergencies.)*

Smoking

You will find most of the cigarette brands sold in Europe in Argentina, but at between one third and half the price. They are sold in all the *kioscos*. However, most hotels and all restaurants are now smoke-free.

Tax-free Shopping

As a foreigner purchasing Argentinian goods, a VAT (Value Added Tax) of 21 percent is applied to the sale of goods, provision of services and import of goods. However, there is a tax refund offered when leaving the country. Many stores offer tax-free shopping (a sticker can be seen on window fronts indicating this) and it doesn't hurt to ask if no sticker is seen; at the point of purchase ask if they are offer tax-free shopping and if so, you will be handed a tax-free receipt which must be filled out and handed at the tax-free refund line at Ezeiza Airport. Be sure to save purchase receipts along with the tax-free receipt for your refunds.

Tipping

In Argentina, it is customary to leave a tip of about 10 percent of the bill in restaurants. In airports and railway stations, porters will also ask for a few pesos as thanks for their services (even if, in fact, you didn't ask for them.) Hotel porters, chamber maids and gas station attendants expect to be tipped. It is however not usual to tip taxi drivers, but it is considered polite to round up the fare to the next peso.

Time Difference

Buenos Aires is one hour ahead of Eastern Standard Time: when it's midnight in Buenos Aires, it's 11pm in New York.

Travel Tip:
At the airport, once your receipt forms are stamped, you will be given the tax refund. Be sure to allow at least an hour before your departure as tax-free refund lines are slow-moving.

PUBLIC HOLIDAYS

January 1:	New Year's Day
Feb 20 & 21 (2012)/ Feb 11 & 12 (2013):	Maundy Thursday and Good Friday
March 24:	National Day of Remembrance for Truth and Justice, established in 2005
April 2*:	Day of Commemoration for the Veterans and Fallen of the Malvinas War
May 1:	Labor Day
May 25:	Anniversary of the 1810 May Revolution
June 20*:	National Flag Day
July 9:	Independence Day
August 17*:	Anniversary of the death of General San Martín
October 12*:	Celebration of Cultural Diversity Day
December 8:	Immaculate Conception Day
November 20*:	National Sovereignty Day
December 25:	Christmas Day

The holidays marked with an asterisk (*) are celebrated on the Monday preceding this date if it falls on a Tuesday or Wednesday, or on the following Monday if it falls on a Thursday, Friday, Saturday or Sunday.

Travel Tip:
Of course for the Spanish learner, picking up "Argentinian Spanish" might seem an adventure all its own. A difference in speech is the use of "y" and "ll," pronounced "zho"; for example, "Yo me llamo" is actually pronounced "zho me zhamo."

Useful Words and Phrases

Everyday Words and Phrases

Do you speak English?
¿Habla ingles? (formal)/¿Hablás ingles? (informal)

Talk slowly please Hable más despacio, por favor.

How do you say that in Spanish/English? ¿Cómo se lo dice en Español/Inglés?

Can you repeat that, please? ¿Puede repetirlo por favor?

I don't understand No entiendo

Hi/hello Hola

Yes Sí

No No

Please Por favor

Thank you Gracias

Goodbye Chau (informal)/ Adiós (formal)

See you soon Hasta luego

Don't mention it De nada

Excuse me (when asking to move past someone) Permiso

Excuse me (after bumping into someone) Disculpe/ Perdón

I'm sorry Lo siento

Good morning Buenos días or Buen día

Good afternoon Buenas tardes

Good evening/night Buenas noches

How are you? ¿Cómo está? (formal)/¿Cómo estás? (informal)

What's up? ¿Qué tal?

I'm fine, thanks Estoy bien, gracias

And you? ¿Y usted? (formal)/ ¿Y vos? (informal)

Cheers! ¡Salud!

Very Muy

Where? ¿Dónde?

Here Aquí/Acá

There Allí/Allá

When? ¿Cuando?

Why? ¿Por qué?

How? ¿Cómo?

Now Ahora

Right now Ahora mismo

Later Más tarde

Today Hoy

Tomorrow Mañana

Next week La semana que viene

Last week La semana pasada

I like it Me gusta

I don't like it No me gusta

My name is... Me llamo...

What is your name? ¿Cómo se llama usted?

Directions

Left Izquierda

Right Derecha

Straight ahead Derecho

I'm lost Estoy perdido (masc.)/Estoy perdida (fem.)

Please write it down Por favor, escríbalo

Can you help me, please? ¿Me ayuda, por favor?

Where is the nearest bank? ¿Dónde está el banco más cercano?

Places

Avenue Avenida

Bank Banco

Bridge Puente

Café Café

Church Iglesia

Drugstore Kiosco

Dry cleaner's Tintorería

Hospital Hospital

House Casa

Launderette Lavandería

Market Mercado

Museum Museo
Park Parque
Post Office Correo
Restaurant
Restaurante/Restorán
Statue Estatua
Square Plaza
Store Tienda/Negocio
Street Calle
Tower Torre

Emergencies
Help! ¡Ayuda!/¡Socorro!
I'm sick Estoy enfermo/a
I need a doctor
Necesito un médico
Where are we?
¿Dónde estamos?
Where is the train/bus station? ¿Dónde está la terminal de micros/estación de trenes?
Where is the police station?
¿Dónde hay una comisaría?
Where is the bathroom?
¿Donde está el baño?
I've lost my wallet
Perdí mi billetera
I've lost my passport
Perdí mi pasaporte

Numbers

0 zero
1 uno
2 dos
3 tres
4 cuatro
5 cinco
6 seis
7 siete
8 ocho
9 nueve
10 diez
20 veinte
30 treinte
40 cuarenta
50 cincuenta
60 sesenta
70 setenta
80 ochenta

90 noventa
100 cien
200 doscientos
1000 mil

Days
Monday Lunes
Tuesday Martes
Wednesday Miércoles
Thursday Jueves
Friday Viernes
Saturday Sabado
Sunday Domingo

Months
January Enero
February Febrero
March Marzo
April Abril
May Mayo
June Junio
July Julio
August Agosto
September Septiembre
October Octubre
November Noviembre
December Diciembre

Colors
Black Negro
Blue Azul
Brown Marrón
Green Verde
Grey Gris
Orange Naranja
Purple Morado
Red Rojo
White Blanco

Transportation
Airport Aeropuerto
Arrivals Arribos
Bus Colectivo
Bus station
Terminal de micros
Chauffeur-driven car
Remise
Coach Micro/Autobus
Departures Partidas
Gas Nafta

Port Puerto
Road Ruta
Ticket Pasaje/Ticket
Timetable Horario
Train Tren
Train station Estación de tren
Taxi Taxi
Where is the nearest bus stop? ¿Dónde está la parada de colectivo más cerca?
Is it direct? ¿Es directo?
Where can I get a taxi? ¿Dónde puedo buscar un taxi?
When does the next train/bus/plane leave? ¿A qué hora sale el próximo tren/autobus/avión?
When does it arrive? ¿A qué hora llega?
A return ticket, please. Un pasaje ida y vuelta por favor.

Shopping
Bakery Panadería
Bookshop Librería
Butcher's Carnicería
Pharmacy Farmacia
Supermarket Supermercado
I'm just looking Solo mirando, gracias
How much is it? ¿Cuánto cuesta?
Can I try it on? ¿Puedo probarme?
How much is this? ¿Cuánto es?
Where can I buy…? ¿Dónde puedo comprar…?
Do you accept credit cards? ¿Aceptan tarjetas de crédito?
Do you have this in a larger size? ¿Tiene esto en un tamaño más grande?
I'll take it Me lo llevo
Large Grande
Small Chico(masc.)/Chica(fem.)
Expensive Caro (masc.)/Cara (fem.)

Open Abierto
Closed Cerrado

Money
Bank Banco
Bureau de change Casa de cambio
Money Dinero/Plata
Cash Efectivo
Credit card Tarjeta de crédito
Stamps Sellos
I would like to change some travelers' checks, please Quiero cambiar unos cheques de viaje por favor
Do you charge commission? ¿Hay comisión?
What is today's date? ¿Qué es la fecha de hoy?
How much does it cost to send a letter to the United States? ¿Cuánto cuesta para mandar una carta al Estados Unidos?

Accommodation
Where is the reception, please? ¿Dónde está la recepción por favor?
Is there a car park? ¿Hay estacionamiento?
Does the hotel have a restaurant? ¿Hay restaurante en el hotel?
Is there an elevator? ¿Hay ascensor?
How much is a single/double room per night? ¿Cúanto cuesta una habitación individual/doble por noche?
Is breakfast included? ¿Se incluye desayuno?
Do you have a room? ¿Tiene una habitación?
With bath/shower Con baño/ducha
A double bed Un matrimonio

MENU READER

The Basics
Menu La carta
Breakfast Desayuno
Lunch Almuerzo
Dinner Cena
Starter Entrada
Main course
Plato principal
Dessert Postre
Short orders Minutas
Oil Aceite
Water Agua
Carbonated Con gas
Uncarbonated Sin gas
Wine Vino
Red wine Vino tinto
White wine
Vino blanco
Beer Cerveza
Tea Te

Cooking Styles
Baked Al horno
Fried Frito
Grilled A la parrilla
Spicy Picante
Rare Jugoso
Medium rare A punto
Well done Bien cocido

Meat
Sirloin steak
Bife de chorizo
Tenderloin Lomo
Rack of ribs
Tira de asado
Rump tail
Colita de cuadril
Chop Chuleta
Sweetbreads
Mollejas
Blood sausage
Morcilla

Liver Higado
Kidneys Riñones
Mixed grill Parrillada
Duck Pato
Lamb Cordero
Veal Ternera
Meatballs
Albóndigas
Sausage Chorizo
Hot dog Pancho

Fish & Seafood
Anchovy Anchoa
Clam Almeja
Crab Cangrejo
Fish Pescado
Fried squid rings
Rabas
Hake Merluza
King crab Centolla
Lobster Langosta
Mussel Mejillón
Octopus Pulpo
Oyster Ostra
Prawn Camarón
Shellfish Mariscos
Sole Lenguado
Squid Calamar
Trout Trucha
Tuna Atún

Vegetables
Beetroot Remolacha
Cabbage Repollo
Carrot Zanahoria
Celery Apio
Chickpea Garbanzo
Cucumber Pepino
Eggplant Berenjena
Green beans
Chauchas
Green peas Arvejas
Leek Puerro

Lentils Lentejas
Lettuce Lechuga
Onion Cebolla
Potato Papa
Rice Arroz
Spinach Espinaca
Squash Calabaza
Sweetcorn Choclo
Sweet Potato Batata
Vegetables Verduras
Watercress Berro

Desserts
Bread pudding
Budín de pan
Cheese Queso
Crême caramel Flan
Thick caramel Dulce
de leche
Ice-cream Helado

Useful Phrases
I would like to see
the menu, please
Quiero ver la carta
por favor
A table for… please
Una mesa para…
por favor
I would like a table
near the window
Quiero una mesa a
lado de la ventana
The check, please
La cuenta, por favor
What flavors do
you have?
¿Qué sabores tienen?
What do you
recommend?
¿Qué nos recomienda?

DISCOVERING
BUENOS AIRES

This *barrio* has several of the city's major avenues, so it's easy to walk and a great jumping-off point for getting to know the city. Monserrat is also the city's earliest *barrio* and its historic center. Thus it contains some of the capital's oldest, most architecturally impressive and important buildings. The neighborhood is crammed with churches, museums and many of Argentina's political institutions.

At Monserrat's heart is the Plaza de Mayo, a giant square lined with famous buildings, including the Casa Rosada, the official seat of the executive branch of the government of Argentina. You'll remember this pink palace as where Evita, and later Madonna, addressed the public.

Heading west from the *plaza* is another of Buenos Aires' major sights, the 10-block Avenida de Mayo.

As the city's major boulevard, the Avenida de Mayo is know for its Art Nouveau and Art Deco architecture, and its French-style cafes and hotels. Make time to check out the Palacio Barolo, one of the Avenida de Mayo's architectural standouts. Bring along your copy of Dante's *Divine Comedy* to see if you can catch all the architectural references to the poem.

After you've finished exploring Avenida de Mayo, another block worth walking down is Manzana de las Luces or the "block of enlightenment." Dating back to 1662, this block originally belonged to a Jesuit community. There are a series of tunnels beneath the Manzana de las Luces that once connected the city's churches. The tunnels were originally part of Buenos Aires' defenses in case of an enemy attack. Today, you can visit the tunnels as part of several tours of the area.

PETER'S TOP PICKS

 CULTURE

Palacio Barolo is a must if you're interested in architecture or literature. Don't forget to revisit Dante's *Divine Comedy* to get the most out of this experience. **Palacio Barolo (p 112)**

 GREEN SPACES

Amid the famous buildings of Plaza de Mayo, you'll find green palm trees and park benches. Take a break in the open *plaza*. **Plaza de Mayo (p 108)**

 SHOP

When I travel I always try to find a local bookstore, and the older the store the more history and the better the selection. Librería del Ávila is considered the oldest bookstore in the city, and shouldn't be missed. **Librería del Ávila (p 114)**

 EAT

Café Tortoni is one of the oldest cafes and this classic spot is my pick for a popular local go-to. Come for the *churros* but stay for the downstairs entertainment. **Café Tortoni (p 111)**

 HISTORY

Architecture is one of my favorite ways to experience history and the Cabildo building dates back to the 18C. **Cabildo (p 109)**

 ENTERTAINMENT

Not only is Teatro Avenida one of the oldest theaters in the city, it's also the place to go for cultural performances. **Teatro Avenida (p 112)**

MONSERRAT, CENTRO, RETIRO AND RECOLETA
Map II

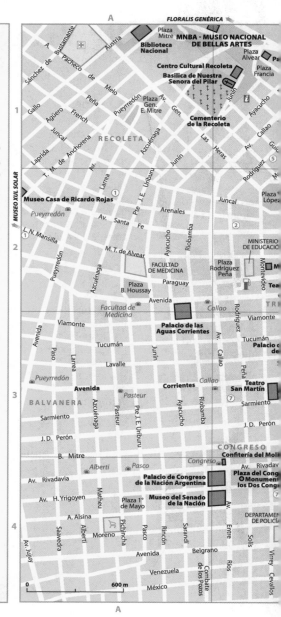

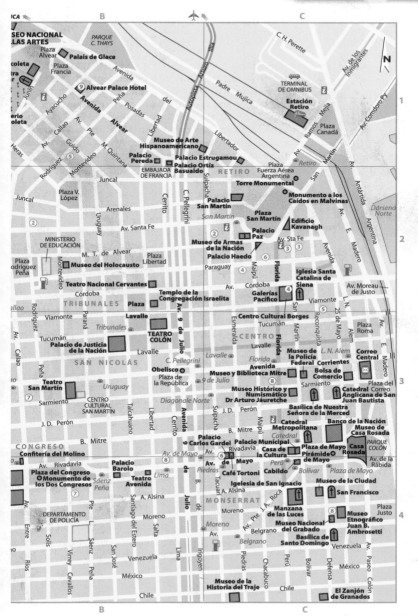

Location:
Demarcated by
Bolívar, Balcarce,
Rivadavia and
Hipólito Yrigoyen.
Subte: Plaza de Mayo
(line A), Catedral
(line D), Bolívar (line E).
Bus nos.: 2, 4, 7, 9,
10, 17, 20, 22, 24, 28,
29, 33, 45, 50, 56, 61,
62, 64, 74, 86, 91, 93,
99, 103, 105, 111, 126,
129, 130, 140, 143,
146, 152, 159, 195.

Plaza de Mayo *and Around*

Map II, C3–4 and Map III, A1–2

Named after the May 1810 Revolution that marked the country's first steps toward Independence, the Plaza de Mayo is seen as the heart of Buenos Aires, from both a historical and symbolic point of view. It was here, on June 11, 1580, that the Spaniard Juan de Garay established a new colony called "Santísima Trinidad y Puerto de Nuestra Señora de los Buenos Ayres," around which the village would develop.

Plaza de Mayo★★

The square serves as a rallying point for most of the city's political gatherings and public demonstrations, notably that of the **Madres de Plaza de Mayo** (the Mothers of the Plaza de Mayo), whose sons and daughters "disappeared" during the Dirty War of 1976-83 *(see The Memory of the Missing on p38)*. Since 1977, wearing white headscarves as a sign of protest, they gather every Thursday afternoon to campaign for justice and the conviction of the officials responsible for the kidnapping, killing and torture of their children. In the center of the square stands the **Pirámide de Mayo**, a 19m/62ft-high obelisk crowned by an allegory to Freedom, which was built in 1811 to celebrate the first anniversary of the Revolution.

Among the plaza's palm trees and park benches, there are also plenty of signs of a typical mode of Argentine expression: graffiti. The slogans you see here often have a strong political flavor, including the names of presidents past and present. It is rare not to find a protest or rally of some sort going on here, and on big occasions, the entire square and surrounding streets are taken over by groups waving flags and beating drums.

Notable incidents have included an attempted *coup d'etat* against President Perón in 1955, when the area was bombed, killing 364, and in 2001 when crowds came out to bang saucepans in protest against the authorities who had overseen the country's economic collapse. The plaza is also the site of pro-government gatherings and public wakes, following the deaths of major public figures, such as former presidents. These days, gatherings tend to be noisy but predominantly peaceful.

Casa Rosada★

Map II, C3 and Map III, A2. ◑ *Allow 1hr. Balcarce 50.* ✆ *(011) 4344 3802. www.museo.gov.ar. Guided tour of the palace (in Spanish). Open Sat and Sun 10am–6pm; museum open Mon–Fri 10am–6pm, Sun 2–6pm.*

Many fortresses succeeded each other on the site where the "Pink House" now stands. The official seat of the executive branch of the government of Argentina is an eclectic building, uniting the Post Office Palace (1873-8), the work of Swedish architect Carlos Kihlberg, and the former Government House, designed by another Swede, Enrique Aberg. In 1894, Italian architect Francisco Tamburini was commissioned to build a great archway to join the two buildings. The new Government House was officially inaugurated in 1898. The building is a remarkable pink color, a tradition that goes back to the presidency of Domingo F. Sarmiento (1873) and that is thought to symbolize the union of the Unitarian and Federalist parties, represented respectively by the colors white and red. Another theory is that the original paint contained cow's blood to prevent damage from humidity.

The guided tour is restricted to the north wing of the palace, which is organized around the elegant **Patio de las Palmeras** (Palm Tree Patio). Notably, it provides access to the sumptuous **Salón Blanco** (white room), where grand official receptions are held, and to the **Salón Norte**, where the government sits. Take one of the two majestic stairs of honor, the Callera Italia or the Callera Francia, to reach the **Salón de los Bustos** (Hall of Busts), which is adorned with 29 busts of Argentinia's presidents.

The building also houses the **Museo de la Casa Rosada** *(entrance on Hipólito Yrigoyen 219)*, which contains various official and personal objects that belonged to the country's various presidents.

Cabildo

Map II, C4 and Map III, A2. ◑ *Allow 30–45mins. Bolívar 65.* ✆ *(011) 4342 6729. www.cultura.gov.ar. Open Wed–Fri 10.30am–5pm, Sat, Sun and public holidays 11.30am–6pm. 1 A$, (no charge on Fri). Guided tour Fri 3pm (no charge), Sat and Sun 12.30pm (3 A$), 2pm (no charge) and 3.30pm (3 A$).*

Built in 1725 to house the seat of government at the time of Spanish colonization, the Cabildo is one of the rare buildings of the 18C to remain standing in Buenos Aires. A witness to the May Revolution and the signing of the country's Declaration of Independence, it was used as a prison from 1821 to 1878, then as a *casa de justicia* (courthouse). It is now home to the **Museo Historico Nacional del Cabildo y de la Revolucion de Mayo**, which recounts the history of the building and of the 1810 Revolution via furniture, paintings and portraits of the first government.

Palacio de Munícipal

Map II, C3. ◗ *Allow 30mins. Bolívar 1.* ✆ *(011) 4323 9400. www.buenosaires.gov.ar. Open Sat 4–6pm, Sun 11am–5.15pm. Free tours.*

Buenos Aires' city hall was built between 1890 and 1893, at the request of the then mayor, Francisco P. Bollini, who felt the city government needed to occupy something more prestigious than the second floor of the police headquarters, where they had been for the past three decades. Plans were scaled back somewhat as the country was in the midst of an economic depression, but the building was later extended. Some of the fittings—expropriated from a next-door mansion—can now be seen in the Casa Rosada.

Catedral Metropolitana★

Map II, C3 and Map III, A1. ◗ *Allow 20mins. San Martín 27.* ✆ *(011) 4331 2845. www.catedralbuenosaires.org.ar. Mausoleum of General San Martín open Mon–Fri 8am–7pm, Sat and Sun 9am–7.30pm.*

It is not at first glance obvious that the imposing Neoclassical façade that stands on the corner of Avenida Rivadavia and Calle San Martín is that of the metropolitan cathedral, Buenos Aires' main Catholic church. The triangular tympanum above the colonnade holds the carvings by French sculptor Joseph Dubourdieu. Its biblical scene portrays the reunion of Joseph with his father Jacob and brothers in Egypt. The interior of the cathedral, which comprises three naves and lateral chapels, is in a Spanish Colonial style. Since 1880, it has housed the mortal remains of the great national hero **General José de San Martín** (1778-1850), known as El Libertador (the liberator), which are guarded by armed grenadiers of the Argentine army.

Banco de la Nación Argentina

Map II, C3 and Map III, A1. ◗ *Allow 20mins. Rivadavia 205.*

The National Bank of Argentina, created in 1891 on the initiative of president Carlos Pellegrini to help the development of the Argentinian economy, was built on the site occupied by the Teatro Colón from 1857 to 1888. However, the imposing building that faces onto the plaza, the work

Travel Tip:

Monserrat was the first *barrio* to have a working subway system. In 1913, Line A launched there and become the first subway in the city of Buenos Aires, as well as the first subway in Latin America and in the Spanish-speaking world. If you're looking to recreate the historic ride, hop on Line A, which runs from Plaza de Mayo to Carabobo. And for added authenticity, the line retains the historic wooden La Brugeoise cars, which were originally built in Belgium for the city's subway and tram lines. The cars now count as the oldest metro rolling stock in commercial service in the world.

of the famous architect Alejandro Bustillo, dates from 1939. The interior has a glass and concrete dome, decorative features and period furniture. The bank runs the **Museo Histórico y Numismático** *(Bartolomé Mitre 326 (first floor); ☏ (011) 4347 6277; open Mon–Fri 10am–3pm)* where exhibits include old coins from the Colonial period.

Avenida de Mayo

Map II, BC4 and Map III, A2

Linking the Casa Rosada and the Palacio del Congreso, the seat of the legislative branch of government, this arterial road is without doubt one of the capital's most beautiful avenues. Wide and liberally shaded, it is lined with smart houses and buildings renowned for their historic and architectural merit.

Casa de la Cultura★

Map II, C3. ◗ *Allow 15mins–1hr for a guided tour. Mayo 575.* ☏ *(011) 4323 9669. www.buenosaires.gob.ar. Guided tour of the Palacio del Gobierno and the Casa de la Cultura, Sat 4pm and 5pm, Sun hourly from 11am–4pm.*

Adjoining the Palacio del Gobierno, the Casa de la Cultura was built in 1896-8 to house the headquarters of *La Prensa*, Argentina's most popular newspaper of the first half of the 20C *(see sidebar below)*. This luxurious, French-inspired building now belongs to the City of Buenos Aires. The cultural center organizes various activities and workshops, and it is accessible for guided tours.

Café Tortoni★★

Map II, C3 and Map III, A2. ◗ *Allow 30–50mins. Mayo 825.* ☏ *(011) 4342 4328. www.cafetortoni.com.ar. Open Mon–Sun 8.30am–1am.*

A bit farther on, this famous cafe is the oldest in the city. Opened in 1858 by a French immigrant, it was named thus after an establishment on the

Location: Starting at Plaza De Mayo and running parallel to Rivadavia, as far as Paraná.
Subte: Perú, Piedras, Lima and Sáenz Peña (line A). Avenida de Mayo (line C).
Bus nos.: 9, 10, 17, 22, 23, 24, 28, 29, 45, 56, 60, 61, 64, 67, 70, 86, 91, 100, 102, 105, 111, 126, 151, 168.

LA PRENSA

If you're a fan of the news and journalist infighting, then take a closer look at the Casa de la Cultura. Less than a block west of the Plaza de Mayo is the former La Prensa building, which once was the home of Argentina's largest newspaper of the same name. Founded in 1869, *La Prensa* was a bastion of conservative thought and openly supported British influence in Argentina. Pressure from a new government headed by Juan Perón and competition from what is now Argentina's largest paper, *Clarin*, eventually pushed *La Prensa* into obscurity and the building was sold over to the State.

ASK PETER...

Q: Are there any free tours of government buildings in Monserrat?

A: Not only are many of Buenos Aires' government buildings open to the public, but also in most cases entry is free and complimentary tours are offered. The Casa Rosada, for example, is open on weekends with free bilingual tours *(1hr)* which take you right through the palace, including into the President's office and out onto the famous balcony overlooking the Plaza de Mayo. Another government building worth visiting is the Banco de la Nacion Argentina. Since this is a functioning bank there is no admission fee, and you can take a look at the massive 50m/164ft dome, the third largest in the world.

Boulevard des Italiens, in Paris, where the Parisian *intelligentsia* gathered. Its Argentinian namesake enjoys the same success and has been frequented by of the country's elite, counting among them Jorge Luis Borges, Luigi Pirandello, García Lorca, Benito Quinquela Martín, Julio Cortázar, Arthur Rubinstein and Carlos Gardel. It has preserved period features, elegant décor, intimate salons, paintings, busts and black and white photographs relating to its long history. Jazz and tango concerts are regularly given in the basement room.

Palacio Carlos Gardel

Map II, C3. ◗ *Allow 30mins or more for a class. Mayo 833.* ✆ *(011) 4345 6968. www.anacdeltango.org.ar. Museum open Mon–Fri, 2.30pm–7.30pm. 15 A$.*

This 19C Italianate mansion was given a new lease of life when it became home to the **National Academy of Tango** in 2000. It now contains the World Tango Museum, a dance studio and a tango library of books and music, as well as the organization's administrative offices. Classes are also offered on site *(Mon–Fri)*.

Teatro Avenida

Map II, B4. ◗ *Allow 10mins. Mayo 1220.* ✆ *(011) 4381 0662. www.balirica.org.ar.*

Inaugurated in 1908, this venue started out showcasing traditional Spanish theater, before moving on to Broadway shows from the 1960s. The grandeur lies on the inside—with its sculpted ceiling and tiered balconies—as the exterior lost much of its drama when the top half, once the Hotel Castilla, was destroyed by fire in the 1970s.

It reopened in 1994, and when Teatro Colón *(see p130)* was undergoing its lengthy renovations from 2006 to 2010, the city's opera program moved here.

Palacio Barolo★★

Map II, B4. ◗ *Allow 10mins–1hr. Mayo 1370.* ✆ *(011) 4381 1885. www.pbarolo.com.ar. Open Mon–Fri 8am–10pm (ground level only). Guided tour Mon and Fri 2pm. 40 A$.*

Inaugurated in 1923, the Palacio Barolo is incontestably one of the more beautiful buildings on the avenue. At one time it was also the tallest in Buenos Aires before being dethroned by the Kavanagh Building in 1935 *(see p135)*. More surprisingly, its architect, Italian Mario Palanti, was inspired by Dante Alighieri's "Divine Comedy": the height of the Palacio (100m/328ft), for example, echoes the poem's

CAFÉ CULTURE
...LIKE A LOCAL

Considered the "truly Spanish" district of Buenos Aires, there are rows of con-gressional buildings on and around Avenida de Mayo, as well as tons of lo-cal restaurants. Pizza and coffee shops line the street and you will find office workers grabbing a quick bite in the middle of the work day. Take a break from touring the impressive architecture, and experience what it's truly like to be a local.

A tip to remember is, if at the end of your meal you raise your hand to signal the waiter to ask for the check, don't be surprised if he brings you another espresso; in Buenos Aires, when raising your hand and gesturing as though you're holding a piece of bread, that's the signal for "another cup of coffee, please" and not the signal for the end of your meal.

Words to remember: espresso = *café*; espresso with milk = *cortado*; half espresso/half milk = *café con leche*; warm milk with a small amount of espresso = *lagrima*.

Café Tortoni *(see p111)*
You might want to stop by the Café Tortoni any time of day to enjoy their legendary coffee and *chocolate con churros* (hot cocoa and *churros*), a traditional Argentine breakfast. One of the oldest cafes in the area, Café Tortoni has been around since 1858. In addition to above average-cafe fare, its basement is a hothouse for poetry and literature, as well as a stage for tango artists.

London City
Avenida De Mayo 599; open 7am–9pm Mon–Fri, 8am–7pm Sat, closed Sun.
If you're looking for a more local option, London City is a step above the average cafe experience. Visit during the morning rush hour to see the city's workers going past on their way to the office. The cafe's selection of pastries and other breakfast options won't break your travel fund.

Museo del Jamon
Cerrito 8, corner of Rivadavia; open Mon–Fri noon–3am, Sat noon–1.30am, Sun noon–midnight.
If you are interested in discovering why Avenida de Mayo is considered the "truly Spanish" part of Buenos Aires, look no further than Museo del Jamon. Although located half a block away from the Avenida de Mayo, it's worth the extra couple steps. Museo del Jamon serves a wide range of Spanish cuisine, including tapas and Liberian ham.

Avila
Avenida de Mayo 1384; open Mon–Sat noon–4pm, 8pm–2am, closed Sun.
Argentina is also well known for its seafood and Avila is one of the best places to find authentic seafood tapas since the 1940s. Set in a dark, traditional atmosphere, Avila has entertainment as well as food, but make sure you plan ahead: reservations are necessary.

Location:
South of the main square as far as Avenida Belgrano. Farther south still, and you'll come to San Telmo.

Subte: Plaza de Mayo and Perú (line A), Catedral (line D), Bolívar (line E).

Bus nos.: 2, 4, 7, 17, 20, 22, 24, 26, 28, 29, 33, 38, 45, 50, 54, 56, 59, 61, 62, 64, 67, 74, 86, 91, 93, 100, 103, 105, 111, 122, 126, 130, 139, 142, 143, 146, 152, 159.

100 cantos; its division into three distinct parts, the three canticas of the book: Hell, Purgatory and Paradise. Today, the building mainly houses offices and only the foyer can be visited; more is, however, accessible by guided tour.

South of Plaza de Mayo

Map II, C4 and Map III, A2

Head just south of Buenos Aires' main square and you'll encounter some of the most beautiful sections of the city, complete with culturally and historically significant churches and other stone buildings.

Manzana de las Luces★

Map II, C4 and Map III, A2. ◗ *Allow 1hr. Entrance via Perú 272.* ℘ *(011) 4342 6973. www.manzanadelasluces.gov.ar. Guided tours only (1hr) Mon–Fri 3pm, Sat and Sun 3pm, 4.30pm and 6pm. 7 A$.*

Demarcated by the streets Bolívar, Moreno, Alsina and Perú, la Manzana de las Luces is one of the oldest blocks of houses *(manzana)* in Buenos Aires, shown on maps since 1580. For over a century from 1661, it was owned by the Jesuits, who notably also built the city's first church, the **Iglesia San Ignacio** *(Bolívar 225)*. After the order's expulsion in 1767, the building soon grouped together many prestigious educational and cultural establishments, which led to its nickname, "the Illuminated Block."

Most of these establishments have now closed or moved, but the **Colegio Nacional de Buenos Aires** *(Bolívar 263)* remains. Many guided tours provide access to this historic site and the tunnels beneath it.

At the intersection of the *calles* Alsina and Perú, the **Mercado de las Luces** (market of lights) *(Sun–Fri 10.30am–7.30pm)* assembles craft and antiques stalls. On the corner of *calles* Alsina and Bolívar, the **Librería del Ávila** *(Alsina 500)* is the city's oldest bookshop, dating back to 1785.

Museo de la Ciudad

Map II, C4 and Map III, A2. ◗ *Allow 30–45mins. Defensa 219–223 (on the corner of Alsina).* ℘ *(011) 4331 9855. www.museos.buenosaires.gov.ar. Open daily 11am–7pm. 1 A$ (no charge Mon and Wed). Guided tour the first Sun of the month at 3pm and the last Sun of the month at 4.30pm.*

If, as it appears, the city museum's role is to preserve an historical record of Buenos Aires and its inhabitants, it has to be said that its collections, which are at least diverse, are hardly fascinating: toys, phonographs, reconstructions of an office of the 1910s, a dining room of the 1950s, the Art Déco bedroom of Myriam Stefford and Baron Biza, etc. Nevertheless, it's worth checking out the **Farmacia de la Estrella** (Star Pharmacy) on the ground floor of the museum, which has retained furniture and decoration from the 1900s.

Basílica de San Francisco de Asis y Capilla de San Roque

Map II, C4 and Map III, A2. ◗ *Allow 15mins. Alsina 380.* ✆ *(011) 4331 0625. www.museofransciano.com.ar. Open Mon–Fri 7.30am–1.30pm, 5–7pm; Sat 5–7pm; Sun 10am–noon, 5–7pm. Museum open Wed–Sun, 11am–5pm.*

Facing the museum, a charming *plazoleta* leads to the **San Francisco Church**. Built around 1730, this sanctuary has been transformed many times and since the early 19C has sported a Bavarian Baroque-style façade. Inside, admire the second-largest tapestry in the world, second only to one in Coventry Cathedral, England. The **San Roque Chapel** stands outside, sharing an atrium with the church. In the square outside are four marble statues by French sculptor Joseph Dubordieu, which personify Astronomy, Navigation, Geography and Industry.

Museo Nacional del Grabado

Map II, C4 and Map III, A2. ◗ *Allow 30mins. Agüero 2502.* ✆ *(011) 4802 3295. www.cultura.gov.ar. Closed for renovation until Spring 2012, call for opening times.*

Created in 1960 from the private collection of professor Oscar Carlos Pecora, the **National Print Museum** assembles some 11,000 items, original engravings, illustrated books and works by Argentine and foreign artists of the 20C. The museum also has a printing workshop and offers various cultural activities. In 2006, its collections had to move from the elegant late-19C residence that had housed the museum for around a decade and are now provisionally installed in the premises of the Biblioteca Nacional. The museum was recently renovated and reopened at the end of 2011.

Museo Etnográfico Juan B. Ambrosetti★

Map II, C4 and Map III, A2. ◗ *Allow 1hr. Moreno 350.* ✆ *(011) 4345 8196. www.museoetnografico.filo.uba.ar. Open Tue–Fri 1–7pm, Sat and Sun 3–7pm. 3 A$. Guided tour Sat and Sun 4pm.*

Created by the Faculty of Philosophy and Arts in 1904, the **Museum of Ethnography** is largely the work of naturalist Juan B. Ambrosetti. His archaeological, ethnographic and anthropological collections assemble beautiful items from around the world, but in particular provide an interesting perspective on the different aboriginal peoples of northwest Argentina, Patagonia and Tierra del Fuego.

Travel Tip:

One Latin American and European tradition is that of a **siesta**. Although it's not common in the large department store/restaurant chains in the big city, smaller neighborhood kiosks and stores observe this special time of day to rest in order to tackle the afternoon duties later on in the day. Siestas are usually an hour and a half long, taken after lunch. Just be sure you won't need anything important like batteries for your digital camera during siesta time.

Juan Bautista Ambrosetti (1865-1917)

Juan Bautista Ambrosetti is a name you'll see throughout Monserrat. His presence is obviously felt at the Museum of Ethnography, which is only natural given that Ambrosetti pioneered anthropology in Buenos Aires. Ambrosetti graduated from the University of Buenos Aires and later led an expedition into the uncharted area of Chaco Province. In the early 20C, Ambrosetti discovered the ruins of Tilcara, an Omaguaca people that has long since vanished into extinction, in the Quebrada de Humahuaca. Those findings earned him an honorary doctorate from the school. In 2003, long after Ambrosetti's death, the area was declared a UNESCO World Heritage Site.

On display in this attractive, 19C townhouse are thousands of ancient artifacts, including masks, weapons, jewelry, pottery and dug-out canoes, plus a range of mummies. This is a respectful museum that was founded to focus attention on indigenous cultures that were fast disappearing due to early settlers and colonization.

Argentina's original tribes are detailed in geographical sequence and although explanations are only given in Spanish, printed English hand-outs are also available.

Basílica de Santo Domingo

Map II, C4. ◗ *Allow 15mins. Defensa 422.* ✆ *(011) 4331 1668. Open Mon–Fri 7am–6pm; Sat during Mass; Sun during Mass, 2.30–4.30pm. Guided tours Sun 3–7pm; call to book. No charge but donation requested for tours.*

Behind Spanish Colonial-style railings, this 18C Dominican basilica, also known as the Iglesia de Nuestra Señora del Rosario, has survived fire and a military attack.

Today two symmetrical towers provide its crown, but originally it was somewhat lopsided, with just one. When cannon balls destroyed the first tower during the British invasions of the early 1800s, it was rebuilt with replica bullet holes added to preserve the history *(look left)*. Outside is the mausoleum of General Manuel Belgrano, the Independence hero who designed the Argentine flag.

MEDICAL TOURISM

A few years ago, medical tourism threw around phrases like "surgical safari" or "breast implants and tango" to promote the idea that folks could combine travel experiences with affordable—and usually elective—medical procedures. After all, if you were going to spend three weeks recuperating from a facelift, why not combine it with a vacation?

Argentina, and especially Buenos Aires, has made a reputation for itself as a go-to destination for cosmetic procedures carried out in modern clinics with cutting-edge technology. Think rhinoplasty, breast augmentation and reduction, even laser-eye surgery. And it's not just tourists getting procedures done, image conscious *porteños* are also taking the plunge.

In recent years, the big business of medical tourism has undergone more stringent regulations. There are now multiple international accreditation programs for hospitals and clinics, so there isn't just one set of standards that you can use as a benchmark. Probably the most common accreditation program that you'll hear about is Joint Commission International (JCI), which requires hospitals and clinics to go through a multi-layered process and be reassessed every three years. Other similar and equally legitimate accreditation programs include the Canadian Council on Health Services Accreditation, Australian Council on Healthcare Standards (ACHSI), and the UK's Trent Accreditation Scheme.

If you are electing to have surgery when you travel, it's your responsibility to double and triple check your clinic's credentials and ask plenty of questions. First talk to specialists in the US to find out the normal procedure and follow-up care timeline. Then ask how long is the estimated recovery time? If recovery is done on an outpatient basis, what is the follow up and the contingency plan in case of emergency? Does the facility have a list of accommodations that are close by? Is the hotel staff accustomed to medical tourists? Is there someone on staff who speaks English and can advocate on your behalf? And do you have a way to contact your doctor?

One caution: if a facility tells you that you can come in for a procedure and fly home the next day, run away—don't walk—and don't look back. After any surgical procedure, you must remember that it's not a good idea to immediately hop on a long flight that forces your body to deal with altitude, pressure and oxygen changes.

Here's an important distinction in my experience: Tourists usually just concentrate on where to spend their money, but for an authentic, more genuine experience consider going to the neighborhoods where locals actually *make* their money.

If Retiro and Monserrat are the cultural hearts of the city, Centro (officially San Nicolás) is Buenos Aires' commercial center. Sandwiched between the *barrios* of Retiro and Monserrat, Centro is a neighborhood in the middle of Buenos Aires where Argentines come to earn money. Even if you're not a business traveler, there is plenty to see and do here.

Be sure to visit Avenida 9 de Julio, an avenue named in honor of Argentina's July 9 Independence Day. This avenue needs to be seen to be believed. It is one of the widest in the world and stretches an impressive 140/153yd and 12 traffic lanes wide. Opposing traffic on the avenue is divided by a gardened median that comes in handy for pedestrians trying to walk from one side of the avenue to the other. Even brisk walkers will find it takes around two traffic lights to cross Avenida 9 de Julio. However, a stop in the middle is a great way to take a moment to grasp the scope of this giant avenue, which runs around 30 blocks from north to south. Along its massive stretch, the avenue hits several major sites including the famous Avenida de Mayo. But perhaps the best known site along the avenue is El Obelisco, a white obelisk that sits in the middle of 9 de Julio. Built in 31 days in 1936, the Obelisco stands 67m/220ft tall and was built to commemorate the 400th anniversary of the first founding of Buenos Aires. The location of the Obelisco is on the exact spot where Belgrano's design of the Argentinean flag was flown for the first time in Buenos Aires.

Two blocks away from the Obelisco is another of Buenos Aires' icons, the Teatro Colón, Argentina's most prestigious cultural institution. The Teatro is most famous as an opera house, but also hosts ballets and classical music concerts.

In addition to its cultural sites, San Nicolás holds the Argentine Central Bank and the National Bank, the country's largest financial institutions.

PETER'S TOP PICKS

 CULTURE

Museo y Biblioteca Mitre is a three-for-one special. You can visit one of the city's historic residences while also seeing one of the most interesting libraries and exploring the museum. **Museo y Biblioteca Mitre (p 122)**

 GREEN SPACES

If you're looking for a break from this neighborhood's administrative buildings, consider Plaza Lavalle, which has three blocks-worth of open green space. **Plaza Lavalle (p 129)**

 HISTORY

Most people head to Catholic churches for Gothic architecture and pageantry, but the Cathedral Angelicana de San Jaun Bautista is the oldest Protestant cathedral in all of South America and well worth a visit. **Cathedral Angelicana de San Jaun Bautista (p 125)**

 SHOP

Calle Florida may be making a hard push for tourist dollars, but the Galería Güemes offers a more civilized and stylish shopping experience. Take note of the Art Nouveau architecture. **Calle Florida (p 120) Galería Güemes (p 120)**

 ENTERTAINMENT

With both theater and opera in this neighborhood, there are many options. Visit the Teatro Colón both to catch the opera and to see the opulent structure. **Teatro Colón (p 130)**

DISCOVERING CENTRO

Location:
Demarcated by the Plaza de Mayo to the south, the *avenidas* Córdoba to the north, 9 de Julio to the west and Eduardo Madero to the east.

Subte: Plaza de Mayo, Perú, Piedras and Avenida de Mayo (line A), L. N. Alem, Florida, Carlos Pellegrini (line B), Catedral, Diagonal Norte and 9 de Julio (line D).

Bus nos.: 6, 22, 23, 26, 28, 33, 45, 50, 54, 56, 61, 62, 91, 93, 99, 109, 115, 130, 140, 146, 152, 155.

Travel Tip:
Haggling for leather on Calle Florida is a popular tourist pastime. However, more tourists means higher prices for leather goods and local trinkets. Walk a couple blocks away from Plaza St. Martín and believe me, you will reap the financial benefits.

Microcentro

Map II, C3 and Map III, A1.

"Microcentro," or "La City," is both the financial and the commercial center of the capital. This is where banks, currency exchanges and corporate headquarters are concentrated, plus some of the city's busiest thoroughfares. When you get caught up in the crowds as they rush to work or from store to store, it is easy to lose sight of the architecture, but this is where you find some of the city's most impressive buildings, hidden among the chain stores. Note that most of the museums in the area are only open on weekdays.

Calle Florida
Map II, C2–4 and Map III, A1. ◖ *Allow 30–50mins.*
The Calle Florida is undoubtedly one of the more famous and lively streets in the district. One block to the west of the Plaza de Mayo, it stretches between Avenida Rivadavia, to the south, and the Plaza San Martín, to the north. This pedestrian street is in fact the city's main commercial thoroughfare. You certainly won't find the most chic or trendy boutiques here, but there are lots of stores selling high-quality leather goods. You'll also find a few historic cafes here, such as Confitería Richmond at no 468, which is sadly set to become a sports store. Note also the old Harrods building at no 877, which was opened in 1914 as the only overseas branch of the renowned London store, but closed following economic difficulties and is no longer owned by its original founder.

There is always a buzz on this road. Expect to rub shoulders with shopaholic Brazilians, touts selling tango tickets and newspaper vendors manning their sidewalk *kioscos*, plus musicians, painters and mime artists providing street entertainment.

Just north of Florida's midpoint is an intersection with another pedestrianized street, Calle Lavalle, which offers more shopping opportunities.

Galería Güemes
Map II, C3 and Map III, A1. ◖ *Allow 20–30mins. Florida 165.* ✆ *(011) 4331 3041. www.galeriaguemes.com.ar. Open Mon–Fri 8am–8pm. Sat 9am–1pm.*
Galería Güemes, which links the *calles* Florida *(no 165)* and San Martín *(no 172)*, is one of a few stylish shopping malls

in the area and a fine example of Art Nouveau architecture. You may still hear it referred to by its old name, Paseo Florida. It was designed by Italian architect Francesco Gianotti, who also designed Confitería del Molino *(see p127)*. Though the arcade dates back to 1915, it was badly damaged by fire and has undergone extensive renovation. It now has a deceptively modern entrance. A tango show takes place in a fabulously restored basement theater, where the genre's number-one legend, Carlos Gardel, once performed *(www.piazzollatangoshow.com)*. There's a lookout point on the 14th floor.

Galerías Pacífico★

Map II, C2 and Map III, A1. ◗ *Allow 20–30mins. On the corner of Florida and Córdoba.* ✆ *(011) 5555 5110. www.galeriaspacifico.com.ar. Open Mon–Sat 10am–9pm, Sun noon–9pm. Guided tour (20 mins) Mon–Fri 11.30am and 4.30pm (English and Spanish).*

More spectacular still, the Galerías Pacífico building has rediscovered the purpose it was built for in the 1890s. Built from 1889 to 1895 and modeled on the Bon Marché department store in Paris, this opulent mall was for a time the commercial headquarters of the railroad. Now admirably restored, it houses famous brand boutiques and is worth a look for its remarkable architecture, particularly the superb frescoes that decorate the central dome, which were completed in 1945 by the painters Antonio Berni *(see below)*, Lino Spilimbergo, Juan Carlos Castagnino, Demetrio Urruchua and Antonio Colmeiro. The gallery is also home to the famous **Centro Cultural Borges** *(entrance via Viamonte)*, which offers many cultural and artistic events (exhibitions, theater, concerts, entertainments, conferences; *see also Entertainment p247)*.

AN ARGENTINIAN PAINTER

Unrecognized outside Argentina, **Antonio Berni** *(1905-81)* is, however, an original and engaging painter, a witness to the events of the 20C. In Buenos Aires, he is one of the five artists who created the spectacular frescoes of the Galerías Pacífico on Calle Florida. Buenos Aires' two great fine art museums, the MNBA and the MALBA, exhibit a large selection of his most arresting works. Throughout his long career, he addressed all the century's great artistic movements, from very moving Realism to the vibrant and caustic humor of Pop Art.

Travel Tip:
With American fast food outposts and limitless souvenir shops, many tourists head to Calle Florida. Yes, you can find a few cheap souvenirs to bring home, but the trip may cost you more than you expect. Pickpockets have been known to operate here, so carry only what you need for the day and keep valuables hidden.

Iglesia Santa Catalina de Siena

Map II, C2. ◗ *Allow 15mins. San Martín 705 and Viamonte.* ℘ *(011) 5238 6040. www.santacatalina.org.ar. Open daily 8am-8pm.*

Writer Victoria Ocampo (1890-1979) wrote about being born just opposite Iglesia Santa Catalina and feeling as though the two of them grew up together, even though the building was actually over 150 years her senior. The construction of the first convent in Buenos Aires began in 1727, following a formal request from priest Dionisio Torres Briceño to King Philip V of Spain. During the second British invasion in the early 19C, the convent was taken over by the foreign troops, who destroyed the holy images and stole religious objects. Later in the conflict, Santa Catalina became a field hospital to treat the wounded of both sides. In March 2001, a restoration project began led by architect Edward Ellis. Inside is an attractive Baroque altar.

Museo y Biblioteca Mitre

Map II, C3 and Map III, A1. ◗ *Allow 30mins. San Martín 336.* ℘ *(011) 4394 8240. www.museomitre.gov.ar. Open Mon–Fri 1–5.30pm. 5 A$.*

The fine, late-18C Colonial residence, where **General Bartolomé Mitre** (1821-1906) lived with his family from 1860 was converted into a museum after his death, the state having bought the house in 1907. It retains beautiful furniture of the period, a **library** of great merit, containing some 53,000 books, maps and documents, and a collection of objects that belonged to this important Argentinian politician and writer. Mitre was the country's president from 1862 to 1868 and the founder of the newspaper *La Nación*.

Museo Histórico y Numismático Dr. Arturo Jáuretche

Map II, C3 and Map III, A1. ◗ *Allow 30mins. Sarmiento 362–364.* ℘ *(011) 4331 1775. www.bapro.com.ar/museo/index2.htm. Open Mon–Fri 10am–6pm.*

Managed by the Banco de la Provincia de Buenos Aires, this little banking museum exhibits old national monetary units, furniture, photographs and equipment related to banking.

Bolsa de Comercio

Map II, C3 and Map III, A1. ◗ *Allow 30mins. Leandro N. Alem and Sarmiento.* ℘ *(011) 4316 7066. http://www.bcba.sba.*

LUNA PARK

Luna Park Stadium, declared an Historic National Monument by Argentina's Secretary of Culture in 2007, occupies a special place in Buenos Aires' cultural history. The Art Deco building downtown has played host to landmark events in Argentine cultural history. Boxer Carlos Monzón, undisputed world middleweight champion, was discovered in the gymnasium here and later fought much of his 87 win career in the ring at Luna Park. Evita Duarte met her future husband and soon-to-be president Juan Perón at a charity event there. The Bolshoi Ballet, Milan's La Scala Orchestra, the Moscow Circus, and the Harlem Globetrotters have all visited the famed venue at one point in its near 100-year history.

The first incarnation of the stadium went up in 1912, on 9 de Julio Avenue where the Obelisco now stands. The American Frederick Ingersoll, responsible for over 40 Luna Parks all over the world, based it on the original Coney Island design. Luna Park was originally an amusement park and outdoor venue for live theater, concerts, and boxing matches. In 1932 it was demolished and relocated 10 blocks away in the heart of downtown Buenos Aires, on the edge of the Puerto Madero neighborhood. Italian businessmen Ismael Pace and former amateur boxer, José Lectoure took over the rights to Luna Park, forging a lasting relationship between the venue and boxing.

In the late 1930s, the Perónist government transformed the venue into what looked like a scene straight out of Berlin, hosting spectacular pro-Nazi rallies that attracted over 20,000 participants. Following the deaths of Pace and Lectoure in the late 1950s, the stadium passed into the hands of Juan Carlos, Lectoure's young nephew and a lifelong boxing fan. Carlos transformed Luna Park into a boxing mecca to rival New York's Madison Square Garden and Atlantic City's Boardwalk Hall. At the height of its popularity, Luna Park attracted the biggest names in boxing, including Mohammed Ali.

Today Luna Park hosts huge international music acts and sporting events, and although it's not known for its acoustics, the stadium is still the city's premier venue for a concert or a good old fashioned fight night.

com.ar/home. Free guided tours (no admission in informal clothing such as shorts) Mon–Fri noon, 2pm and 4pm (30mins). Take identification to Sarmiento 299, first floor.

The Buenos Aires stock exchange was founded in 1854 and has had various headquarters across the city center, from its original spot in a house owned by Independence hero José San Martín to its 19C location in front of the Casa Rosada. The Beaux-Arts building where it has come to rest was built in 1913-16 by Alejandro Christophersen, who also designed the fabulous **Palacio San Martin★** *(see p137)*. In the 1970s, it was given a modern extension by architect Mario Roberto Álvarez.

Museo de la Policía Federal

Map II, C3 and Map III, A1. ◗ *Allow 30mins. San Martin 353, 7th and 8th floor.* ℘ *(011) 4394 6857. www.cpf.org.ar. Open Mon–Fri 2–6pm.*

Upstairs in a rather nondescript building, this police museum looks at the history of the Argentine force and its criminal investigations. There are displays of police weapons, uniforms through the ages, fingerprinting techniques and, at the back, some grizzly crime scene photographs that aren't for the weak stomached. ◗

Basílica de Nuestra Señora de la Merced and Convento San Ramón

Map II, C3 and Map III, A1. ◗ *Allow 15mins. Reconquista and Perón.* ℘ *(011) 4343 9623. Open Mon–Fri 9am–7pm.*

A little slice of peace in the heart of the financial district, this church has origins that date back to the early 17C, when its first incarnation was a mud-and-clay chapel. A convent was soon built at its side and various renovations took place during its early years, until finally the crumbling original chapel had to be knocked down. In 1721, the foundation stone was laid for the current incarnation. The Baroque altarpiece and pulpit you see inside today were created by craftsman Tomás Saravia.

During the English invasions, it was occupied by the defending forces and it was from here that military leader Santiago de Liniers directed troops. It was also used as a hospital for injured soldiers during 1820s conflict with Brazil, and later was orphanage and a center for deaf-mutes. When Napoleon's ille-

---

DEMONSTRATIONS IN LA CITY

The financial nerve-center of Buenos Aires, La City is not all about old, beautiful architecture and bustling sidewalks. The area became the focal point of Argentina's financial instability in the 1980s, when hyperinflation drastically damaged the country's economy. In 2001, the area was the sight of civic unrest as housewives took to the streets and participated in *cazerolazo* pot-banging demonstrations, showing their displeasure with the savings-withdrawal policy implemented on their bank accounts.

gitimate son, Alejando Florián Colonna Walewice-Walewski, came to Buenos Aires to negotiate with Governor Juan Manuel de Rosas on behalf of the French government in 1847, his premature baby daughter was baptized here. Sadly, she died before reaching two months old and was buried in Recoleta cemetery.

Catedral Anglicana de San Juan Bautista
Map II, C3 and Map III, A1. ◐ *Allow 15mins. 25 de Mayo 282, between Sarmiento and Perón.* ☏ *(011) 4342 4618. www.catedralanglicana.com. Open Wed 1–3pm, Fri 1–2pm, Sunday 10–11.30am.*

Dating back to 1831, this is the oldest non-Catholic church in the country and the oldest Protestant church in the whole of South America. In February 1830, Governor Juan Manuel de Rosas allocated the land for the temple and by April the first stone was laid, following a commission by the architect Richard Adamser, who adopted neo-Doric stylings. Remodeled over the years, it took on its final form in 1931 when its interior was modified with oak cladding, The organ dates from 1895 and was electrified in 1924.

Avenida Corrientes
Map II, A-C3 and Map III, A1. ◐ *Allow 30mins. Spanning west from Av. E Madero, between Lavalle and Sarmiento.*

Another important street, the Avenida Corrientes is perhaps one of the city's busiest, and therefore noisiest. It stretches over some seventy blocks between Puerto Madero and the district of Chacarita. Although distressingly unstylish, it nevertheless swarms with life by day and by night as it is here that are found most of the capital's theaters—the Maypo, the Gran Rex, the Ópera, the Avenida, the San Martín, the Astral, the Multiteatro and the Metropolitan—as well as cinemas, bookstores, cafes and restaurants.

At the eastern end of the Avenida Corrientes, the building of the **Correo Central** *(Sarmiento 151)*, also known as the Palacio de Correos y Telecomunicaciones (Post and Telecommunications Palace), was designed by French architect Norbert Maillart and opened in 1928. If watching a play in Spanish is beyond you, enjoy another quintessential *porteño* experience on Avenue Corrientes by popping into one of its famous pizza restaurants *(see Where to Eat p241)*. To do this in true local style, order by the slice and eat it at the bar. Try the Fugazzeta, topped simply with a thick layer of mozzarella and onion.

Travel Tip:
Centro is a good place to exchange your Benjamins and turn them into Pesos. Walking to a bank like Banco Ciudad is your best option *(Avenida Cordoba 675; open daily (including holidays) 10am-7pm)*. Banco Ciudad is the place to get the best exchange rate in town and this branch specializes in tourist help, requiring nothing but a passport to exchange American dollars and travelers' checks.

Map II, B3-4.

Location:
Demarcated by
Rivadavia, Hipólito
Yrigoyen, Entre Ríos
and Combate de
Los Pozos.
Subte: Congreso
(line A).
Bus nos.: 2, 5, 6, 7, 12,
29, 37, 50, 60, 64, 75,
86, 99, 105, 109, 115,
124, 150, 155.

Congreso

There is no official *barrio* called Congreso, but you will still hear the name used by locals. The area fell into great disrepair over the years and, by the 1990s, much of the gravitas of the central plaza was lost when it was used as a makeshift football pitch. In 2006, a renovation project began to clean it up. It is a place to visit by day while workers mill around, as at night the streets can seem quite desolate.

Plaza de los Dos Congresos

Map II, B4. ◗ *Allow 15mins.*
The district around the Plaza de los Dos Congresos is one of Buenos Aires' civic centers, dominated by the imposing profile of the National Congress. To the west of the square, the **Monumento de los Dos Congresos**, crowned with an allegory of the Republic on the March, celebrates the centenary of the Assembly constituted in 1813 and the Declaration of Independence of 1816. Sadly, it has been fenced off since 2006 due to repeated vandalism. Also to be admired, in the center of the square, are the replica of Rodin's *The Thinker* and the monolith marking kilometer zero, from which all distances are calculated for the country's roads.

Palacio del Congreso de la Nación Argentina★

Map II, A4–B4. ◗ *Allow 1hr. Entrance via Yrigoyen 849.* ☏ *(011) 4010 3000. Guided tour Mon, Tue and Fri 11am, 4pm (in English) and 11am and 5pm (in Spanish). Take identification.*
If the frontispiece of the metropolitan cathedral is inspired by the Palais Bourbon in Paris, the Argentine National Congress, which houses the Chamber of Deputies and the Senate, clearly resembles the Capitol in Washington. Inaugurated in 1906, the seat of Argentina's legislative branch of government is the work of Italian Victor Meano. It is topped by an imposing bronze dome some 80m/262ft tall in Greco-Roman style.
The first joint session of the Chamber of Deputies and the Senate was opened by President José Figueroa Alcorta in May 1906. In true Buenos Aires style, however, the building was not actually completed until 1946.

Museo del Senado de la Nación

Map II, A4–B4. Yrigoyen 1708. ☏ *(011) 4010 3000. Open Mon–Fri 10am–6pm.*
Just a stone's throw from the Palacio del Congreso, this museum has a collection of furniture, photographs, paintings and documents related to the Senate and its senators, including a copy of the Constitution of Argentina drafted in 1994.

Confitería del Molino★

Map II, B4. On the corner of Rivadavia and Callao.

This somewhat bizarre, Art Nouveau building with a windmill on the top is the source of much intrigue. It can't fail to capture your attention, even though it is next to one of the grandest buildings in town. An old café dating back to 1917, it has been empty since 1997, although its fairly filthy exterior makes this period of abandonment look even longer. It was built by Italian architect **Francesco Gianotti** *(see Galleria Güemes p120).*

Unfortunately, it is not possible to enter so you just have to imagine the interior, filled with marble, ceramic and stained glass all imported from Italy. Alternatively, watch Madonna's *Love Don't Live Here Anymore* video, which was filmed here during its last year before closure. A rainy day is best for spotting the gold tiles on the tower, as they glisten when wet. In its heyday, everyone from Eva Perón to Carlos Gardel frequented the cafe. It was set on fire during a military coup in 1930 and reconstructed. There have been various campaigns to reopen it over the years.

Tribunales

Map II, B2–3 and Map III, A1.

The Avenida Roque Saenz Peña, also known as the Diagonal Norte, links the Plaza de Mayo to the Plaza Lavalle and around it is the Tribunales sector, which, as can be guessed from its name, houses the Buenos Aires tribunal and everything to do with justice. The area is bordered on the west side by giant central throughway, Avenida 9 de Julio.

Avenida 9 de Julio★ and Obelisco★

Map II, B2–3 and Map III, A1. ◗ *Allow 20mins. Central point (or Plaza de la República) demarcated by Lavalle, Irigoyen, Samiento and Cerrito.*

The Diagonal Norte cuts across the **Avenida 9 de Julio** (Avenue of July 9), which at 140m/153yd wide is one of the widest avenues in the world. It hardly needs to be said that it's impossible to cross it in one go: make the most of each stop at the lights to appreciate the incredible view that stretches out for almost 4km/2.5mi. Named in honor of the day of Argentinian Independence, July 9 1816, its construction was begun in 1937 and it was created by the Franco-Argentinian architect and landscape designer **Carlos Thays** *(see p194).*

Travel Tip:

In the States, a yellow light means slow down, but in Buenos Aires, lights also turn yellow before they go from red to green. This serves to let everyone know that a green light is coming and gives drivers a chance to really start accelerating before the light actually turns green. So if you hear drivers revving up their engines on a yellow light don't become too alarmed.

INDEPENDENT (OFF BROADWAY) THEATERS ...LIKE A LOCAL

Theaters are a huge industry in Buenos Aires, particularly in the San Nicolás area. You can always head to the Avenida Corrientes or "the street that never sleeps," which plays host to Broadway plays. But locals know there is more to see beyond these extravagant performances. Instead, check out the many independent theaters, known as "off Corrientes."

Like all small theaters, the productions are much less showy than the average Broadway play. But if you are looking to practice your Spanish or see some truly authentic stories acted out on the stage, look no further than this area.

Prices for these independent theater shows vary from US$10 at small theaters to US$100 at more widely known ones. Here are some of the best independent, or "off Corrientes," theaters you should explore while in the area:

Teatro el Vitral
Rodriguez Pena 344.
The amazing historical setting has this theater in an old mansion just off the main strip. This small independent theater presents a range of theatrical performances, including musicals and one-man acts.

Teatro Astral
Av. Corrientes 1693.
Although this is one of the main revue theaters in the area, it should not be missed! The cabaret-style shows are full of leggy star attractions with some great can-can moves. This theater also runs the huge Broadway hits.

El Camarin de las Musas
Mario Bravo 960.
This is, literally, an underground theater. Many of the plays presented at this arthouse theater are based on local books and literature.

COLLATERAL TRIBUTE

Although the name of San Nicolás is hardly ever used except in an official manner to refer to the district more commonly known as El Centro, the *barrio* was called this in memory of the Church of San Nicolás de Bari that formerly stood at the intersection of Avenida Corrientes and Calle Carlos Pellegrini. It was in this church that the Argentinian flag was first raised in 1812, and yet it was one of the collateral victims of the construction of Avenida 9 de Julio in 1937. In its place now stands the Obelisco of Buenos Aires.

Today it cuts its way through the heart of the city, but it hasn't always been this way—back in 1940 it was only five blocks long and was more of a plaza than an avenue. It was another 10 years until the buildings between Cerrito and Carlos Pelligrini were leveled to extend the avenue. At Plaza de la República, the iconic **Obelisco★** rises 67.5m/ 221ft into the air.

The work of architect Alberto Prebisch, it was inaugurated in 1936 in commemoration of the fourth centenary of the city's first settlement. On each of its four sides is inscribed a key date in the history of Buenos Aires: the first settlement of the city in 1536, the second in 1580, the first time the Argentinian flag was hoisted in 1812 and the naming of Buenos Aires as the country's capital in 1880. Its Rationalist aesthetic has long been a source of controversy and it came within an inch of being demolished.

Plaza Lavalle

Map II, B2–3. ❍ *Allow 15mins. Demarcated by Córdoba, Talcahuano, Libertad and Lavalle.*

Plaza Lavalle is one of the city's main squares, pleasantly shaded by 100-year-old trees and dotted with various statues and monuments, including the one built in honor of the pro-Independence general Juan Lavalle (1797-1841). The square occupies the equivalent of three blocks, separated by the *calles* Tucumán and Viamonte, and covers an area of more than 4ha/9.9 acres. It is lined with some of the city's most prestigious administrative and cultural buildings.

Templo de la Congregación Israelita

Map II, B2. ❍ *Allow 45mins. Libertad 761.* ✆ *(011) 4123 0832. www.templolibertad.org.ar. www.museojudio.org.ar. Museum Tue–Thu 3–6pm, Fri 3–5pm. 30 A$. Bring identification.*

Location:
Demarcated by Tucumán, Talcahuano, Lavalle and Uruguay.
Subte: Carlos Pellegrini (line B), Diagonal Norte (line C), 9 de Julio and Tribunales (line D).
Bus nos.: 5, 6, 22, 24, 26, 28, 29, 33, 54, 56, 61, 62, 64, 74, 75, 91, 93, 99, 100, 105, 106, 111, 126, 130, 132, 140, 143, 146, 152, 195.

Travel Tip:
Avenida 9 de Julio is one of the world's largest avenues measuring 140m/153yd wide, with more than 9 lanes each side. It's grandiose and impressive but it's also deadly. Argentina has the highest rate of road deaths in Latin America (approximately one person is killed every hour) and this is a particularly dangerous stretch.

Travel Tip:
If you don't have the
time or the budget
to see a show at the
Teatro Colón, you still
shouldn't miss seeing
the building, which
is considered to be
among the five best
concert venues in the
world. Take a tour *(see
opposite)*; just keep in
mind that the general
staff at the theater
finish work around
two, so book an earlier
tour so you don't
miss any behind-the-
scenes activity.

The first synagogue in the city, built in 1897, was modi-fied extensively in 1932, drawing on Romantic and Byzan-tine influences. Today it serves one of the largest Jewish communities in the world. It also has a small museum on site, the **Museo Judío de Buenos Aires Dr. Salvador Kibrick**.

The collection was donated by the man of the same name, who was a member of the congregation. His be-longings have since been added to by other benefactors. On display are *sidurim* (books of prayers), old maps of the colonies, replicas of synagogue windows from Toledo in Spain and documents detailing Argentina's first Jewish immigrants.

Palacio de Justicia de la Nación

Map II, B3. ❍ *Allow 1hr. Talcahuano 550.*
✆ *(011) 4114 5791. www.csjn.gov.ar. Free guided tour Friday 2.30pm (Spanish). Call in advance and bring identification.*

To the southwest of the square, the seat of judiciary power and the Supreme Court of justice covers a whole block. This imposing Neo-classical building was designed by the architect Norbert Maillart. The main hall houses a monumental sculpture, Justice, by Rogelio Yrurtia. It is also known as the Palacio de Tribunales, or simply Tribunales.

Teatro Colón★★★

Map II, B3 and Map III, A1. ❍ *Allow 1hr. Libertad 621, on the corner of Tucumán.* ✆ *(011) 4378 7127. www.teatrocolon.org.ar. Guided tour from Tucumán 1171, in English 11am, midday , 1pm, 2pm. 60 A$.*

On the other side of the square—and taking up an entire block—is the famous Teatro Colón, one of the most prestigious opera houses in the world. Founded in 1857, it was originally sited on the Plaza de Mayo and moved to the Plaza Lavalle only in 1908. Three architects were in charge of

EL BAJO

Centro is known for its banks and financial significance, but there is a smaller, sketchier neighborhood located within it that houses some of the area's more popular bars and restaurants. The area El Bajo (which means "the low point") used to be the city's red light district until recent years when hipster bars started popping up, bringing in tourists and young locals alike. El Bajo got its less-than-desirable reputation because of the sailors who used to make port in nearby Puerto Madero and head to El Bajo looking for a good time. The owners and investors that are now opening up bars and restaurants in this area are calling it "Nuevo Bajo" (New Bajo).

its construction, the Italians Francisco Tamburini and Victor Meano, then the Belgian Julio Dormal, which doubtless explains its eclectic style, a mixture of neo-Renaissance Italian and French Baroque.

After a lengthy renovation project, which spanned the best part of four years, following numerous delays and complications, the theater finally reopened in 2010, just in time for the nation's bicentenary. The outside may have stoic majesty, but it is the **interior★★★** that really sends jaws crashing to the floor. Here you are greeted by Italian marble staircases, antique furniture and delicate stained-glass ceilings.

The phenomenal 2,500-seat main auditorium has tiers reaching up to the gods and is crowned with an immense dome, decorated with a fresco by 20C artist Raúl Soldi in an earlier renovation project. The very top level—known as "paraiso" (paradise)—has standing room for a further 1,000 and tickets sell for just a few pesos.

Visitors who don't manage to catch a performance can at least take advantage of the tours, which include the main auditorium, plus backstage, and costume and props workshops.

Known for its remarkable acoustics, the Colón also has its own philharmonic orchestra, choir and ballet company.

Teatro Nacional Cervantes

Map II, B2. ◗ *Allow 30mins. Córdoba and Libertad.*
✆ *(011) 4815 8817. www.teatrocervantes.gov.ar.*
Open (box office) Wed–Sun 10am–9pm. Museum open Mon–Fri 10am–6pm. Guided tours Wed 2.30pm and 3.30pm.

A bit farther on, the Teatro Nacional Cervantes, which opened in 1921, is another important theater in the capital and makes a splendid sight on the corner of a commercial street. It was built with collaboration from the city's high society and King Alfonso XIII of Spain.

In 1961, a fire ripped through it, nearly destroying the entire building and renovations have been slowly progressing over the decades, with scaffolding often still fixed to the elaborate frontage.

As well as putting on a variety of plays, musicals and dance shows, both classic and contemporary, the theater also screens movies, often with series based on special themes, such as the works of a great Argentinian actor or director. The **Museo Nacional del Teatro** *(Córdoba 1199)* contains costumes, scripts and photographs of stars, while presenting a history of Argentinian theater.

ASK PETER...

Q: I'm curious about buying tickets to the Teatro Colón.

A: Seeing a show at Teatro Colón is one of the quintessential experiences of Buenos Aires, but it can also be a bit tricky. Most travelers find it simplest to go through a travel agency to buy tickets, but it's possible, not to mention less expensive, to do this on you own. There are two ways to buy tickets: in person and online. Teatro Colón sells tickets on its website: https://www.tuentrada.com/colon/Online/. The only issue with buying tickets online is that many performances are not listed on the theater website. If you want the full range of events, it's worth stopping in at the Teatro Colón box office. The Teatro periodically offers free shows that are not advertized online.

The *barrio* of Retiro may be small, but it's well worth a visit. Within this neighborhood is Buenos Aires' main plaza, and two very different sub-neighborhoods.

As you'll read, Retiro is known for the Plaza San Martín, which is the most famous pedestrian walkway in all of Buenos Aires. Along with many of the parks in the city, landscaper Charles Thays was involved in the design. If you're looking for a green space within the city, consider that Thays filled the Plaza San Martín with more than 350 trees, using regional species like ceibos, gomeros, ombues, tipas, jacarandas, palos borrachos and tilos. Tourists may be seen in the southwest corner of the *plaza* taking photos in front of the giant bronze equestrian statue of the *plaza's* namesake—Argentinean Independence hero Don José de San Martín. But the *plaza* is also a real local experience. The *plaza's* central location makes it a popular local hangout. Throughout the week, you can find *porteños* using the *plaza* to sunbathe, have a picnic, play soccer or simply relax on the grass.

Around the *plaza* are some of the city's most exclusive properties and palatial mansions that hold museums, embassies and government ministries. Standouts in this area include the Marriot Plaza Hotel, one of the most famous hotels in Buenos Aires, and the Kavanagh Building, once the tallest building in South America. Equally impressive is the Estación Retiro, a complex of railroad terminals at the northern end of Plaza San Martín. The English-style station is the gateway to the northern *barrios* of Buenos Aires and the largest public transportation hub in the city.

PETER'S TOP PICKS

 HISTORY

Want a different way to
learn about Argentine
history? The historic
weapons museum,
Museo de Armas de la
Nación, has weapons
dating from the 12C
to the present day and
the collections at the
Palacio San Martín has
everything from pre-
Columbian pottery
to 20C art. **Museo de
Armas de la Nación
(p 139) Palacio San
Martín (p 137)**

 GREEN SPACES

If you're only going to go
to one park in Buenos
Aires, make it Plaza San
Martín. It's one of the
city's most famous green
spaces and a good place
to take a break. **Plaza San
Martín (p 134)**

 CULTURE

Estación Retiro is more
than a commuter hub, it's
also national monument.
Note that the design
is more historic than
unique; it's modeled
after London's famous
Crystal Palace, destroyed
by fire in 1936. Another
standout cultural
highlight you should visit
in the neighborhood is
the Latin American Art
Museum. **Estación Retiro
(p 134) Museo de Arte
Hispanoamericano Isaac
Fernández Blanco
(p 142)**

 EAT

If you want a quick bite
as you pass through
Retiro, consider stopping
in the Estación Retiro.
You can find fast
food that fills up local
commuters, as well as
a lovely historic cafe.
Estación Retiro (p 134)

Location: The heart of the Retiro district, between San Martín and Ramos Mejia.
Subte: San Martín and Retiro (line C).
Bus nos.: 3, 5, 6, 7, 9, 10, 17, 20, 22, 23, 26, 28, 33, 45, 50, 54, 56, 59, 61, 62, 67, 70, 75, 86, 91, 92, 93, 100, 101, 106, 108, 109, 111, 115, 126, 129, 130, 132, 140, 142, 143, 150, 152, 195.

Travel Tip:

"Che boludo, veni aca!" If you're wondering why so many Argentinians can't seem to go a sentence without including a *che* or a *boludo* in there, don't bother, just do as the Argentines do (but be sure to practice with caution). To an Argentine, *che* has three uses: it can mean "hey you," it can mean "dude" or "buddy," and lastly, it may simply be used as a meaningless utterance to keep a conversation going. *Boludo* on the other hand, must be practiced with caution; a *boludo* is either a jerk/idiot or a meaningless name used amongst friends.

Plaza San Martín *and Around*

Map II, C1-2

Plaza San Martín is at the heart of a neighborhood called Retiro (meaning "retreat" in Spanish), named after a monastery that once lay on its spot in the late 17C. Today, it is a busy transportation hub, home to the city's flagship train station and a vast bus terminal. The area is frequented on a daily basis by a huge cross-section of life, including smartly dressed office workers, tourists from the numerous nearby hotels and residents of the nearby Villa 31, one of the city's most established shanty towns. Keep safe by not straying past the bus station down Avenida de Los Inmigrantes and by protecting your belongings from pickpockets.

Plaza San Martín★

Map II, C2. ◗ *Allow 20 mins.*

Designed by the landscape architect **Charles Thays** *(see p194)*, this large and symbolic square is built around a grand statue of General San Martín, the so-called "liberator" of Argentina, who has been captured here in bronze, looking dominant on horseback. Liberally shaded with palm trees, gum trees and giant magnolias, the plaza is typically filled with workers from nearby offices reclining on the grass during their lunch breaks, while families use the lawn for games at the weekends. In recent years, Argentina's big international soccer games—such as the World Cup and the Copa América—have been shown here on big screens. Before receiving its late 19C makeover, the area had been a slave market, bullring and fort.

Estación Retiro

Map II, C1. ◗ *Allow 15mins. Ramos Mejía 1358.*

Opened in 1915, this grand, British-built station was inspired by London's Crystal Palace, with its huge steel framework shipped over from Liverpool. In 1997, it was declared a National Monument. It's typically heaving with people trying to make a living, from commuters heading to the neighboring business district to the immigrant street vendors peddling their wares on the sidewalk.

If you're hungry, keep a lookout for the fast-food outlet by the right of the exit as you walk in; it is admirable less for its average *panchos* (hot dogs), but more for providing work to disabled employees. The station also has a nicely renovated **cafe**, with ornate plaster columns and a stained-glass roof, which is a great spot for people-watching. Retiro station is the end point for many suburban lines and the C line of the *subte* metro system. There are a few long-distance services too.

Edificio Kavanagh

Map II, C2. ⚫ *Allow 15mins. Florida 1065.*
Plaza San Martín is dominated to the south by the astonishing stepped profile of the **Kavanagh Building**, a 120m/394ft, 32-story residential building. It was built in 1936 at the request of millionaire Corina Kavanagh. The story goes that Kavanagh wanted to marry a son of the aristocratic Anchorena family, but, as she was a member of

---

VILLA 31

Every major city in Latin America has its *villas miseria* (shanty towns or slums), and although Buenos Aires is an upper-middle income city, it has its share of big-city woes. The shanty towns of Latin America first appeared at the beginning of the 20C and started to grow substantially during the 1930s as immigrants from Europe began to arrive in the country. Today, government initiatives, gentrification and new construction projects have reduced the number of shanty towns in central Buenos Aires, making Villa 31 the last. Beyond the Estación Retiro in the northern part of the *barrio*, Villa 31 is a sub-neighborhood of makeshift settlements next to the freeway, home to an estimated 30,000 people. Standing in stark contrast to the opulence of southern Retiro, nowhere else in the city does the divide between the haves and the have-nots feel so pronounced.

In the early 1970s, an activist named Emma Almiron began working on ways to help the marginalized people of Villa 31 with a knitting cooperative. Knitting has not only become a hobby in this area, it has actually become a means for survival. Women meet every Thursday to learn how to knit or continue their creations together, providing a source of income, a much-needed support network and a sense of self-worth. The women are paid between 15 and 30 pesos for their knitted sweaters and it allows them to provide for their families. You can help the women with their efforts by purchasing sweaters or making a donation to help Emma Almiron continue with her project. Email Emma at emma@villa31.org and check out http://www.villa31.org for more information.

ASK PETER...

Q: As one of Buenos Aires' largest parks, does Plaza San Martín have free activities?
A: Many locals gather at Plaza San Martín, but don't count on organized activities. Instead, think of casual pickup soccer games, picnics and the like. As one of the central points in the city, the park has played host to a series of free exhibits. In 2009, the park hosted the United Buddy Bears exhibit, an international arts exhibit originating in Berlin and featuring over 350 fiberglass bears. The newspaper *Clarín* also hosted a large-scale journalistic photo exhibition in the park.

THE ANCHORENAS

"As rich as an Anchorena" was the phrase heard in Buenos Aires in the early 20C. The family of the same name was one of the biggest landowners in the entire country, owning almost 400,000ha/988,000 acres. Their power and influence was further enhanced by some astute marriages. Among their clan was Tomás Manuel de Anchorena, one of the politicians who signed the nation's Independence treaty in 1816; Aaron Anchorena, the first person, along with Jorge Newberry, to cross the River Plate in a balloon in 1908; and Matriarch Mercedes Castellanos de Anchorena, who proudly built her own church in the neighborhood, the Basílica del Santísimo Sacramento (San Martín 1039) in 1916. Originally living near Plaza de Mayo, they, like many families, moved farther north and left their mark on the Retiro area by creating the fabulous **Palacio Anchorena**, later renamed **Palacio San Martín★** *(see p137)*. The palace became known for its illustrious receptions, with distinguished guests—President Roque Saenz Peña was among regular visitors. The family was like royalty in the area and it is said they came to view Plaza San Martín as their own private garden. It is, therefore, easy to imagine their horror when a young upstart decided to undermine their status by building the **Kavanagh Building** in their supposed backyard *(see above)*.

Like many rich families of the time, their fortune disintegrated when the Great Depression hit in the 1930s. Look out for their tomb in Recoleta Cemetery.

the *nouveau riche*, she was deemed unsuitable. To spite them, she ploughed all her fortunes into building one of the most shockingly modern buildings the city had ever seen and with it took away the thing the Anchorena family prized the most: their view of the church they built— the Church of the Holy Sacrament—which was previously visible from their mansion, **Palacio San Martín★** *(see below)*. The church is now hidden almost completely from view. The Art-Deco apartment block is said to resemble a ship at sea and it points towards the River Plate.

Palacio San Martín★

Map II, C2. ❷ *Allow 35mins for tour. Arenales 761.* ✆ *(011) 4819 8092. www.mrecic.gov.ar. Guided tours Wed and Thu 2.30pm.*

Palacio San Martín serves as the ceremonial headquarters for the Ministry of Foreign Relations, having been acquired by the state in 1936. It was originally known as the Anchorena Palace, after the prestigious family who built it between 1905 and 1909 in its ornate Beaux-Arts style. It was designed by architect **Alejandro Christophersen** (1866-1946), who was born in Spain, trained in Paris and Antwerp, and later settled in Argentina. His eclectic take on the *hôtel particulier* has little modesty to it and was designed to make a statement. Behind a Neoclassical entrance are three residences, organized around a ceremonial courtyard and an impressive staircase.

The palace houses works by Argentine and American artists of the 20C, such as Antonio Berni, Pablo Curatella Manes, Lino Enea Spilimbergo, Roberto Matta and others. There is also a pre-Columbian collection, featuring pieces of pottery, stone and metalwork from the country's northwest.

Palacio Estrugamou

Map II, C1. ◗ *Allow 5mins. Esmeralda 1319*

Huge iron gates keep passersby from wandering into this purely residential building, but it is worth noting for being another example of how, after Independence, Argentina sought to lose its ties with Spain and looked instead to France. Curving around the corner and taking up almost an entire block, this landmark building was commissioned in 1924 by landowner Alejandro Estrugamou.

Divided into four sections, it is arranged around a patio, which is adorned with a bronze copy of the iconic Winged Victory of Samothrace. Many of the materials used in its construction came from France. The mansard roof and multiple balconies are typically French. The style is similar to other buildings in the neighborhood, such as **Palacio San Martín★** *(see above).*

Palacio Paz★★

Map II, C2. ◗ *Allow 1hr 30mins. Santa Fe 750.* ✆ *(011) 4311 1071. www.palaciopaz.com.ar. Guided tour (Spanish) Wed–Sat 11am, Tue–Fri 3pm; (English) Wed and Thu 3.30pm. 35 A$.*

On the corner of Avenue Santa Fe and Calle Maipú, this imposing building—also known as **Palacio Retiro**—is one of the city's most deluxe palaces and a witness to Buenos Aires' *grand époque.* Built in the early 20C, it belonged to **José C. Paz**, a politician, journalist and the founder of the newspaper La Prensa. Paz worked at the Argentinian Embassy in Paris from 1885 until 1893, and the heavy influence the city had on him is clear.

When Paz came to commission his family home in Buenos Aires, he decided he wanted to create something on a par with the Louvre and employed French architect Louis Sortais to help realize his dreams. The resulting legacy building has all the hallmarks of a classic French palace—from the indomitable frontage to the Louis XIV-inspired interior décor, which includes lashings of gold leaf.

Sadly Paz died in 1912, two years before the palace was completed. Sortais, who carried out the entire project without visiting Argentina, also died before his work was finished.

Travel Tip:

Believe it or not, Argentina is experiencing one of the strangest economic crises around. There is a coin shortage in Argentina affecting everyone: store owners refuse to sell goods to those who do not have exact change; taxis have to round up or down depending on the fare amount; store owners display signs *No hay monedas* ("We have no coins"). So any change that comes into your possession, hold onto for dear life; especially since the most popular form of transportation in Buenos Aires are city buses, which only accept coins.

ARGENTINA'S NATIONAL FLAG

You'll see the national flag of Argentina everywhere you go in Buenos Aires, but few people make time to understand its symbolism. Argentina's history is, of course, integral to the design of the flag; however there are conflicting theories as to its origin.

The Argentinian flag is described as a triband flag with two horizontal bands of light blue at the top and bottom and a white band in the middle. The design is completed with the yellow Sun of May in the center.

But how did this intricate flag come about? Manuel Belgrano, a military leader who took part in the wars of Independence, created the flag in 1812. The flag was first raised in the city of Rosario during that same war; the site now holds the National Flag Memorial.

Belgrano began to take interest in the flag when he noticed that both the royalists and patriots in Argentina were using Spain's official colors, yellow and red. The use of the flag was not initially accepted as it was considered an Independence act. Belgrano's original design was declared the national flag four years later on July 20, 1816 by the Congress of Tucumán, shortly after Argentina's Declaration of Independence from Spain.

The Sun of May, which is a replica of the first Argentine coin, was not officially added to the flag until 1818. The flag with the sun emblem is considered the official ceremonial flag, whereas the flag without the sun is considered the ornamental flag. The ornamental version is always raised below the official ceremony flag, but both are considered the national flag.

The colors are widely believed to represent devotion to the Virgin Mary. The mother of Christ is usually presented dressed in white and light blue clothing. Belgrano was a devote Catholic and the Virgin Mary was the patron of the Commerce Consulate of Buenos Aires during the Belgrano era.

Although this theory is widely accepted, many recent historians assert that the colors were simply taken from the coat of arms of the House of Bourbon, the Spanish royal family.

Containing 140 rooms and covering 12,000sq m/130,000sq ft, it was the largest home in the city when built, and allegedly it still is. It is not technically a home though today, having been bought by the state in 1938. Its use is now divided between a society for retired military officers, known as the Círculo Militar, and to display the collection of the **National Arms Museum** *(see below)*.

To fully appreciate its architectural magnificence, take the guided tour of the reception rooms. Highlights are the ballroom, which is inspired by the Gallery of Mirrors at the Palace of Versailles and has views out onto Plaza San Martín, and the circular Grand Hall of Honor, with its stunning domed roof.

Palacio Haedo

Map II, C2. Santa Fe 690.

Forming a triangle at the corner of Florida and Santa Fe, this unusual building was built in the 1870s by the aristocratic Haedo family. It is had a series of reformations over the years. First it looked more like an Italianate castle, when it was largely out on a limb as one of the first high-class residences in the area. Later it got the neo-Gothic makeover that still characterizes it today.

The property was later bought by the Banco Popular Argentino and it changed hands again, in 1942, when the national government turned it into the headquarters for the National Parks Administration (APN), which still uses the building today. The APN are proud of their headquarters and, at the turn of the 20C, fought off a private company seeking to buy it. Some renovation work is needed to repair the tired frontage and, at the time of going to press, scaffolding covered the exterior up to the first floor.

Museo de Armas de la Nación

Map II, C2. ◑ *Allow 45mins. Santa Fe 702.* ✆ *(011) 4311 1071. Mon–Fri 1–7pm. 10 A$. Guided tours available with advance booking.*

For enthusiasts, this museum contains an important collection of South American weaponry and relates the history and technical evolution of weapons throughout the world, from the 12C to the present day. Guns, rifles, pistols and swords stand to attention behind glass cases. "Here rest the arms that forged the nation," reads a sign above a room showcasing weapons from the Independence wars, alongside oil paintings depicting the big battles. There is also an interesting little collection of miniature soldiers

Travel Tip:
A good and inexpensive way to experience Buenos Aires is by public transportation—the *colectivo* (bus). You can go everywhere and explore the entire city. Sounds great, right? Well here's a little tip if exploring the city by *colectivo*; *colectivos* are a collection of independently owned operators, which means they don't follow normal public transportation guidelines.

Bus stops, for one thing, are nonexistent (or at least very hard to spot)—you just estimate a bus stop every two blocks or so and wait between 5–10 minutes as *colectivos* frequently pass by; to ensure the bus stops for you, flag it down by raising your arm up and signaling the driver you want to board. Another word of advice—purchase the *Guia T*, a small book including bus routes and city maps.

Travel Tip:
If your wife has
dragged you from
one historical tour
to another, you
might ditch the
next museum and
take a real man's
tour: J.R.'s Classic
Hombre Tour. You'll
spend half the day
exploring different
neighborhoods
(Belgrano, Caballito
and Congreso) where
you'll visit a traditional
barber's shop for a
haircut and straight
razor shave (the
works!); next stop is
a cigar store where
you'll relax with a
nice glass of Scotch
and a Cuban cigar;
and lastly, get fitted
for your very own
custom hat. The tour
is available Tuesday
through Saturday
in the mornings
and afternoons, and
remember, for the
morning of the tour,
don't shave!

from across the ranks, dressed in imitation military regalia. You won't learn much about the country's history here, as the information is generally reduced to labels showing dates and model details. The museum's size is deceptive, with rooms snaking on and on. Right at the back, there is a surprising collection of Japanese Samurai swords and costumes.

Monumento a los Caídos en Malvinas

Map II, C2. ◉ *Allow 10mins.*
Plaza San Martín. Florida and Libertador.

The black marble panels in this horseshoe-shaped cenotaph lists the names of the Argentinian soldiers who died during the 1982 war against the British for governance of the Islas Malvinas, known in Britain as the Falkland Islands *(see p41)*. An eternal flame burns over a metallic rendering of the islands and it is guarded by representatives of the Army, the Navy, and the Air Force, on rotation. If you pass by at 8am, you may see the Argentinian flag being raised. The memorial was inaugurated in 1992 and it is no coincidence that is facing the square formerly known as Plaza Britanica, later renamed Plaza Fuerza Aerea Argentina (Argentina Air Force Square).

Torre Monumental

Map II, C2. ◉ *Allow 30mins.*
Libertador 49. ✆ *(011) 4311 0186.*

At the foot of Place San Martín, directly facing the imposing monument erected in honor of the soldiers who died during the Malvinas/Falklands War, is the ex-*Torre de los Ingleses* (English Tower), renamed Torre Monumental after the 1982 war against the United Kingdom. The 75.5m/247ft structure is often said to resemble Big Ben, although anyone familiar with the original will see that the similarities are loose. This red-brick, copper-roofed clock tower was a gift from the British community of Buenos Aires in 1910 to commemorate the centenary of the Revolution of May 1810. The bells are replicas of those from Westminster Abbey and the building is decorated with British symbols—the Scottish thistle, the English rose, the Welsh dragon and the Irish shamrock. An inscription by the door reads (in Spanish): "To the health of the Great Argentine people, from the British residents, May 25, 1810–1910." Sadly, the viewing tower and museum at the top are currently not open to the public.

BEST VIEWS OF THE CITY...LIKE A LOCAL

If you want a great view of the city, head to the roof. The Art Deco-style Kavanagh Building is located right next to the Marriott Hotel and it's a local favorite. Although it's mainly used as an office building, what many people don't know is that you are allowed to go up to the roof, and it has one of the best panoramic views of the entire city.

Located a short distance away from the Kavanagh Building is the Palacio Barolo, a landmark office building located on Avenida de Mayo. When first completed in 1923, it was the tallest building in the city, but was quickly superceded by the Kavanagh Building in 1935. Although the building is nothing special on the inside—it's mainly law offices—it has one of the best views of the most iconic street in Argentina. At night, after the building is closed, you can even get a guided tour of the structure. Check it out every Monday and Thursday from 4pm to 7pm and make sure you get to the top for some spectacular views.

Another spectacular view, although admittedly a little more touristy than the others, is from the Torre Monumental (the so-called English Tower). Located in the heart of Retiro, this Elizabethan-style building represents a little piece of Britain in the middle of the city. In the past, you've been able to go up the tower and get spectacular views of the city, as well as learn a bit of the history behind the tower and what it means to locals. It's not currently open, but there is tourist information at the foot of the tower and they might be able to give you information about its reopening.

It's not necessarily something a local would do, but take it from the locals, one of the best places to stay in Retiro (and arguably Buenos Aires) is the Marriott Plaza Hotel. Although it's a chain, don't overlook it. It was the first five-star hotel in Buenos Aires and to this day is still one of the most historical hotel buildings in the city. It also has fabulous views. Make sure you stay in one of the Vista Plaza rooms, which have an amazing view of Plaza San Martín and makes for a great place to people-watch. Some of the hotel suites also have rooftop terraces, so if you're in the mood for a little luxury, be sure to book a suite and enjoy incredible views over the city.

Location:
Suipacha 1422,
between Libertador
and Esmeralda.
Subte: San Martín
and Retiro (line C).
Bus nos.: 5, 6, 7,
9, 10, 17, 22, 23, 26,
28, 33, 45, 50, 56, 60,
61, 62, 67, 70, 75, 91,
92, 93, 100, 101, 106,
108, 111, 115, 129,
130, 132, 143, 150,
152, 195.

ASK PETER...

Q: Where can I find cheap leather without falling into any tourist traps?

A: Visit Centro de Cuero in Retiro for your one-of-a-kind find. Here you will find *fabricantes de cuero* (manufacturers) who will not only give you the best deals in town (deals that are given to vendors, after a little haggling of course) but will also personally tailor your own leather jacket, and have it delivered to your hotel room a week later, all for the tidy sum of about US$200.

Museo de Arte Hispanoamericano Isaac Fernández Blanco★★

Located in the Palacio Noel, a superb example of the neoColonial architecture that was in vogue in the 1920s, this museum houses a splendid collection of **Spanish Colonial art** from the 16C to 19C (furniture, silverware, goldwork, sacred objects, paintings and ceramics). It focuses on various South American cultures, most of which contributed to the building of the *criolla* identity, the first Argentinian identity.

Map II, B1–C1 ◗ *Allow 1–2hrs. Suipacha 1422.*
(011) 4327 0228/72. www.museos.buenosaires.gov.ar.
Open Tue–Fri 2–7pm, Sat, Sun and public holidays 11am–
7pm. 1 A$ (Free Thu). Guided tour (in Spanish): Sat and
Sun 3pm and 5pm.

Moving away from the obsession to try to recreate Paris on the River Plate's shores, architect **Martin Noel** (1888-1963) was considered one of the leading figures who helped kick-start the first wave of nationalism. He trained in France and traveled widely in Europe and South America, before deciding to bring together a mixture of traditions and styles into the design of his palace, which was finished in 1922. Inside the courtyard, but before going into the main building, note the Lima-style balconies, the Arequipa gateway and the Andalusian garden—today incongruously backed by a string of skyscrapers. Inside the building has some fabulous carved doors and tiled floors, plus a painted ceiling that imitates the work of the Jesuits in Córdoba.

In 1936, Noel sold the house, and all the art within it, to the state for a token sum and, in 1943, it was amalgamated with the extensive collection amassed by a *porteño* engineer **Isaac Fernández Blanco**, who used an inherited fortune to buy fabulous objects from all over Latin America.

The museum's main focus is looking at how native cultures and Colonial traditions blended. It includes a mix of works, from Cuzco school paintings to Spanish furniture.

To the left of the main hallway is a display of Guarani and Jesuit iconography. Upstairs looks at the creation of the *criolla* identity and the importance of the Virgin Mary as an

THE IMMIGRANTS' HOTEL

By the railway lines, alongside Avenue Libertador, stands a four-story, red-brick structure that looks like a forgotten warehouse, but is actually one of the most significant buildings in the whole country. From 1911 to 1953, **El Hotel de los Inmigrantes** (Immigrants' Hotel) was the first stop for those coming off the boats from Europe to begin their new lives in the southern hemisphere. It's the equivalent of New York's Ellis Island and, similarly, there are plans to turn it into more of an attraction. The building was previously used as a museum—hence word *museo* painted in large white letters on the front—but it is currently closed for a major renovation project. At the time of going to press, a reopening date had not been set. The hotel was part of a complex constructed to offer accommodation, advice and services to the newcomers. After having their luggage checked and passing a medical examination, they were given five days' free board here. The building could sleep 4,000 people, with up to 250 people per room in dormitory bunks.

There were interpreters on site, a job center, a branch of the Banco de la Nacion Argentina to change foreign currencies and a well-equipped hospital for treating those who were made ill by the long journey. One of the main rooms had a display of agricultural machinery and, during the day, men were given lessons on how to use them. After closing, it became a place for Argentinians to trace their roots. A database of almost four million arrivals has been collected here—listing each entrant's age, civil status, profession and religion—and it is continually being added to. As one of the officials working on the project said, "Almost no one in this country has grandparents who were [indigenous] Argentinian". A vast percentage will, however, have had a relative who has passed through these doors.

artistic muse. There is also a recreation of some extravagant living quarters in Potosí, Alto Perú (present-day Bolivia), when the city's silver mines were at the height of production, and a bedroom from the times of the viceroyalty of the Río de la Plata. The basement holds a collection of Spanish ceramics in what used to be in the building's kitchen, along with a room showcasing various objects from 19C Argentina.

All the signs are in Spanish, making it tricky for those who don't read the language, but it is worth a visit purely to see the building and the workmanship of many of the items speaks for itself.

Palacio Noel was damaged by the 1992 bombing of the Israeli Embassy next door. Twenty-nine civilians were killed in the attack and 242 were injured. Today, a memorial plaza stands at the spot, with a plaque in both Hebrew and Spanish.

DISCOVERING
SAN TELMO★★
AND PUERTO
MADERO★

It always surprises me how much Puerto Madero and San Telmo have in common. Despite the fact Puerto Madero is one of the newest neighborhoods in Buenos Aires and San Telmo is one of the oldest, they share a similar sort of glamour.

Puerto Madero was originally the main port of Buenos Aires. Many of the luxury hotels, offices and bistros found in this district are housed in refurbished brick warehouses along former dockyards. Trendy and expensive, Puerto Madero's waterfront real estate is the priciest in all of Buenos Aires if not all of South America. It's also considered the safest part of the city. Though this high-end *barrio* may lack some of the color of older neighborhoods, it is pedestrian-friendly and is a local favorite for an afternoon stroll. You can take a walk or a bike ride along the docks, or wander through the open boulevards of the neighborhood. There are also plenty of cafes and restaurants from simple fast food to exotic international dishes. During the day, the area attracts businessmen from nearby San Nicolás, while at night Puerto Madero hosts the city's elite. A barrio almost completely on the water, it makes sense that some of its best places are not on land. Puerto Madero has two floating museums, both based in old Navy training vessels.

If Puerto Madero is modern Argentina, the tiny *barrio* of San Telmo, southeast of Puerto Madera, is Buenos Aires' past. The entire neighborhood is so historically significant that it is considered a National Historic Monument, since many of the major events in Argentinian history happened here. San Telmo retains most of the features of old Buenos Aires: narrow cobblestone streets, ancient trees and *faroles* (street lamps). Originally this area was home to the rich and powerful of Buenos Aires, who owned large estates called *quintas*. A yellow fever outbreak in the late 1800s drove those families from the area into Retiro and San Martín. The majestic European-style Colonial mansions were abandoned, and become occupied by a new group, low-income immigrant families. Most recently, the neighborhood has gone through another incarnation and now these mansions hold art galleries, artisan workshops, tango halls and restaurants.

PETER'S TOP PICKS

 CULTURE

This guide is full of places to see and dance the tango, so for a truly bizarre tango monument, check out the Monumento al Tango, a large public sculpture that resembles the accordion-like instrument that fuels tango music.
Monumento al Tango (p 155)

 GREEN SPACES

Go from park to ecological reserve: the Parque de las Mujeres Argentinas and Parque Micaela Bastidas link to the Reserva Ecologica Constanera Sur.
Reserva Ecologica Constanera Sur (p 157)

 HISTORY

On the outside, El Zanjón de Granados appears to be an abandoned mansion, but historians went deeper and found a network of underground tunnels that you can now explore. **El Zanjón de Granados (p 149)**

 STAY

The Faena Hotel in Puerto Madero is the locals' choice for its bar and restaurant, so why not consider spending the night there too?
Faena Hotel (p 235)

 EAT

Going local means going to the market. Instead of stopping at a cafe, consider stopping at Mercado de San Telmo to check out the food stalls and the old-school seltzer dispensers.
Mercado de San Telmo (p 147)

 ENTERTAINMENT

If you want to see tango and street performances while you get in a little shopping, check out the Plaza Dorrego during the Sunday antiques fair.
Feria de San Telmo (p 147)

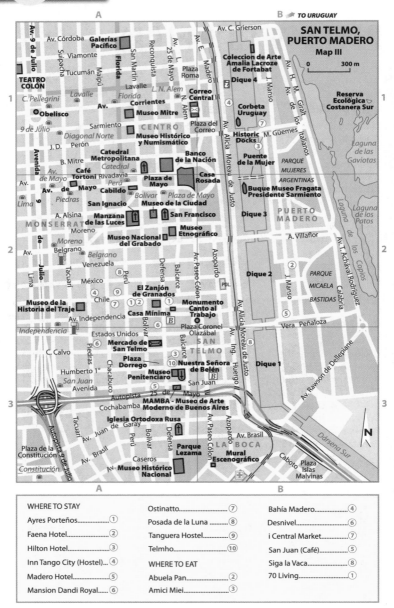

San Telmo, Puerto Madero — Map III

WALKING TOUR

Plaza Dorrego★ *and Around*

The lively heart of San Telmo, Plaza Dorrego, is also one of the oldest squares in Buenos Aires. It is surrounded by cafes and restaurants, with plenty of outdoor seating for the sunny days that come all year round.

Feria de San Pedro Telmo★★ and Mercado de San Telmo

Map III, A3. ◯ *Allow 1–1.5hrs. Feria: Plaza Dorrego; www.feria desantelmo.com; open Sun 10am–5pm. Mercado: Defensa 970; www.mercadodesantelmo.com; open 10am–7pm.*

The square livens up even more on Sundays, when the **Feria de San Telmo** assembles more than 250 crafts and antiques stalls, with street entertainment laid on by mime artists, painters, musicians and tango dancers. On Sunday evenings at around 6pm, the square turns into an outdoor *milonga*, where tango dancers of all abilities strut their stuff in the open air. A block to the north of the square, the **Mercado de San Telmo** (San Telmo market) *(entrance via Defensa, Bolívar, Carlos Calvo and Estados Unidos)* is a vast metal and glass-roofed structure. Behind its Italian-style façade is a hidden food market, with plenty of intriguing stalls selling only-in-Argentina souvenirs, such as retro signs, old soda siphons and *filete* artwork.

MATÉ; ARGENTINA'S NATIONAL DRINK

The earthy, grassy taste (it tastes a bit like green tea) comes from the *yerba maté* plant that is toasted, dried, packaged and aged for 6 to 18 months; the *maté* "cup" is made from a dried-out gourd. Once the *yerba maté* is prepared, hot water and a *bombilla* is added; a *bombilla* is a metal straw with fine holes on one end (to help you avoid getting a mouthful of *yerba maté* when you suck on it) and a gold-colored spout on the other end which stays cool enough to touch your lips. *Maté* is more than a drink in Argentina, it is a way of life. Mr. Mate in San Telmo is a unique establishment serving *yerba maté* for locals and tourists alike to enjoy, just be sure not to go Mondays, as it's closed.

» *Make your starting point Defensa 970, the indoor market. After exploring it fully, head back out the way you came in and turn right down Defensa until you hit Plaza Dorrego. If it's a Sunday, there will be plenty of stalls and entertainment along the way.*

Travel Tip:

After spending the day looking for treasures, the Feria de San Pedro clears out and Plaza Dorrego is transformed into a tango dance hall. It's time to let loose and show off your tango skills in this free and informal outdoor space known as a *milonga*. Locals, tourists and tango-ists extraordinaire all come out to take part in this fun festival of dance. So put on your dancing shoes and enjoy the vibrant San Telmo culture.

147

Travel Tip:
Guided by Australian beer connoisseur Chris Canty, you can't miss this one-of-a-kind beer tour. The 3-hour tour starts at 7pm Tuesdays and Fridays; covering four pubs, the beer lover's tour showcases Argentina's best craft beer from regions including Cordoba, La Plata and outer Buenos Aires. For 80 A$ (US$22) you get six craft beers and a bite to eat (either *choripan* or a burger); not bad for a night on the town.

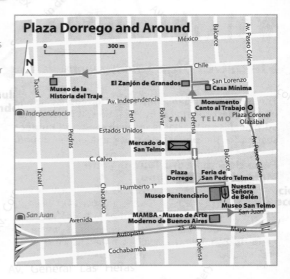

Plaza Dorrego and Around

» *At the corner of the plaza, just next to Plaza Dorrego Bar, turn left down Humberto Primero until you see Iglesia de Nuestra Señora de Belén on your right.*

Iglesia de Nuestra Señora de Belén

Map III, A3. ◗ *Allow 20mins. Humberto Primo 340.* ✆ *(011) 4361 1168. www.parroquiasantelmo.org. Open Mon–Fri 8am–midday, 4–8pm, Sat 9am–1.30pm, 4–8pm, Sun 8am–8pm.*
The parish church of San Pedro Telmo is a heterogeneous mix of Neoclassical, Baroque and post-Colonial styles. This was doubtless not the intention of the first architect, the Jesuit Andrés Blanqui, when construction began in 1734, but the church remained unfinished after the expulsion of the Jesuits in 1767 and was later modified several times. It houses the little **Museo San Telmo** *(open Sun 3.30–6.30pm, guided tour 4pm).*

» *Hop to the Penitentiary Museum at no 378.*

Museo Penitenciario

Map III, A3. ◗ *Allow 30mins. Humberto Primo 378.* ✆ *(011) 4361 0917. Open Wed–Fri 2.30–5.30pm, Sun 1–7pm. 2 A$. Guided tour (Spanish) Sun 2.30pm, 4pm and 5.30pm.*
Converted from an 18C former Jesuit monastery that later became an almshouse and then a women's prison, this penitentiary museum relates the evolution of the Argentinian prison system through photographic archives and reconstructions of prison cells, as well as through various items, secret weapons and clothing made or worn by the prisoners.

Museo de Arte Moderno de Buenos Aires (MAMBA)★

Map III, A3. ❍ *Allow 1hr. San Juan 350. ☏ (011) 4342 3001. www.museodeartemoderno.buenosaires.gob.ar. Open Mon–Fri noon–7pm, Sat, Sun and holidays 11am–8pm. (1 A$, Tue no charge.)*

Not to be confused with the MALBA *(see p188)*, this is the city's brand new modern art museum. After five years and a $15m investment, it held its soft opening in December 2010, with further renovations still underway. The beautiful red-brick building was once a tobacco factory and the number 43 that you see repeated across the frontage was the brand of cigarettes produced here. The original museum project was founded in 1956 and over the years it has accrued over 7,000 works of Argentinian art from the 20C and 21C.

» *Backtrack ever so slightly onto Defensa, turning left away from the plaza. Take the first left onto San Juan.*

Monumento Canto al Trabajo

Map III, A2. Paseo Colón 800.

Situated in a small plaza by the indomitable structure of the Engineering Faculty of the University of Buenos Aires, this larger-than-life bronze sculpture is by Rogelio Yrurtia, Argentina's answer to Auguste Rodin. Unveiled in 1927, the "Ode to Work" depicts 14 figures—men, women and children—dragging a large boulders and is a tribute to the efforts of the working classes.

» *Carry on down San Juan and take the second left onto Paseo Colon. Continue left until you reach the Monument Canto al Trabajo.*

El Zanjón de Granados★★

Map III, A2. ❍ *Allow 30mins–1hr. Defensa 755. ☏ (011) 4361 3002. www.elzanjon.com.ar. Guided tours only (30mins or 1hr) Mon–Fri hourly 11am–4pm (40 A$), Sun every 30mins 1pm–6pm (40 A$). Tours of Casa Minima, Fri 4pm (30 A$, 30mins). Tours in English if requested in advance.*

This early 19C aristocratic residence, abandoned by its owners at the time of the 1871 yellow fever epidemic, was converted into a *conventillo (see box on p150)*. It was not until the 1980s that its more complicated past was revealed, when an amateur historian dug deeper—quite literally—and discovered more than 150m/164yd of underground tunnels.

The Zanjón was a gorge that ran though this part of the city during the 1500s. By delving along its old route, many relics from the country's founding years have been unearthed and are now on display. As you travel through the different levels, you get the sense of peeling back history, which informed guides help bring to life. Not only is

» *The road just after the huge university faculty is Av. Independencia; turn left onto it and walk until you hit Defensa; then turn right this time up to no. 755.*

A BOHEMIAN DISTRICT

At first inhabited by port workers, **San Telmo** became filled with increasingly rich families during the course of the 19C. In 1871, a yellow fever epidemic drove out this wealthy population and saw them taking refuge farther north, in the districts of Retiro, Recoleta and Palermo. Their abandoned homes were converted into *conventillos*, overcrowded residential blocks, where immigrant families, who had recently disembarked in Buenos Aires, lived in poverty. The district, once bourgeois, became bohemian. Tango took its first steps here. Long seen as poor and unsanitary, the neighborhood experienced a revival during the 1960s, when artists began to set up studios. Thereafter, an increasing number of galleries, bars and restaurants opened up, following in the footsteps of these pioneers.

it one of the most important archaeological sites in the city, it also throws a mean party, with regular concerts and events.

Casa Mínima

» Almost opposite El Zanjón de Granados is a small passageway, San Lorenzo, which is just off Defensa between Independencia and Chile. Casa Mínima will be on your right.

Map III, A2. ◗ Allow 5mins. Pasaje San Lorenzo 380. Accessible by guided tour from El Zanjón de Granado.

This intriguing house is famed for being the skinniest property in the city, its frontage measuring less than 2.5m/8.2ft wide. One theory is that this tiny sliver of land was given to a liberated slave in the 1800s; it is more likely, however, that aggressive building in the area simply ate into the original plot. Take a souvenir snap outside, or get between its narrow walls by joining the tour from **El Zanjón de Granados★★** *(see above)*. There are plans to turn it into a museum, but, at the time of going to print, renovations were not finished.

Museo Nacional de la Historia del Traje

» Back on Defensa, turn left down Chile. The final museum is just over four blocks down here. You can stop for refreshment at Café La Poesía (Chile 502).

Map III, A2. ◗ Allow 30mins. Chile 832. ℰ (011) 4343 8427. www.funmuseodeltraje.com.ar. Open Tue–Sun 3–7pm. Guided tour in Spanish Sat and Sun 5pm.

This modest **costume museum** contains clothing and accessories from the 17C to the present day, which are presented successively in temporary thematic exhibitions. It's based out of an attractive 19C house, with an internal patio and stained-glass windows, an historic monument in itself and perhaps the main attraction.

MARKETS
...LIKE A LOCAL

Whenever someone asks for the number-one way to have a local experience, head straight to the market. Buenos Aires has a variety of markets that are not only interesting and culturally diverse places to sightsee, but, if you look further than the tourist souvenirs and bric-á-brac, they also offer great deals on fresh foods, antiques and handicrafts. Wander around, soak up the atmosphere and grab some authentic Argentinian food. Get to know the vendors and participate in a local tradition that's been around for centuries.

One of the oldest markets in the area can be found in San Telmo—the **Mercado Municipal**. It's a thriving indoor food market that has been around since the 1890s. You'll find tons of local fruit, vegetables, fish and various meats to buy and enjoy. The market itself is an historic experience. Designed by Italian architect Juan Antonio Buschiazzo, the building was restored at the end of the 20C.

San Telmo is also home to the famous antiques fair on Plaza Dorrego, the **Feria de San Telmo**, which every Sunday attracts locals and tourists alike. Looking for something unique? Look no further than the antiques fair, selling heirlooms, jewelry and treasures. One caution, in the past decade the market has transformed from traditional antiques to more kitsch and souvenirs. Intermixed with the shopping are street performances and tango, both on the square and on nearby Defensa.

Another popular market with the locals is the **Feria de Mataderos**, an arts and crafts market, located in the southwest of Buenos Aires near Avenida de los Corrales. Described as the place "where city and country meet," this market is more than just food, it's also a great place to find handmade jewelry, leather, and wood carvings, all by local merchants. All in all the market is a more traditional and local experience than the Mercado Municipal, but you'll also find some entertainment. The market features a stage where local musicians play traditional music and gauchos appear to show off their horsemanship.

Location:
Demarcated by
the Defensa and
the *avenidas* Brasil,
Paseo Colón and
Martín García, Parque
Lezama marks the
boundary between
the districts of San
Telmo and La Boca.
Subte: Constitucion
(line C), plus a seven-
block walk.
Bus nos.: 4, 9, 10, 17,
22, 24, 28, 29, 33, 39,
45, 46, 53, 61, 62, 64,
65, 70, 74, 86, 93, 126,
129, 130, 143, 152,
159, 168, 195.

Parque Lezama *and Around*

Map III, AB3.

According to some historians, the park occupies the site where the first colony was established in 1536. A bronze statue of the founder, Pedro de Mendoza, stands on the corner of Defensa and Brasil.

Mural Escenográfico Parque Lezama

Map IV, A1. ◗ *Allow 10mins. Almirante Brown 36.*

Created by a group of artists working with local theater group Catalinas Sur, this colorful, three-dimensional mural captures life in the working-class neighbourhood of La Boca, using reclaimed materials from an old *conventillo (see p150)*. Among the cartoon-like caricatures that grace the deliberately ramshackled frontage are Italian immigrants, various sailors, accordion players and a dog in a Boca Juniors soccer jersey. There are also some famous faces, including "number 10" soccer player Maradona and tango legend Carlos Gardel.

Iglesia Ortodoxa Rusa

Map III, A3. ◗ *Allow 15mins. Brasil 315.* ℘ *(011) 4361 4274. www.iglesiarusa.org.ar. Open for visits except during services, Sat 6pm and Sun 10am.*

Taking visitors by surprise on the north side of the square are the five star-covered, turquoise domes of the Iglesia Ortodoxa Rusa de la Santísima Trinidad. In the 1890s, the small Russian community petitioned Tsar Alexander III for funds to build the first Orthodox church in South America. The 17C Muscovite-style church was inaugurated in 1904 and is adorned with icons sent by Tsar Nicholas II from St Petersberg.

Museo Histórico Nacional

Map III, A3 and Map IV, A1. ◗ *Allow 20mins. Defensa 1600.* ℘ *(011) 4307 2301. www.cultura.gov.ar. Open Wed–Sun 11am–6pm.*

The park owes its name to José Gregorio Lezama, a rich Buenos Aires merchant (1802-89), whose attractive Italianate mansion today houses the National History Museum. Having enlarged and reorganized its collections, it reopened all its rooms in 2010. The museum takes a traditional approach; on display are pre-Colombian relics, giant historic paintings, and items owned by important figures in Argentina's political and military past.

LITERARY CONNECTIONS

If you've ever read **Jorge Luis Borges**, you might already be familiar with San Telmo, which is featured in several of Borges' short stories. Now an internationally renowned artist, Borges rose to prominence in the 1960s when he won the first-ever awarded Prix Internation-al, a short-lived international literary prize, which he shared with Samuel Beckett. Ten years later, Borges won the Jerusalem Prize, an award given to writers who feature themes of human freedom. As a result of his fame, Borges' works have been translated into many languages and have been distributed all over the world.

A loyal citizen of the city, Borges once wrote, "To me, it seems a mere tale that Buenos Aires had a beginning: I judge her to be as eternal as water and air." Then in his short story El Sur, Borges de-scribes the San Telmo *barrio* as "an older, more solid world."

In *The Aleph*, another famous short story by Borges, the author describes how he discovered, under the 19th step of a basement staircase somewhere along Juan de Garay Street to be exact, the point where all things in the universe converge. In other words, en-lightenment.

If you're looking for a place to soak up Buenos Aires' literary side, in San Telmo you will find **La Poesia** *(Chile 502)*, which was a buzzing literary cafe that closed in the 1980s. Reopened under new man-agement in 2008, the cafe retains it's literary history. In fact, the cafe's wooden tables even have brass plaques that mention the writers who went to the cafe in its earlier incarnation.

Another literary cafe well worth a visit began as a bookstore in 1938. **Clásica y Moderna** *(Callao 892)* now serves up coffee, tea, Argen-tinian wine and cocktails in what has been a center of the intel-lectual community in Buenos Aires ever since the 1930s. Politicians, writers, and artists passed through its doors, gathering to chat and share ideas amongst one of the most comprehensive collection of books on the humanities, philosophy, and literature. Following a revival and modernization in the 1980s, Clásica became a hot spot for book presentations, lectures and cultural meetings—featuring the likes of Isabel Allende, Juan José Sebrili, Abelardo Castillo and David Viñas.

Location:
The four docks of
Puerto Madero
run alongside Av.
Alicia Moreu de
Justo, to the east.
The Costanera Sur
ecological reserve
marks the area's
western border.
Subte: L. N. Alem
(line B).
Bus nos.: 4, 6, 20,
22, 23, 26, 28, 33, 50,
56, 61, 62, 74, 91, 93,
99, 105, 109, 115,
126, 129, 130, 132,
140, 143, 146, 152,
159, 180, 195.

Puerto Madero★

*Map III, B1-2-3. Word of advice: To cross the speedway
that runs alongside the port as far as Puerto Madero by
foot, go down from the San Telmo district via Av. Belgrano,
from Microcentro via Av. Corrientes or from Retiro via Av.
Córdoba. Incidentally, you can also take the Tranvía del Este
tramway, which runs along Av. Alicia Moreau de Justo, from
Independencia to Córdoba.*

**You will need plenty of imagination if you want to find
in Puerto Madero any of the port atmosphere of Old
Buenos Aires, which was renowned for tales of rich car-
goes and immigrants arriving full of hope. Here, there
are no quays cluttered with pallets and moorings, no
great rusting hulls. Instead, everything is impeccably
shipshape. A very successful urban renovation turned
the area into the city's newest and sleekest neighborhood. Today, the only vessels that haunt the great
docks are old sailing ships transformed into museums
and a flotilla of smart yachts. A business district and a
meeting place for modern yuppies, it may not be the
most atmospheric spot in town, but the wide esplanades provide a pleasant place for a waterside stroll
or a meal on an outdoor terrace.**

Historic Docks★

Map III, B1-2-3. ◗ *Allow 30mins. Dique 1–4.* ✆ *(11) 4515
4600. www.puertomadero.com.*
Constructed in the late 19C, these docks faced problems
from the start. Almost as soon as they were finished, they
were outdated and unable to cope with the cargo boats'
increasing size. When the area was abandoned and opera-
tions were moved north, left behind were decaying factories, half-sunk ships and algae-covered water. It was hardly
the sort of place you'd expect Hilton Hotels to move into.
Hence the shock most *porteños* felt when such plans were
announced in the late 1990s, as part of an ambitious regeneration project. The plan was realized by restoring and
converting the old red-brick warehouses that lined the
docks. Along with a few cranes that have been preserved
in situ, it is these that give the four huge docks *(diques)*
their character.
On the east side, landing platforms welcome pleasure
crafts, while the west quays serve as docks for two old sailing ships. On both sides, the high-reaching, ultramodern

skyline demonstrates the project's ambitions, as does the ceaseless construction work.

For a port city, Buenos Aires often seems somewhat disconnected from its river and there are few places, apart from here, where you can have a drink overlooking the water. The area is a hit with wealthy *porteños*, who value the area's security and hole-free sidewalks, and who see owning an apartment here as the ultimate status symbol.

By the waterside, there are plenty of upmarket restaurants, along with some less upmarket ones (including a Hooters), plus a small number of velvet-rope nightclubs and bars. Patrons tend to dress in designer clothes and do not balk at the inflated prices.

Perhaps the most notable renovation is on the east side of the docks, where an 100-year-old mill has been turned into a luxury hotel and apartment complex, the immodestly named Faena Hotel and Universe *(see p236).*

Just behind the Faena Hotel (where Azucena Villaflor meets Avenida de los Italianos) is the **Monumento al Tango**, which resembles a giant *bandonéon*, the accordian-like instrument that is central to the genre.

Corbeta Uruguay★

Map III, B1. ◯ *Allow 15mins. Dique 4. ✆ (011) 4314 1090. Open daily 10am–7pm. 2 A$.*

Built in England in 1874, this corvette was commissioned by President Sarmiento for the Argentine army. She served in the expedition to Antarctica to rescue the Swede Otto Nordenskjöld, who found himself trapped by glaciers during an exploratory expedition in 1903. A 46m/151ft-long, three-masted sailing and steam ship, she was used mainly

THE FIRST SHANTY TOWNS

As with megacities across the world, the divide between rich and poor in Buenos Aires is growing. The first *villas miserias* (shanty towns) appeared at the beginning of the 20C, around the industrial zones, inevitably trailing poverty and social tension in their wake. Built out of whatever materials are to hand, these improvised settlements of sometimes precarious multi-leveled shacks are home to the city's poorest residents. Apart from one close to Retiro bus station *(see p135)* most of these are in the far outskirts. The decision to either clear or urbanize the *villas* is always a hot topic at election time.

ASK PETER...

Q: Where can I find an authentic night out in Puerto Madero?

A: Hotel Faena may be a hotel, but it is also the locals' choice for its bar and restaurant. Locals head to the bar, which might have a live band, or relax in small lounge-style rooms. Wine lovers should look out for the wine list at El Mercado—it's a splurge but worth it. The hotel Rojo Tango is small and exclusive. Check out the show that tells the history of tango. Be sure to dress up before you head over; this is a place to see and be seen and sneakers will not win you many friends.

in defense, as her capacities were reduced in high seas. Subsequently converted into a training ship, the Uruguay has been a museum since 1967.

Buque Museo Fragata Presidente Sarmiento★★

Map III, B2. ◗ *Allow 15mins. Dique 3.* ✆ *(011) 4334 9386. Open daily 10am–7pm. 2 A$.*

More impressive than her little sister the Uruguay, this fine, 85m/279ft-long, **three-masted frigate** can reach a speed of 13 knots. Between 1899 and 1938, she served as a training ship for the Argentinian Navy, during which time she made 37 trips on all the oceans of the world. She also participated in the opening ceremonies of the Panama Canal. According to legend, it was the sailors of the Sarmiento who first took the tango to France, where it was embraced with extraordinary passion and went on to win acclaim worldwide. The ship has been turned into a museum, showcasing artifacts collected on its voyages. It's worth the nominal entrance fee just for a walk around the deck and to see the restored living quarters. Among the usual charts and maps, the oddest memento on board has to be the embalmed body of a dog that was once the ship's mascot.

Puente de la Mujer★

Map III, B2. ◗ *Allow 10mins. Dique 3.*

It's impossible to miss the elegant white profile of this footbridge, built in 2001 by the Catalan architect **Santiago Calatrava**. It owes its name (meaning "Woman's Bridge") to the decision by the authorities to name the roads in the district after important woman in the country's history, in contrast to elsewhere in the city where almost all roads are named after men. The bridge may look like a sharp wishbone laying down on the water's edge, but its slanting form is supposed to resemble the asymmetric angles created by tango dancers. Notice that the central section is pivotal, designed to let ships pass.

Coleccion de Arte Amalia Lacroze de Fortabat★

Map III, B1. ◗ *Allow 30mins. Olga Cossettini 141, Dique 4.* ✆ *(0)11 4310 6600. www.coleccionfortabat.org.ar. Open Tue–Sun 12–9pm. 15 A$. Guided tours 3pm and 5pm (Spanish). Audio guides are available in English. The building also contains a riverfront cafe.*

One of Argentina's wealthiest women, María Amalia La-

AMALIA LACROZE DE FORTABAT

The businesswoman and philanthropist Amalia Lacroze de Fortabat is the Brooke Astor of Argentina. The patroness of the Arts serves as the Chairperson of Loma Negra Compania Industrial Argentina S.A., an industrial conglomerate that includes the largest cement and concrete producer in the country, as well as a number of other industrial, energy, and communication concerns. Her net worth of US$2 billion makes Ms. Fortabat Argentina's wealthiest woman. She is also in possession of a sizeable art collection, much of which is housed at the Fortabat Art Collection.

croze de Fortabat, opened this gallery in 2008 to share highlights of her US$280 million private art collection. Running parallel with the waterfront, the modern building was designed by Uruguayan architect Rafael Viñoly and is notable for the curved aluminum panels, which move in response to the sun, so the works can always be viewed in good light, yet without being damaged. The museum celebrates the work of Argentine and international artists. If you want proof of how well connected this particular collector is, take note of the Andy Warhol work: it's a portrait of the woman herself. Argentinian artists to look out for are Antonio Berni and Carlos Alonso, who moved from Surrealism to Social Realism, and Social Realism to New Realism, respectively. The most talked about inclusion, however, is an oil painting by Joseph Mallord William Turner, called "Juliet and her Nurse," which was painted in the artist's last years and led to accusations of senility, as he placed Shakespeare's heroine in Venice rather than Verona.

Reserva Ecológica Costanera Sur★

Map III, B1–2. ◑ *Allow 1–2hrs Tristán Achával Rodríguez 1550.* ☏ *(011) 4893 1597. www.buenosaires.gov.ar. Open Tue–Sun 8am–5.30pm (Apr–Oct); 8am–6.30pm (Nov–Mar).* On the river side of Puerto Madero, two parks, the **Parque de las Mujeres Argentinas** (Argentine Women's Park) and the **Parque Micaela Bastidas**, provide the link to a vast ecological reserve. In the corner of the second park by the reserve's entrance, you'll find the statue Las Nereidas *(Avenida Padre Migone and Tristán Achával Rodríguez)*, created by the tucumano sculptor Lola Mora, which depicts the Birth of Venus. When it was first unveiled in 1903, the female nudes provoked such controversy that the artist fled Buenos Aires and retired to Salta in the northwest. At the turn of the 20C, the **Promenade de la Costanera**

Travel Tip:

The two-story steel-and-glass structure includes two exhibition halls, a library, an auditorium, offices and a cafe-restaurant overlooking the Puerto Madero docklands. The exhibition halls are divided into seven galleries: the family gallery, landscapes, international art, modern art and the Antonio Berni gallery.

PORT DEVELOPMENT

Curiously, although Buenos Aires is Argentina's only large port of entry, it was not until the 19C that it was truly developed. Until the 19C, the flat, marshy banks of the Río de la Plata prevented ships from docking and unloading took place via an irksome flurry of barges. Recognizing a need for change, local businessman Eduardo Madero came along with a plan, and not for the first time.

Growing needs

In the mid-to-late 1800s, Madero made numerous approaches to the authorities with proposals for a new port behind Plaza de Mayo. Finally, he got serious—teaming up with British engineer Sir John Hawkshaw and getting funding from London's Barings Bank—and in 1882, he received government approval. The work lasted from 1887 until 1897, but Madero died before it was completed, having fled to Italy due to a financial crisis.

The story took a further sad turn when, barely ten years later, the basins and equipment were already rendered obsolete due to the ever-growing size of the ships. The state, therefore, turned to the plan that had been proposed 20 years earlier by the city planner Luis Huergo, the Puerto Nuevo, which is still operational today, just north of Puerto Madero, on the banks of the Río de la Plata.

A revival

Abandoned, Puerto Madero declined little by little until it became no more than an unsanitary zone of deserted warehouses, ruined quays and industrial wastelands. One renovation plan followed another throughout most of the 20C, but all were unsuccessful, due to conflicts of interest and political rivalries.

Finally, in 1991, a competition was launched to transform and restore the district. To renovate the old brick warehouses and establish green spaces, the outlays were huge. Despite a slow-down due to the recession at the end of the 1990s and the economic crisis of 2001, many offices, businesses, luxury hotels and restaurants moved into the area. The Pontifical Catholic University of Argentina took up residence here and the construction of Futurist towers radically changed the *porteño* horizon. Among the tallest are the twin towers of Château Puerto Madero and the Mulieris and Renoir towers (170m/558ft). The district has become the capital's most expensive one. Yet the most recent economic crisis has slowed down constructions and dampened enthusiasm. The district has its own little tramway, which was financed by a French company as a sort of bonus after the signing of an agreement for a future high-speed railway that will link Buenos Aires with the cities of Córdoba and Rosario. The economic crisis of 2009 has meant, however, that while the tramway remains operational, the high-speed trains will have to wait for better times….

THE CITY AND ITS RIVER

Buenos Aires' identity as a port is not evident to visitors at first sight, as the city seems to have completely turned its back on the **Río de la Plata**. However, the capital's development as a trading center and the river's crucial role in exporting meat and agricultural products led to the development of important harbor facilities in the 19C. Unfortunately, successive economic and political crises jeopardized this industry. Later, during the second half of the 20C, the divide between the city and its port was accentuated with the increase in road traffic along the major avenues that border the city center on the side of the river. The renovation of the Puerto Madero district came at just the right moment to restore Buenos Aires' maritime identity.

Sur was hugely popular during the summer months. People would bathe in the river and beach tents could be seen all along the banks. Pollution got the better of bathing from the 1950s and the embankment became a dumping ground for construction debris. However, as time went by, grass and trees started to grow on top, as if nature was reclaiming the 350ha/865-acre space. Many developers then saw the area's potential and sought to buy, but in the mid-1980s it was declared protected land. **Footpaths** (Laguna de Los Patos, 3.3km/2mi; Camino del Río, 2.2/1.4km) run around the reserve and its four little lagoons. You can follow the banks of the Río de la Plata all around its periphery and take in the view of the gleaming towers of Puerto Madero, which provide a great contrast to the wild grasses you are standing among.

Plenty of locals come down here to jog, cycle, stroll or simply to nuzzle up to their loved ones like teenagers. At weekends, and on most weekdays in summer, you can hire a bike from one of the stalls by the entrance. The area is also a renowned spot for birdwatching, with over 200 species making their home here at various times of year. There is strictly no swimming in the river, although some people do sunbathe on the small stretches of beach on hot days.

It's customary for Argentines to come to this area at the weekend to drink *maté* and buy a *choripan* (beloved sausage sandwich) from one of the unfussy vans that line the promenade. Midweek days are much more peaceful, but they do lack the atmosphere you find from watching locals at play on a typically busy Sunday.

Free guided tours of the reserve are offered at the weekends and on holidays, at 10.30am or 3.30pm *(Spanish only, no reservation needed)*. Once a month, there is a three-hour nocturnal tour *(Spanish only)*; dates are posted on the website and you need to book ahead as they are extremely popular.

Travel Tip:

The ecological reserve is a perfect spot for a jog, bike ride (bikes are available for rent) or just to stroll with the locals looking at the hundreds of species of birds. With all the wildlife, you'll also encounter a few unexpected critters—mosquitoes. Remember to pack lots of bug repellent.

159

DISCOVERING
LA BOCA★

The English translation for La Boca is "the mouth," and this neighborhood gets its name not only from its location at the mouth of the River Riachuelo, but also from its history as the entranceway for immigrants to Argentina. Buenos Aires' main harbor during the 1800s, this southeastern *barrio* was the entry point for all ships coming in from Europe and the first home to many of the immigrants who came to the city.

Perhaps because of its eclectic background, La Boca is completely different from the other *barrios* of Buenos Aires. Its houses are bright and extravagant, painted in a patchwork of colors. The common explanation behind these funky paint jobs is that the working-class residents of La Boca would use leftover paint found at the docks to decorate their homes. In addition to its colorful houses, La Boca is also known as the birthplace of tango. Want to see authentic tango dancing? On Sundays, stroll the streets of La Boca, especially the famous El Caminito, to see tango dancers, singers and buskers.

Soccer fans will also find plenty to do in La Boca. Soccer, or *fútbol,* is like a religion to Argentinians, and one of the world's best-known soccer clubs, Boca Juniors, is based in La Boca. The Boca Juniors' stadium, known as La Bombonera or "the chocolate box," is one of the *barrio's* big attractions, as is its adjoining sports museum. Seeing a game at La Bombonera can be intense—the entire stadium sometimes shakes from the jumping of excited fans—but for aficionados, this is one of the world's great soccer experiences.

La Boca is a working-class district (care should be taken away from the main strip of El Caminito), and it lacks the palaces and mansions found in other parts of the city. However, the neighborhood is not without its own cultural centers.

The Museo de Bellas Artes de La Boca houses the works of the famous Argentinian painter Benito Quinquela Martín and other modern Argentinian artists. Nearby, Fundación Proa also houses an impressive array of Latin American art and artifacts, and has an active social event calendar you'll want too look into.

PETER'S TOP PICKS

 CULTURE

The iconic El Caminito is the most colorful street in the city, and a unique Buenos Aires must-see. Benito Quinquela Martín might just be the patron saint of El Caminito; see his seascapes at the Museum of Fine Arts.
El Caminito (p 163).
Museo de Bellas Artes de la Boca Benito Quinquela Martín (p 165)

 HISTORY

For a new way to explore the history of La Boca, check out the Museo Historico de Cera where you can learn the history of the neighborhood through waxwork recreations of the *barrio's* famous residents.
Museo Historico de Cera (p 167)

 EAT

For lunch, I like to pop into the cafe at the Fundacion PROA. Have a quick bite, then visit the galleries and library. For an evening meal, Il Matterello is a wonderful family friendly Italian restaurant hidden in the back streets. **Fundacion PROA (p 165) Il Matterello (p 244)**

 ENTERTAINMENT

La Boca is home to the Boca Juniors soccer team. Try to score seats to a match at La Bombonera or take a tour of the iconic stadium. **La Bombonera (p 167)**

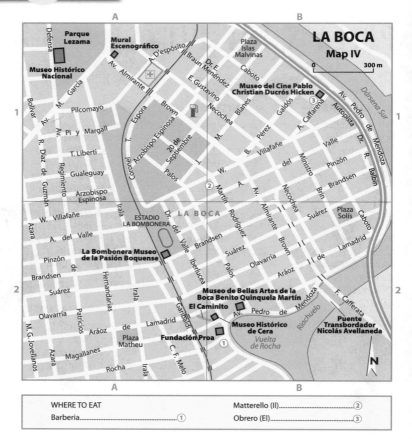

WHERE TO EAT

Barbería .... ①

Matterello (II) .... ②

Obrero (El) .... ③

TOURIST TANGO

Impromptu tango shows on the street are very common in La Boca. Don't be surprised if you happen to be in the area in the middle of the day and everyone suddenly stops to watch a group of street performers break into tango. Interestingly, tango is predominantly a tourist dance now in Buenos Aires. Many *porteños* who actually dance tango for enjoyment are older, whereas the younger generation is turning to the *cumbia*, a dance of African origin that has been gaining momentum in Latin America. Many *porteños* who study tango go on to teach and perform *milonga* at restaurants and bars throughout Buenos Aires.

El Caminito★★ *and Around*

Map IV.

La Boca always was, and still is, a working class neighbourhood. It's not the most desirable part of town and yet it consistently finds itself on the front of postcards and guidebooks, thanks to one small road in its south corner. During the daytime, El Caminito (little walkway) comes alive with crowds of visitors, who come to admire its multi-colored houses, museums and tango displays. It's a very popular stop-off for tour groups but, be warned, beyond El Caminito and its close environs, the area does have a reputation for street crime. You're advised not to wander farther afield and to keep a close check on your belongings. However, if you follow these guidelines, you'll be one of countless tourists who visit safely every day.

El Caminito★★

Map IV, B2. ⊙ *Allow 30mins. Between Garibaldi, Araoz de Lamadrid, del Valle Iberlucea and Magallanes.*
If Disney did Buenos Aires, it would look a lot like this. Brought to you in full Technicolor, this little street aims to tick all the tourism boxes within a stretch of a few yards, from souvenir shopping and tango displays to having your photo taken with a man masquerading as Maradona. Although its iconic ramshackle houses clad in corrugated iron panels were originally decorated using leftover paint from the shipyard, now their bodywork is kept constantly repainted for the benefit of tourism. Nonetheless, a quick pitstop here makes for some good photo opportunities,

CAMINITO, A SCENIC WALKWAY

Named in honor of the famous tango song by Juan de Dios Filiberto, who hailed from the district, **El Caminito★★** *(see opposite)* is aptly named, because this "little footpath" stretches only about 100m/330ft between the *calles* Garibaldi, Araoz de Lamadrid, del Valle Iberlucea and Magallanes. With its brightly painted corrugated-iron houses, this open-air museum is the main "attraction" of La Boca and one of Buenos Aires' iconic images. The old *conventillos* *(see p150)* that were once packed with immigrants are now teeming with restaurants and souvenir shops.

Location:
Running diagonally between the block demarcated by Dr. del Valle Iberlucea, Magallanes, Garibaldi and Aráoz de Lamadrid
Bus nos.: 20, 25, 29, 33, 46, 53, 64, 86, 152, 168.

ASK PETER...

Q: Are taxis a good way to get around Buenos Aires?
A: Most taxi drivers are hard working and honest, but of course, as will all cities, some caution is advised. Try to take cabs with the words Radio Taxi above; you can easily identify these by their black body and yellow trim. Radio Taxis are affiliated to a radio taxi company and deemed more secure, as opposed to independent drivers who might rip you off. Be sure to carry small bills, as coins are scarce in Argentina. Try not to hand over large bills of 50 or 100 pesos, as one (not common) scam is to take it, refuse it, and hand back a counterfeit bill.

THE ITALIAN DISTRICT

La Boca is traditionally a blue-collar district, mainly populated by Italian immigrants who arrived in Argentina at the end of the 19C. Coming mostly from the town of Gênes, they disembarked at La Boca (the mouth), Buenos Aires' true natural port, where they decided to settle.

A naval beginning

Situated at the mouth of El Riachuelo ("the Little River"), a tributary of the Río de la Plata, the *barrio* essentially developed around port activity. A few blocks east of El Caminito, beside the river, La Boca's industrial past is palpable. The waters of the Riachuelo are straddled by the impressive steel-and-cement structure **Puente Nicolás Avellaneda**, which stands alongside the disused Puente Transbordador.

The metal workshops and shipyards that set up on either bank of the river needed workforces, and those workers lived in flimsy wooden or corrugated-iron houses that were built on stilts to escape the frequent floods. Gradually, they began to paint the façades with paint left over from the boats and an original patchwork of vivid colors built up. La Boca thus developed, a little away from Buenos Aires. In the 1887 census, it was said to have 25,000 inhabitants.

The time of renaissance?

The Argentinian painter **Benito Quinquela Martín** (1890-1977), who was born and lived in La Boca, is one of the most famous and popular figures of the district, where he was quite a philanthropist. He is to thank, in particular, for transforming El Caminito. He invited the locals to come and paint his house with their leftover paint from the shipyard. Soon it was covered in a colorful mosaic that was soon emulated on many other houses in the district. Little by little, various social and cultural institutions emerged, while tango naturally found its place in the areas cafes.

The República de La Boca

You will doubtless have noticed, on your arrival, the sign proudly declaring "Bienvenidos a la República de La Boca." This independence is not, of course, official; the aim is, above all, to preserve the cultural heritage of this unique district. However, it is reminiscent of a strange episode in La Boca's history: in 1882, following a long general strike, a group of immigrants from Gênes actually proclaimed a secession of La Boca from Argentina and raised the flag of Gênes. The Argentinian government was quick to respond, however: the rebellion was rapidly suppressed and the president Julio Argentino Roca himself removed the rebels' flag.

and if you can't capture the scene well enough yourself, there are plenty of artists on hand, ready to sell you their interpretations via collage or photograph.

The alleyway itself is full of colorful characters, from buskers to larger-than-life sculptures of famous figures, such as Carlos Gardel. A small arts and crafts fair runs up its middle and down to the edge of the Riachuelo river, where you can buy jewelry, *maté* gourds and the usual memorabilia, while numerous tango dancers offer displays in the cafes or on the street. Be prepared to fend off a glut of playful waiters trying to coerce you into their establishment, and note that those dressed up and offering to be in your photos will expect a tip.

Museo de Bellas Artes de La Boca Benito Quinquela Martín★

Map IV, B2. ◗ *Allow 30mins. Pedro de Mendoza 1835.*
☏ *(011) 4301 1080. Open Tue–Sun 10am–6pm. 5 A$.*

The painter **Benito Quinquela Martín** *(see opposite)* is known above all for his port scenes, which marvelously reproduce the harsh and virile ambiance of Buenos Aires' quays. Thanks to the patronage of, among others, the then President of the Republic, he gained a reputation at the end of the 1920s and many great museums bought his paintings. In 1933, he bequeathed land for a building that would house a primary school, a museum, his studio and an apartment.

The visit starts with a rather isolated room that exclusively contains figureheads. The 25 sculptures, mostly dating from the 19C, come mainly from studios in La Boca and highlight the district's maritime identity. Next is a succession of small rooms in which are hung, beside port scenes by Quinquela Martín, paintings by 20C Argentinian artists such as Pío Collivadino (1869-1945), Raúl Soldi (1905-94) and José Arcidiácono (1910-82). The end of the visit encompasses the works that Quinquela Martín bequeathed in 1968, some 50 engravings and, in particular, **27 impressive pictures** that recreate the arduous, working-class atmosphere of the old port. You can also see his study, preserved in its original state. Finally, make sure you go up to the terrace for a panorama of the port.

Fundación PROA★

Map IV, B2. ◗ *Allow 45mins. Pedro de Mendoza 1929.*
☏ *(011) 4104 1000. www.proa.org. Open Tue–Sun 11am–8pm (last entry 7pm). 10 A$. Guided tour (1hr) in Spanish:*

Travel Tip:
Don't go to La Boca at night. Cliché, right? Look at it this way, La Boca, particularly El Caminito, is one of the most flamboyant neighborhoods in the city. It's a photographer's dream to capture the colorful bohemian feel of the neighborhood, but once you leave Caminito, you're venturing into authentic La Boca, a working-class neighborhood with high crime. Photographing La Boca is therefore best done during the day.

FÚTBOL IN ARGENTINA

Football (soccer) is a popular sport all over Argentina, but it can be argued that the most popular team resides in the Buenos Aires neighborhood of La Boca. The Boca Juniors are one of the world's best known football clubs and people flock from all around the world to catch of glimpse of the popular sport *(for more about Buenos Aires' teams, see p255).*

Football in Argentina has a long and colorful past, which has led to Argentina being one the most enthusiastic footballing nations in the world, with more than 90 percent of the population showing allegiance to a particular team. In the early 1880s, the widely-held founder of Argentine football, Alexander Watson Hutton, began teaching football at St. Andrews School, where he was a teacher.

The Buenos Aires Football Club was founded in 1868 by two English immigrants, Thomas and James Hogg. In 1891, Hutton established the Association of Argentine Football League, the first non-British league in the nation. Argentinian football remained largely amateur for many years. During the early 20C, a large number of new clubs formed all over the country. More than 300 teams would play in various amateur tournaments and local championships.

In 1930, 18 teams decided to form a professional league, which would run alongside the amateur league until 1934 when the amateur league finally fell apart. Since then Argentina has had a huge presence on the international football stage, hosting the FIFA World Cup in 1978. In 2004, the men's Argentinian Olympic Team won gold at the Athens summer Olympic games and defended its title, winning again at the 2008 Beijing summer Olympic games.

Football is not just about the men; women are starting to make their presence known on the football field. In 1991, the Argentine Football Association established a national league for women, the *Campeonato de Fútbol Feminino*. Like the men, the women have teams for River Plate and Boca Juniors. Though not yet as skilled as the men, the women are starting to gain international recognition. The team qualified for the World Cup in 2007 and prior to that, they won the *Campeonato Sudamericano Femenino* (a top continental competition) in 2006.

Tue–Fri 5pm, Sat 3pm, and Sun 3pm and 5pm. Free access to the bookshop and cafe.

At the heart of this curious district, which once attracted artists and avant-gardists, this foundation dedicated to contemporary art presents temporary exhibitions showcasing internationally renowned artists. It was founded in 1996, but since November 2008 has occupied superb new premises that encompass four exhibition galleries on three floors, an auditorium, a specialist library and a cafe with a lovely terrace. Past exhibits include a major show of work by French Surrealist Marcel Duchamp and Louise Bourgeois' giant spider sculpture, *Maman*.

Museo Histórico de Cera

Map IV, B2. ◯ *Allow 30mins. Dr Enrique Del Valle Iberlucea 1261. ✆ (011) 4301 1497. www.museodecera.com.ar. Open Mon–Fri 11.30am–6pm (7pm in summer), Sat, Sun and public holidays 11am–6pm (8pm in summer). 10 A$.*

Created on the first floor of one of the first stone-built residences in the district—a boldly colored, Italian Renaissance-style building—this little waxworks museum recounts the history of La Boca through its most iconic figures. It's not Madame Tussauds—especially as you won't recognize many of the faces—but it is fun to visit, when in the right frame of mind. Founded in 1980 by an artist and taxidermist, it is proudly the only waxwork museum in the country.

LOS MILLIONARIOS

Attending a Boca Juniors–River Plate *superclasico* game is on the list of 20 things to do before you die, according to the *Observer* newspaper in Britain. For a little history, know that the rivalry between the teams is over 100 years old. Back in the day, both teams played in La Boca. Then, in 1923, River Plate moved uptown to nicer surroundings, earning themselves the nickname "Los Millionarios." You can see the rivalry alive and well when the teams play today and River fans arrive at La Bombonera with clothes pegs on their noses. Interestingly, for the 2011-12 season, the *superclasico* was not played for the first time in many years. Because of financial woes and losses, River Plate was relegated to the lower leagues, so the two teams did not meet up for the traditional game of the year.

ASK PETER...

Q: What is the best of the bunch of tourist restaurants near El Caminito?

A: Very close to El Caminito, at Magallanes 845, La Barrica Restaurant and Bistrot, with live tango performances, cannot be missed. At night make sure you take a cab directly to the restaurant and call a cab from the restaurant without walking too far outside. Trust me, it will be worth it.

Travel Tip:
Boca Juniors and River Plate are fierce rivals, so it's no surprise that each side takes their colors very seriously: Boca blue and yellow, River red and white. Be cautious of wearing rival colors on match days. A River Plate jersey, or anything red and white, is not likely to make you many friends when Boca Juniors are playing.

GOING TO A GAME
...LIKE A LOCAL

Going to a *fútbol* (soccer) game in Buenos Aires is a once-in-a-lifetime experience, although getting there could be a little tricky as you must fight your way through the thousands of local fans on any given game day. Even if you're not a huge football fan, the emotion from the fans in the stadium provides more than enough drama to warrant the price of a ticket.

Tickets to league games can be quite pricey, but are available at many different locations. The football season runs from the beginning of August to the end of December, so if you are interested in seeing a game, make sure to plan a trip in the second half of the year.

Aim for tickets to a River Plate home game as their stadium is the biggest in Argentina and therefore you are most likely to find available tickets. Boca Juniors have a very small stadium and tickets are basically sold out in advance each year to season-ticket holders.

One of the best places, as a tourist, to get tickets to a game is through your hotel concierge. Hotels very often offer tickets, along with tours and transportation to some of the biggest games in the area. It's all about the experience and the hotels do coordinate all the logistics for you.

If you speak Spanish, you can find tickets and information on attending games at this website: http://www.gofootball.com.ar/.

Tip: La Boca's La Bombonera, a.k.a. Estadio Alberto J. Armando, has a capacity of 49,000, and even then tickets are especially hard to find. So if you're one of the unfortunate ones without a ticket, el Museo de la Pasion Boquense is your last hope of experiencing the inside of the stadium and learning about Boca's rise since its inception in 1905. The museum offers daily stadium tours from 10am–6pm for $12 A$ each or $20 A$ for both. Visit www.museobo-quense.com for more information.

La Bombonera★

Map IV, A2. ❍ *Allow 2hrs. Brandsen 805.* ✆ *(011) 4362 1100.*
www.museoboquense.com. Museum: open daily 10am–6pm, 35 A$.
Stadium tour (1hr): 11am–5pm, combined ticket 50 A$.

A mythic place, La Bombonera stadium houses an attractive modern museum that is entirely dedicated to the **Boca Juniors** team, established in 1905 and 23 times champions of Argentina.

A collection of items and souvenirs relates its history and the careers of its most illustrious players, including **Maradona** and **Batistuta**. Interactive screens, videos and various multimedia exhibits invite visitors to relive the centenarian club's most thrilling moments. To finish, aficionados will want to take the guided tour, which gives access behind the scenes of the stadium and allows you to set foot on the field of this temple of soccer, even if you are not able to mix with supporters on the day of a match.

Legend has it that the team's first players chose its blue-and-yellow colors by saying they would take their inspiration from the next boat to arrive in port: the flag of a Swedish boat came into view. Note that the Coca Cola sponsorship logos on the top of stadium are in black and white; this is because the team received very special permission from the soft drinks giant so as not to employ the colors of arch-rivals, River Plate, who play in red and white *(see p255)*.

For soccer fans, or anyone who appreciates a good spectacle, there is nothing like sitting among the crowds of La Bombonera—meaning chocolate box, named for its compact shape—on match day, as the stands vibrate under the weight of fans jumping on the spot and celebratory paper streamers fly into the air. The easiest, albeit not the cheapest, way to secure tickets is through a tour operator *(see p76)*.

Museo del Cine Pablo Christian Ducrós Hicken

Map IV, B1. ❍ *Allow 30mins. Agustín R. Caffarena 49.* ✆ *(011) 4303 2882.*
www.museodelcine.buenosaires.gov.ar. Open Mon–Fri 11am–6pm. Sat,
Sun and holidays 10am–9pm. 1 A$. Wed free.

Named after a researcher, essayist, historian and collector specializing in film—when he died in 1969, his widow donated his collection of cameras, projectors, films and photos to kick-start this museum. It's the only museum dedicated to Argentinian cinema, and is full of memorabilia and equipment used through the decades. There is an extensive in-house library for those with time to browse. The museum's archives caught the world's attention in the late 2000s when it was found to be in possession of a long-lost 30 minutes of footage from Fritz Lang's *Metropolis*, the silent sci-fi classic said to be one of the most groundbreaking films ever made. To be extra safe, you may want to take a taxi.

Most people first visit Recoleta to see the cemetery. The 5ha/13-acre Cementerio de la Recoleta is one of the most famous cemeteries in the world, and much of that celebrity is because it is the final resting place of Evita Perón. However, Recoleta is so much more than a cemetery—it's really for the living, not the dead.

Beside the cemetery is the Basílica of Nuestra Señora del Pilar, one of the oldest churches in the city. The basilica's Spanish Colonial architecture is impressive and even those who are not religious can enjoy sitting in on services here.

Buenos Aires is often called the Paris of South America, and nowhere is this more apparent than the French-style residences, large gardens, squares and broad avenues of this neighborhood. With all this beauty, it's not surprising that Recoleta is also one of the priciest of Buenos Aires' *barrios*. Most of the city's luxurious hotels are located in Recoleta. The hotel prices are predictably steep, but you'll have outstanding service as well as a unbeatable location next to many of the *barrio's* national monuments.

If you don't have the pesos to stay here, Recoleta is best visited on weekends when street performances, art exhibits and sport events are taking place. You'll definitely want to check out the neighborhood's newest monument, the Floralis Genérica, a 25m/82ft-tall aluminum and stainless steel statue of a blooming flower. The flower opens and closes its giant petals with the rising and the setting of the sun.

To see equally impressive sculptures, visit Argentina's principal art museum, the Museo Nacional de Bellas Artes. As well as astounding permanent and temporary exhibitions of International and Argentinian Art, the museum boasts an extensive collection by French sculptor Auguste Rodin. Rodin's work can be found at various locations throughout Buenos Aires, but an impressive collection is housed here, including the 1899 marble masterpiece, *La Terre et La Lune*.

Cementerio de la Recoleta Photo: © BILDGENTUR-ONLINE/age fotostock

PETER'S TOP PICKS

 CULTURE

Biblioteca National is architecturally interesting, though it might not be appealing to diehard traditionalists. The outstanding Museo National de Bellas Artes is a must-see. **Biblioteca National (p 181) Museo National de Bellas Artes (p 176)**

 GREEN SPACES

You might not think of a cemetery as a green space, but Cementerio de la Recoleta was built on a former garden and is a wonderful place for a stroll. **Cementerio de la Recoleta (p 179)**

 SHOP

Designer row Avenida Alvear is a must, if only to window shop and dream. **Avenida Alvear (p 174)**

 EAT

It's not a cheap eat, but afternoon tea at the glamorous Alvear Palace Hotel is a memorable experience. Few can stay at the hotel, but here's a way to have one of Buenos Aires' chicest experiences. **Alvear Palace Hotel (p 174)**

 ENTERTAINMENT

The renovated Centro Cultural Recoleta hosts an art gallery and exhibition halls. Concerts are held here and films are regularly screened. Drop in and see what events are happening during your stay. **Centro Cultural Recoleta (p 180)**

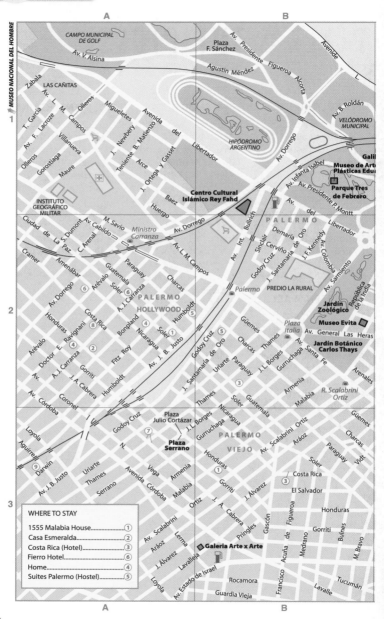

MUSEO NACIONAL DEL HOMBRE

A **B**

CAMPO MUNICIPAL DE GOLF

Plaza F. Sánchez

Av. V. Alsina

Av. Presidente Figueroa Alcorta

Avenida

Agustín Méndez

Zabala

LAS CAÑITAS

Av. L. M. Campos

Olleros

Migueletes

Avenida

del

Libertador

Av. B. Roldán

T. García

Av. F. Lacroze

J. Newbery

Teniente B. Matienzo

VELÓDROMO MUNICIPAL

HIPÓDROMO ARGENTINO

Villanueva

Olleros

Gorostiaga

Maure

Arce

J. Ortega y Gasset

Galil

Museo de Art Plásticas Edu

Av. Infanta Isabel

Av. Presidente P. Montt

Baez

Av. Dorrego

Parque Tres de Febrero

INSTITUTO GEOGRÁFICO MILITAR

Huergo

Centro Cultural Islámico Rey Fahd

Av.

del

Ciudad de La Paz

M. Savio

Av. Cabildo

Ministro Carranza

Av. Dorrego

PALERMO

Libertador

Cramer

S. Dumont

C. Arenal

Av. L. M. Campos

Av. Int. Bullrich

Demaría

Sinclair

Cerviño

de Oro

J. F. Kennedy

J. Salguero

Av. del Libertador

Amenábar

Guatemala

Paraguay

Charcas

Godoy Cruz

J. Santamaría de Oro

J. F. Kennedy-Colombia

Av. Dorrego

Arévalo

Soler

A. J. Carranza

PALERMO HOLLYWOOD

Humboldt

Palermo

PREDIO LA RURAL

Av. Sarmiento

República de la India

Honduras

Costa Rica

Bonpland

Nicaragua

Soler

Güemes

Jardín Zoológico

Museo Evita

Arévalo

Doctor E. Ravignani

Fitz Roy

Av. J. B. Justo

Godoy Cruz

Charcas

Thames

Plaza Italia

Av. General Las Heras

Jardín Botánico Carlos Thays

Gorriti

J. A. Cabrera

Humboldt

J. Santamaría de Oro

Uriarte

Paraguay

J. L. Borges

Gurruchaga

Santa Fe

Arenales

Av. A. J. Carranza

Av. Córdoba

Coronel

Thames

Soler

Guatemala

Armenia

Malabia

R. Scalabrini Ortiz

Loyola

Godoy Cruz

Plaza Julio Cortázar

J. L. Borges

Gurruchaga

Nicaragua

PALERMO VIEJO

Av. Scalabrini Ortiz

Güemes

Charcas

Aguirre

Plaza Serrano

Honduras

Araóz

Paraguay

Vidt

Darwin

Uriarte

N.

Av. J. B. Justo

Thames

Serrano

Vega

Avenida Córdoba

Armenia

Malabia

Gorriti

J. A. Cabrera

Ortiz

J. Álvarez

Costa Rica

El Salvador

Soler

Honduras

Av. Scalabrini

Lerma

Pringles

Gascón

Figueroa

Medrano

Gorriti

Bulnes

M. Bravo

Araóz

J. Álvarez

Galeria Arte x Arte

Francisco Acuña de

Tucumán

Loyola

Lavalleja

Rocamora

Lavalle

Av. Estado de Israel

Guardia Vieja

WHERE TO STAY

1555 Malabia House	①
Casa Esmeralda	②
Costa Rica (Hotel)	③
Fierro Hotel	⑥
Home	④
Suites Palermo (Hostel)	⑤

A **B**

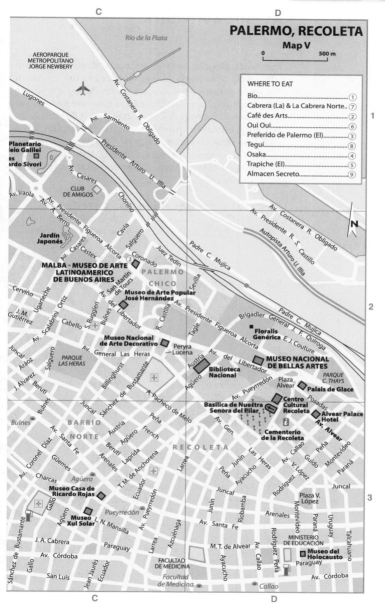

PALERMO, RECOLETA
Map V

0 — 500 m

Río de la Plata

AEROPARQUE
METROPOLITANO
JORGE NEWBERY

Lugones

Av. Costanera R. Obligado

Av. Sarmiento

Presidente Arturo U. Illia

Planetario
leo Galilei
es
ardo Sívori

Av. Casares

Av. Iraola

CLUB
DE AMIGOS

Av. Costanera R. Obligado

Av. Presidente R. S. Castillo

Autopista Arturo U. Illia

N

Chonino

Av. Casares Castex

Av. A. Berro

Av. Presidente Figueroa Alcorta

Cavia

Salguero

Jardín
Japonés

Coronado

Juez Tedín

Padre C. Mujica

**MALBA - MUSEO DE ARTE
LATINOAMERICO
DE BUENOS AIRES**

San Martín de Tours

**PALERMO
CHICO**

Cerviño

Ugarteche

Scalabrini Ortiz

Av. del Libertador

**Museo de Arte Popular
José Hernández**

Sevilla

Tagle

R. Castilla

Av. Presidente Figueroa Alcorta

Brigadier General J. F. Quiroga

Padre C. Mujica

E. J. Couture

J. M.
Gutiérrez

Cabello

S. Bustigel

Bulnes

**Floralis
Genérica**

Juncal

Aráoz

Salguero

Av. Scalabrini Ortiz

**Museo Nacional
de Arte Decorativo**

Av. General Las Heras

Peryra
—Lucena

Av. del Libertador

**MUSEO NACIONAL
DE BELLAS ARTES**

J. Álvarez

Berutti

**PARQUE
LAS HERAS**

Billinghurst

Sánchez de Bustamante

Austria

Agüero

**Biblioteca
Nacional**

Av. Pueyrredón

Plaza
Alvear

*PARQUE
C. THAYS*

Palais de Glace

Bulnes

**BARRIO
NORTE**

Juncal

Peña

A. Pacheco de Melo

Av. Gen.

**Basílica de Nuestra
Senora del Pilar**

**Centro
Cultural
Recoleta**

Posadas

**Alvear Palace
Hotel**

Av. Alvear

Av. Coronel Díaz

Av. Santa Fe

Güemes

Austria

Agüero

French

Berutti

Arenales

Laprida

**Cementerio
de la Recoleta**

Av. Callao

RECOLETA

Las Heras

Peña

Junín

Ayacucho

Guido

V. López

Peha

Montevideo

Paraná

Charcas

Agüero

**Museo Casa de
Ricardo Rojas**

T. M. de Anchorena

Ecuador

Larrea

Peña

Juncal

Junín

Riobamba

Rodríguez

Plaza V.
López

Juncal

Gallo

Pueyrredón

L. N. Mansilla

Av. Pueyrredón

**Museo
Xul Solar**

Av. Santa Fe

Montevideo

Paraná

Uruguay

Sánchez de Bustamante

J. A. Cabrera

Paraguay

Larrea

Azcuénaga

Av. Córdoba

Jean Jaurés

Ecuador

**FACULTAD
DE MEDICINA**

M. T. de Alvear

Ayacucho

Av. Callao

Rodríguez Peña

**MINISTERIO
DE EDUCACIÓN**

**Museo del
Holocausto**

Talcahuano

Gallo

San Luis

*Facultad
de Medicina*

Callao

Paraguay

Av. Córdoba

Location:
Spans from Cerrito to
Libertador, between
Posadas and Pte M.
Quintana.
Subte: San Martín
(line C)
Bus nos.: 5, 10, 17,
37, 38, 39, 41, 59, 60,
61, 62, 67, 75, 92, 93,
95, 101, 102, 106, 108,
110, 124, 130, 152.

Travel Tip:
If you want the same
designer shops as
Avenida Alvear but
in one condensed
experience, then
head to Retiro's Patio
Bullrich shopping
mall. In the 1860s,
the building was
conceived as an
auction house for
cattle and livestock—
far from the high
end goods for sale
today. The building
was reinvented
100 years later as a
designer hub. There
are over 89 stores
including Christian
Dior, Christian Lacroix,
Diesel, Ferragamo
and more. There's
also a gift shop for
the Teatro Colón and
a four-screen movie
theater.

Avenida Alvear★

Map II, B1 and Map V, D3.

The most elegant part of Recoleta stretches out on either side of Avenida Alvear, which links the square of the same name with Plazoleta Carlos Pellegrini, where the sumptuous *palacios* Ortíz Basualdo and Pereda *(see below)* are to be found. Constructed in 1885, this wide avenue is one of the most beautiful in the capital, lined with wealthy Haussmann-style residences, haute-couture boutiques (Armani, Hermès, Valentino, Louis Vuitton) and palaces that house some of the city's most luxurious hotels.

Palacios Ortíz Basualdo and Pereda

Map II, B1. ◗ *Allow 15mins. Cerrito 1399.* ✆ *(011) 4515 7030. www.embafrancia-argentina.org.Arroyo 1130.* ✆ *(011) 4515 2400. www.brasil.org.ar.*
Now the French and Brazilian embassies, these Belle Époque palaces are among the most famous of the grand buildings along the avenue. Palacio Basualdo was designed in the Beaux-Arts style in 1912 by French architect Paul Pater. It became the French Embassy in 1939 and narrowly escaped demolition in the late 1970s when work was being done to make way for the expansive Avenida 9 de Julio. Palacio Pereda, which became the Brazilian Embassy in 1943, is a copy of Palais Jacquemart-André in Paris. Other grand palaces of the same era to look out for include the Palacio Duhau, which has been recently converted into the Park Hyatt Hotel *(Alvear 1661).*

Alvear Palace Hotel★

Map II, B1 and Map V, D3. ◗ *Allow 15mins, or longer for tea. Alvear 1891.* ✆ *(011) 4808 2100. www.alvearpalace.com. Open daily.*
Before this grand structure made its mark, Buenos Aires did not have a five-star hotel that wasn't part of an international chain. The Alvear Palace was designed as a statement to the world, one that showed off the city's confidence, ambition and high style. When a hotel describes itself as a palace and has 12 ballrooms, you get the idea of the type of clientele it seeks to attract and curious tourists won't be disappointed by the grandeur of its lobby.
Building work commenced in 1922 and took ten years to complete. One of the best stories in its history is that a guest

FRENCH INFLUENCE

French architecture is throughout the upper class *barrio* of Recoleta. As many of Buenos Aires' wealthiest residents moved to the outer *barrio*, they brought some of their European influences with them. Starting at the end of the 19C a number of Parisian-style buildings were built, often by French architects to mirror their home country. Most of the actual materials were also brought over from Europe, including French chandeliers, marble staircases and bronzed iron to get the most authentic feel.

Some of the most noteworthy Parisian architecture still remains along Avenida Alvear. The historic buildings include the Palacio Dahua, formerly owned by the Duhau family; the Fernandez Anchorena Palace and the very luxurious (and French!) Alvear Palace Hotel, which is world-famous. Check out the hotel and the historic design for high tea.

Construction for the Avenida Alvear was spearheaded by the then Mayor, Torcuato de Alvear, for whom the boulevard is named. The mayor modeled the street after Paris and Baron Haussmann. Unfortunately, due to an economic crisis and a failing real estate market, many of the French buildings were demolished and replaced with more economically sound buildings. Other historic buildings have been repurposed as stores. The boulevard houses Fendi, Valentino, Hermes and other designer stores.

The mansions and estates were torn down in favor of buildings that allowed for more people in smaller spaces, however you will still be able to see many of the French structures sprinkled throughout the modern apartment buildings, giving this area an old-time feel in an otherwise modern city. To see the modern architecture of this *barrio*, take a look at the National Library of Argentina—one of the more controversially modern buildings.

Interestingly, the French influence can even be seen in some modern designs. Although the buildings have been updated, much of the interior decoration and exterior landscaping has retained its French influence. Famed landscaper Charles Thays used many Parisian outdoor styles in his work.

once brought in an elephant for his daughter's birthday. Non-guests can book brunch, dinner or afternoon tea—elephants not included.

Location:
Libertator, between Agüero and Pueyrredón.
Bus nos.: 10, 17, 37, 41, 59, 60, 61, 62, 67, 92, 93, 95, 102, 108, 110, 118, 124, 130.

Museo Nacional de Bellas Artes (MNBA)★★★

Map V, D2.

This impressive museum, housed in a building dating from 1870, possesses some very fine permanent collections, notably paintings. It also organizes quality temporary exhibitions. Visitors are able to trace back the history of international art (ground floor) and discover the birth and maturation of Argentinian art (first floor).

◯ *Allow 2–3hrs. Libertador 1473.* ✆ *(011) 5288 9900. www.mnba.org.ar. Open Tue–Fri 12.30–8.30pm, Sat and Sun 9.30am–8.30pm. Audioguide 35 A$ (English and Spanish).*

International art

Rooms 1 and 2 display European **sacred art from the 13C to the 16C**. Of particular note are the beautiful German processional cross made from gold, bronze and stones (13C), the Italian Renaissance paintings (15C), the anecdotal but surprising Italian majolica *Holy Family* (15C), the *Mystic Marriage of Saint Catherine* by Veronese and the *Nativity* by Tintoretto. Also to be admired is Patinir's *Flight into Egypt*.

The Hirsch collection (room 3) is devoted to the **art of the 16C and 17C**, with sculptures such as the *Éducation de la Vierge* (France, 16C), with its finely worked drapes, and a beautiful series of Flemish and German paintings, including the *Birth of Mary* (early 16C) by Jacob Cornelisz van Oostsanen and a *Holy Family* by Rubens.

Room 4 highlights **Spanish painters**, such as El Greco and his *Jesus on the Mount of Olives* (1605-10) and Zurbarán and his *Meditating Monk* (1632). Note, too, a fine Fortuny depicting a *Procession to the Church of Santa Cruz in Madrid on a Rainy Day*. As far as sculpture is concerned, don't miss the *Angel with the Head of Saint Jean the Baptist*, by Alonso Cano. The visit continues with **Italian, Flemish and Dutch painters** (rooms 5 to 7). Notice here the minute detailing and the delicate work of the light on the still life and interiors. Among the most notable works are *Diana Returning from the Hunt* by Hendrick van Balen and a *Dutch Interior* by

Hendrick Martensz. Among the Italians, admire the Guardi *vedute* (view painting) of Venice. And from the English, *Boy Reading* by Joshua Reynolds. The French are represented by Corot and Gustave Courbet. A special space is reserved for **Francisco Goya**, with a *War Scene* (1808), which evokes the most famous works of Prado in Madrid, a series of engravings and some somber paintings that were harbingers of his famous black period.

French 19C and 20C art is particularly highlighted in the following rooms (12 to 14), with works by Rodin, the Impressionists and post-Impressionists. Don't miss Manet's *Nymphe Surprise* (1861), Pissarro's *Woman in a Field* (1882), Gauguin's *Vahiné no te Miti* (1892) and *Baigneuses en Bretagne* (1887), Van Gogh's *Le Moulin de la Galette* (1886), Monet's *La Berge de la Seine* (1880), or the vibrant *En Observation* (1901) and the subtle *Portrait de Suzanne Valadon* (1885) by Toulouse-Lautrec. Of note, too, is a lovely series of paintings by Degas, including *Deux Danseuses Jaunes et Roses* (1898), *La Toilette Après le Bain* (1888) and *Arlequin Danse* (1890).

The European avant-garde is also well represented (rooms 20 to 22), by artists as varied as Carrá, Kees van Dongen, Giorgio de Chirico, Paul Klee, Wassily Kandinsky, Diego Rivera, Modigliani, Tsuguharu Foujita, Chagall, Picasso and Fernand Léger.

The two final rooms (23 and 24) are devoted to art from the **second half of the 20C** from Europe and North America, notably by Mark Rothko, Antoni Tápies, Antonio Saura, Franz Kline, Alberto Burri, Pierre Alechinsky, Jackson Pollock and Jean Dubuffet.

Slightly isolated, the **Guerrico collection** (rooms 16 and 17) exhibits paintings, *maté* services, Spanish combs and fans, netsuke, pill boxes and snuff boxes. The only regrettable thing is the lack of commentaries and dates of the exhibits.

Argentinian art

On climbing the stairs to the next floor, note the two works by Antonio Berni (1905-81) and Antonio Seguí (1934-) facing you. To follow the artistic evolution of Latin America, begin your visit of this floor in room 100, which presents **Pre-Colombian art of the Andes**, from 1500 to the Spanish colonization. Don't miss the textiles, next to the pottery, including stunning lace from the south coast, which shows the technical mastery of the Chancay culture.

Next move on to the **Conquest of Mexico** tablets, made

ASK PETER...

Q: Can you recommend any weekend hot spots we should try?

A: You might find that places you would overlook during the week transform into popular destinations on the weekends. The Plaza Francia near the NMBA is a perfect example. During the week most people rush by, but on Saturday and Sunday, the Plaza Francia fills with local artisans selling crafts and food. If you're looking for a place to listen to local bands and people-watch, this should be your weekend destination. While you're there, buy a pack of freshly roasted sugar peanuts or almonds.

A FORMER WORKING-CLASS DISTRICT

Recoleta's history goes back to the beginning of the 18C, when the monks of the Recollect monastery, members of the Fransiscan order, moved to these lands and built the Iglesia del Pilar (1732), one of Buenos Aires' oldest churches. All around the monastery, plots of land were allocated to great landowners. Then an abattoir and a salting tub were built, attracting small farms, which were followed by working-class housing and taverns, where laborers, but also thugs, came to listen to music, drink and gamble. After nightfall, the district's cart tracks, quite deserted, were hardly safe to use. The place remained very working class until, in 1871, a yellow fever epidemic affected the southern districts of Buenos Aires. The wealthy families who lived in San Telmo were forced to flee farther north, notably here, to Recoleta, which, thanks to its more elevated position farther away from the river, was less affected by the disease. They finally settled here, while the working classes, who had become undesirable neighbors, migrated in the other direction, partly to the south, where they occupied the abandoned houses of the more wealthy. The district was then developed through building major roads and elegant, private mansions in the French style. Before long, the famous Avenida Alvear had become the capital's most chic address.

from painted araucaria wood inlaid with mother-of-pearl, which tell the story of the conquistador Cortés and of Moctezuma, the last Aztec emperor.

Next is **The Argentina of Traveling Painters** (room 102), which shows the country as it was seen by painters who arrived here from abroad. As Argentina's own arts scene grew, we discover a greater variety, of portraits, landscapes and genre paintings (room 103). The small room 104 holds the María Luisa Bemberg collection, devoted mainly to **Uruguayan painters**, most of whom worked in Europe.

The following rooms provide an understanding of the artistic orientation of the country, with a collection of domestic scenes that give a view of daily life. Note in particular *Sin Pan y Sin Trabajo* (Without Bread or Work) (1894) by Ernesto de la Cárcova, *La Hora del Almuerzo* (Lunch break time) (1903) by Pío Collivadino, *Waking of the Maid* (1887) by Eduardo Sívori or *La Costurera* (The Dressmaker) (1906) by José Antonio Terry. In contrast, the landscapes and epic scenes, like those of North American painters of the same period, depict the New World: *La Vuelta del Malón* (1892) by Angel Della Valle. Among the witnesses to working-class life, note *Las Lloronas* and the *Los Gauchos* series by Cesáreo Bernaldo de Quirós.

At the same time, influenced by what was happening in Europe, painters such as Eduardo Sívori, Martín Malharro, Pío Collivadino (*El Riachuelo*, 1916) and Justo Lynch (*Día gris*, 1919), like the Impressionists, worked on portraying light.

The huge room 107 features **contemporary artists** and the different trends that were affecting Argentinian creation during the second half of the 20C and the early 21C. Here we find the same great movements observed in Europe: Figurative, Symbolist, Surrealist, Cubist, Geometric, Abstract, Realist Neo-Figurative, Pop Art, Postmodern, Conceptual art… Noteworthy artists include Antonio Berni, Antonio Seguí, Xul Solar, Kenneth Kemble, Luis Felipe Noé, Rómulo Macció, Jorge de la Vega, Carlos Alonso, Luis Fernando Benedit, Nicolás Garcia Uriburu….

Recoleta Cemetery★★ *and Around*

Map V, D2–3.

The main attraction of this high-class neighborhood— and a must-see for any visitor to the city—is the cemetery. Cafes and restaurants have cropped up along its sides to take advantage of the numerous visitors.

Cementerio de la Recoleta★★

Map V, D3. ◗ *Allow 1hr. Junín 1760.* ✆ *(011) 4803 1594. Open 7am–5.45pm. Guided tour (in Spanish) Tue–Sun 9.30am, 11am, 2pm, 4pm; (English) Tue and Thu 11am.*

As renowned as Père Lachaise cemetery in Paris, Recoleta's cemetery contains the tombs of many famous Argentinians: politicians, military figures, writers, artists and scientists. Opened in 1822, it was the city's first public cemetery. It occupies the garden of the former Recollect monastery and includes, in its 6ha/14.8 acres, 4,800 marble tombs decorated with statues. Enter through its Neoclassical gates with Grecian columns and it appears to be a small town in itself, with little avenues lined with some of the grandest

Location:
Demarcated by Junín, Vicente López and Azcuenaga.
Subte: Callao (D line), plus 9-block walk.
Bus nos.: 10, 17, 37, 41, 59, 60, 61, 62, 67, 92, 93, 95, 101, 102, 108, 110, 118, 124, 130.

UPPER CLASS CEMETERY

Many of the affluent families in Buenos Aires, along with dignitaries and other state officials, are buried in the Recoleta Cemetery. But the now-affluent Recoleta wasn't always that way. During the 1870s, an epidemic of yellow fever spread across Buenos Aires. Many upper-class residents fled San Telmo and Monserrat and moved to the northern part of the city, creating an area of upper-class families. Since many of the families made their homes there, the cemetery became the final resting place for many of them. The cemetery is picturesque, with many old buildings and monuments honoring those buried inside.

tombs you will see, incorporating stained-glass windows and huge winged angels. Styles range from Art Deco to Gothic Revival, among many others. Some tombs remain looking fresh; others have fallen into disrepair, allowing you an eerie glimpse at a coffin that peeks through crumbling walls. Even if most of the names won't mean much to the average visitor, you will doubtless still be fascinated by the extravagant lengths the city's elite went to in order to fortify the legacy of their deceased.

Even though every tomb is different, the avenues are like a maze and it's easy to lose your bearings. If—like many tourists—you want to find the final resting place of Evita, look at the map by the gate and note that she is buried under her maiden name in the Duarte family vault.

A small crowd and fresh flowers usually mark the spot.

Basílica de Nuestra Señora del Pilar★

Map V, D3. ◗ *Allow 20mins. Junín 1904.* ☏ *(011) 4806 2209. www.basilicadelpilar.org.ar. Church: open daily 8am–10pm. Museum: open Mon–Sat 10.30am–6.15pm, Sun 2.30–6.15pm. 4 A$.*

The beautiful white church adjacent to the cemetery is one of the oldest in the city. Inaugurated in 1732 and dedicated to the Lady of the Pillar (the Virgin Mary and the patron saint of the Spanish town of Zaragoza), it has a very restrained Colonial style with a beautiful Baroque interior. Its museum contains paintings, silverware, books, furniture and liturgical garments from the 14C to the 19C.

Centro Cultural Recoleta

Map V, D2. ◗ *Allow 30mins. Junín 1930.* ☏ *(011) 4803 1040. www.centroculturalrecoleta.org. Open Mon–Fri 2–9pm. Sat–Sun 10am–9pm. Science museum: www.mpc.org.ar.* ☏ *(011) 4807 3260. Open daily 3.30–7.30pm. 20 A$.*

Behind this pink-painted frontage, you can find art exhibitions and occasional concerts. See the website for the current program. It also houses an interactive science museum, which claims to be aimed at anyone from age 4 to 100. Dating back to the 1700s, the building was designed by Jesuit architects and was later given an Italian twist. Over its long history, it has been a homeless shelter, a mental asylum, a prison and an agricultural school.

Palais de Glace

Map V, D2. ◗ *Allow 30–40mins. Posadas 1725.* ☏ *(011) 4804 1163. www.palaisdeglace.gob.ar. Open Tue–Fri noon–8pm,*

NATIONAL LIBRARY

The Biblioteca Nacional took a long time to build—think 30 years. The unique and controversial structure falls in line with the Brutalist architectural movement. Brutalism doesn't take it's name for brute strength or brute force. Instead it come from the French *béton brut* or raw concrete. In additional to favoring concrete, the Biblioteca emphasizes the repetition of geometrical shapes. The library holds nearly five million books and documents including a first edition of *Don Quixote*, a 1455 Gutenberg Bible and a copy of Dante's *Divine Comedy*.

Sat and Sun 10am–8pm. Guided tour (in Spanish) Sat and Sun 4pm and 5pm.

Opened in 1911, this former ice rink—hence its name—later converted into a ballroom, is now home to the National Office of Fine Arts. It also hosts the National Exhibition of Fine Arts and presents a collection of more than 1,000 works illustrating different disciplines—painting, sculpture, engraving, drawing, printmaking, watercolor, photography, ceramic art and textiles—displayed in temporary exhibitions that change monthly.

Biblioteca Nacional

Map II, A1 and Map V, D2. ◗ *Allow 30mins. Agüero 2502.* ℘ *(011) 4808 6040. www.bn.gov.ar. Open Mon–Fri 9am–9pm, Sat–Sun noon–7pm.*

Sitting up on its own perch, this stark concrete building was built in 1960s Brutalist style and caused some controversy among traditionalists. The project was awarded to winners of an architectural competition, but various complications meant it was not officially finished until 1992. It is built on the site of the former presidential residence, where Eva Perón died, and which was demolished by the new government so that it would not become a place for Evita pilgrimages. There are some great views of the city from the reading room.

Floralis Genérica

Map V, D2. ◗ *Allow 10mins. Plaza de las Naciones Unidas, on the corner of Figueroa Alcorta and Austria.*

The work of Argentinian architect Eduardo Catalano, this wonderful 23m/75ft tall floral sculpture created in 2002 was designed to open its steel petals each morning and close them again as night falls.

ASK PETER...

Q: Where can I go for a picnic lunch in the area?

A: A great place to hang out and enjoy some of the best of Buenos Aires culture is Plaza Intendente Alvear, locally referred to as Plaza Francia (which is actually across the street by the NMBA). Don't miss the enormous rubber tree—it's 15m/50ft wide! It's the kind of tree you would associate with the Amazon, right in the middle of ritzy Recoleta. Plaza Intendente Alvear is also the beginning of a series of parks that run from here all the way to the *barrio* of Belgrano. If you're looking for a great way to get from one neighborhood to another, try taking the "park" route.

LA BIELA
...LIKE A LOCAL

A little piece of history in the middle of trendy Recoleta, La Biela is a favorite among locals of all backgrounds. Executives, artists and famous politicians all visit this little cafe, which serves breakfast, lunch, ice-cream and pastries.

Originally opening as a grocery store in 1850, it wasn't until 60 years later that the cafe became a local treasure. La Biela alledgedly earned its name from an incident in the 1950s involving racing car driver Roberto "Betito" Mieres. Mieres and buddies were out carousing one night when Mieres' car broke down. Legend has it that Mieres brought the defunct *bielas* (connector rod) to the cafe and suggested that it change its name to La Biela Fundida, which means the "melted connecting rod." The cafe became a hot spot for racing car champions and today black and white photos of Argentinian drivers, along with other sporting memorabilia, hang in the large dining room.

Try and get a spot outside on the terrace, sitting underneath a huge gum tree and with a spectacular view of Basílica de Nuestra Señora del Pilar. It's a view you will never forget, but it's also one you may have to pay for... the restaurant has been known to charge more to sit outside.

La Biela is one of the city's most important cafes; in fact the government have declared it a "notable bar" and a protected landmark. Perhaps the protected landmark status has allowed the restaurant to coast on the food as many of the dishes are standard fare. Although, take note that this is one of the few cafes to offer a traditional iced coffee. Also worth ordering are the *picadas*, sampler plates large enough to share with a group.

Outskirts of the Neighborhood

Map V, C3–D3.

Recoleta also extends over Avenida Santa Fe, where you will find a scattering of other less well-known attractions, dotted bet-ween residential streets and commercial establishments.

Museo Xul Solar

Map V, C3. ◗ *Allow 30mins. Laprida 1212.* ✆ *(011) 4824 3302. www.xulsolar.org.ar. Open Tue–Fri 12–8pm, Sat 12–7pm. 10 A$. Guided tour Tue and Thu 4pm, Sat 3.30pm.*

Painter, sculptor, writer and musician **Oscar Agustín Alejandro Schulz Solari**, known as Xul Solar (1887-1963), was an eccentric and versatile artist, multilingual and well versed in religions, astrology and the occult. He was a friend of Jorge Luis Borges and also an illustrator of his books. The museum exhibits 86 paintings, as well as various esoteric instruments and objects that belonged to one of the most unusual representatives of the South American avant-garde.

Museo Casa de Ricardo Rojas

Map V, C3. ◗ *Allow 30mins. Charcas 2837.* ✆ *(011) 4824 4039. www.cultura.gov.ar. Open Mon–Fri 10.30am–6pm. Closed for renovations until mid-2012.*

Ricardo Rojas (1882-1957) was a prominent writer, poet and teacher from Tucumán in the country's far north. He is best known for his biography of Independence hero José de San Martín. On display here are Roja's personal effects, including thousands of books, but the main attraction is probably the building itself, which fuses European and indigenous influences behind an intricate façade that would look more at home in Arequipa, Peru.

Museo del Holocausto

Map II, B2 and Map V, D3. ◗ *Allow 40mins–1hr. Montevideo 919.* ✆ *(011) 4811 3588. www.museodelholocausto.org.ar. Open Mon–Thu 11am–7pm, Fri 11am–4pm. 10 A$.*

Buenos Aires has the largest Jewish community in Latin America and also the largest museum commemorating the Holocaust. This space was conceived to enhance remembrance and understanding. Past exhibits have included 1938 Germany through the eyes of an Argentinian doctor and a look at Adolf Eichmann's years spent living under an assumed name in Buenos Aires.

Location:
To the south of the main road, Av. Santa Fe.
Subte: Agüero (line D).
Bus nos.: 12, 39, 64, 152.

Travel Tip:
In the city where dinner is served between 10pm to midnight, it is customary to have a drink of *Fernet con Coca* to keep you going into the night. The bitter taste of Fernet mixed with the sweet flavor of Coke combines for a "perfect" drink. Preparation is simple: in an ice-filled glass, mix one part Fernet with two parts Coke and enjoy.

The Northern *barrio* of Palermo is so big that it's actually split into different boroughs—Palermo Chico, the trendy Palermo Viejo, the downtown area of Northern Palermo and the gastronomic zone in Las Cañitas. With that much ground to cover, it's hard to know where to begin.

Each piece of Palermo couldn't be more different. Palermo Chico is the historic home to Argentina's elite. Today the neighborhood's Colonial mansions and estates hold foreign embassies, educational centers and museums. Palermo Viejo, meanwhile, splits into the sub-neighborhoods of Palermo Soho and Palermo Hollywood. Palermo Soho, like its American counterpart, is artistic and bohemian. It borders the Plaza Cortázar, a meeting point for artists and designers, and the location of a weekend craft fair. Most of Argentina's television and movie production studios can be found in the refurbished warehouses of Palermo Hollywood. For shopping, Northern Palermo is the neighborhood to go to, especially the Alto Palermo Shopping Center, the city's swankiest shopping mall. Las Cañitas at the far right corner of the city was once best known for its military base and polo field. In the past few years, the neighborhood has been gaining more attention for its food. Get this: Las Cañitas has more restaurants than any other *barrio* in Buenos Aires.

But what sets Palermo apart from other neighborhoods is not its size or the diversity of its neighborhoods, but the abundance of its trees and parks. Palermo is home to the Parque Tres de Febrero, the Argentinian equivalent of Central Park. Covering 80ha/198 acres on the northwest side of the city, the Parque Tres de Febrero was designed by French landscaper and architect, Charles Thays, who modeled it after Paris' Bois de Boulogne and London's Hyde Park. The park may have an Old World feel, but you'll find plenty of native plants like lapachos, tipas, palos borrachos and jacarandas within it. If you're looking for a place to kick back with the locals, especially on a sunny weekend, this is the place to go.

In addition to the main park, Palermo has countless smaller plazas, a zoo and a traditional Japanese garden, and a botanical garden, which is not only famous for its 8,000 species of plants, but also for its large population of domestic cats. Pet lovers will enjoy seeing these felines making themselves at home.

Botanical Garden, marble sculpture of a woman, in a pool
Photo:© APEIRON-PHOTO/Alamy

PETER'S TOP PICKS

 CULTURE

The three million people who have visited the Latin American Art Museum and cultural center MALBA cannot be wrong. **Museo de Arte Latinoamerico de Buenos Aires (p 188)**

 GREEN SPACES

Palermo is know as the green district of the city. Check out Parque Tres de Febrero to find out why. In additional to having some of my favorite Japanese food, Palermo also has the largest Japanese-style garden outside Japan. **Parque Tres de Febrero (p 191) Jardín Japonés (p 193)**

 HISTORY

Evita's legacy is preserved at the Museo Evita. **Museo Evita (p 193)**

 STAY

My pick for Palermo hotel is so comfortable and accommodating, I'm not at all surprised that it's called Home. **Home (p 239)**

 SHOP

A good bookstore experience is hard to beat and Libros del Pasaje has books in English and French as well as Spanish. Make time for a coffee in the cafe while you're browsing. **Libros del Pasaje (p 256)**

 EAT

Las Cañitas has more restaurants than any other part of the city. The whole neighborhood is worth eating your way through. Also, one of my favorite Japanese restaurants is in Palermo. For interesting fusion and some of the best Peruvian and Japanese food, head straight to Osaka. **Las Cañitas (p 196) Osaka (p 246)**

 ENTERTAINMENT

Sometimes the best entertainment is to get dressed up and spend the night at the club. Go late and head to the Nicerto Club to dance the night away. **Niceto Club (p 195)**

WALKING TOUR

Palermo Chico★
Map V.

To the east of Palermo, adjoining Recoleta, Palermo Chico (Little Palermo) is the area that is home to Buenos Aires high society. There are numerous palaces and luxury residences to be admired here, some of which have been converted into museums. This tour takes in three of them and gives you a feel for the neighborhood. It can be easily added on to a visit to the adjacent sights of Recoleta *(see p170)*. Do be sure to check the opening days of the museums before setting off.

» *The nearest subway station (Bulnes) to the starting point is ten blocks away, so you'd do best to arrive by taxi or bus (10, 21, 37, 38, 41, 59, 60, 67, 92, 93, 95, 102, 110, 118, 130).*

Museo Nacional de Arte Decorativo★★
Map V, C2. ◗ *Allow 1hr 30mins. Libertador 1902.* ℘ *(011) 4801 8248. www.mnad.org. Open Tue–Sun 2–7pm. Jan–Feb, Tue–Sat. 5 A\$. (Free Tue). Guided tour Tue–Fri 2.30pm, 15 A\$ (English).*

With cherubs looking down from the roof and an entrance flanked by grand Neoclassical pillars, this enormous, French-inspired palace is a testament to the opulence that reigned in Buenos Aires at the beginning of the 20C.

The former residence of a fabulously wealthy Argentinian-Chilean family (Alvear and Errázuriz), it was built between 1911 and 1917, on the plans of French architect **René Sergent**, who designed Nissim de Camondo's private mansion in Paris.

Matías Errázuriz, the owner, a diplomat, had visited all the European capital cities. Returning to his country, he wanted to bring together the best of all that he had seen to provide an apt setting for the works of art that he had brought back with him. This explains the place's grandeur and the curious mixture of styles. To add to the visit's appeal, the furniture, works of art (El Greco, Fragonard, Corot, Manet, Rodin) and porcelain provide a fascinating exploration of decorative arts.

Ground floor
The **vestibule and foyer** are in the Neoclassical style, a mixture of imitation stone, coffered or molded ceilings, and Louis XVI-style decorative details, with allegories of the arts.

The large **drawing room** relies on the Renaissance style. Huge and two storys tall, it forms the central axis of the house. Note the five grand chandeliers, the inlaid parquet floor, the stained-glass windows, the chimney, the tapestries and the paneling inspired by the English Tudor period. There is also a painting by El Greco and Rodin had been commissioned to produce the fireplace, until plans were disrupted by WWI.

The **dining room** is inspired by Versailles, to which has been added a taste of the Baroque. Here the couple entertained Buenos Aires' and international high society.

Go through the winter garden to reach the ballroom, which is full of Rococo elegance with its curved lines, pale colors, gilding and many mirrored panels.

The **lady's drawing room**, with its 18C furniture, would have suited Marie-Antoinette, thanks to its cosy privacy, armchairs, painted wood paneling and soft furnishings. Moreover, its chandeliers are also inspired by Versailles. Notice the work by Fragonard and a beautiful Rodin.

The **master of the house's study**, designed by a French decorator, marries oak with red velvet, to which are added 19C paintings (including by Manet and Corot), Japanese laquerwork and pieces of Chinese jade.

ASK PETER...

Q: Where can I get some authentic Argentinian designs and clothes?
A: Plaza Serrano, which is located in Palermo Soho, is home to some of the most stylish people in all of South America. In fact, the bars and restaurants around the *plaza* temporarily close on Saturday and Sunday to become a showroom for designers who use the space to sell clothing and other cheap accessories. This gets hectic, but is not to be missed!

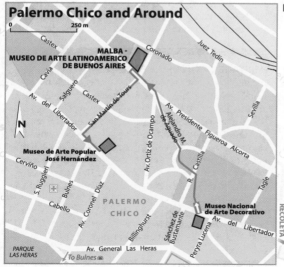

Palermo Chico and Around

187

First floor

The **tapestry gallery**, which forms a mezzanine around the large drawing room, shows, as its name indicates, French and Flemish tapestries from the 16C to the 18C, including scenes from the life of Christ (Tournai, 16C). It leads to private apartments, because each person had, in addition to his or her bedroom, a salon, dressing room, bathroom and toilet. **Matías Errázuriz's small private salon** was entirely decorated in Art Deco style by Catalan painter Josep María Sert: admire his four paintings on the theme of human comedy. The **master's antechamber and bedroom** contain furniture and objects from the period from Louis XVI to Napoleon Bonaparte. The **family drawing room**, which was the place to meet informally, houses a collection of miniatures and small European portraits (16C-19C).

Museo de Arte Latinoamerico de Buenos Aires (MALBA)★★★

Map V, C2. ● *Allow 1hr 30mins–2hrs. Figueroa Alcorta 3415.* ℘ *(011) 4808 6500. www.malba.org.ar. Open Wed–Mon, 12–8pm (9pm Wed), last entry 30mins before closing time. 22 A\$ (10 A\$ Wed). Restaurant.*

Built around the Costantini collection (first shown at the MNBA), this museum, which opened in September 2001 in a bright, well-designed building, has as its goal to show 20C Latin-American art, through all its trends, from Mexico to Argentina via the Caribbean. During its first decade this

» *Come out of the museum and turn left on Libertador, cross over the crossing and walk through the small park—Plaza Chile— past the children's playground. Cross over the mini-roundabout, past the grandfatherly statue of Independence hero José de San Martín. Before hitting the main road, turn left onto sidestreet Alejandro M de Aguado for a glimpse of grand residences and embassies. Follow it round, bearing right, until you come back to the main road, Presidente Figueroa Alcorta. On the other side, you will see the MALBA museum, almost at the foot of a giant skyscraper (10mins).*

HERITAGE OF THE BELLE ÉPOQUE

The district owes its name to its first owner, a Sicilian named Juan Domínguez Palermo. On his arrival in Buenos Aires, at the end of the 16C, the site was just swampland *(los bañados)* and for a long time it was just an area of small properties. Around 1830, things began to change when the city's governor and Argentina's first dictator, Juan Manuel de Rosas, had an imposing Colonial residence built here, putting Palermo on the map of desirable places. The pretentious house was abandoned when the Rosas fled into exile, then demolished at the end of the 19C, but, under Domingo Faustino Sarmiento's presidency, the district had begun its transformation, inspired by the great green spaces of the Belle Époque. Frenchman **Charles Thays** *(see p174)* played a central role in this conception.

privately owned, nonprofit gallery has been visited by over three million people and gained acclaim worldwide. The building is smaller than founder Eduardo Costantini originally wanted and can accommodate only 40 percent of his collection, so an expansion project is in the works. The museum's 1910s and 1920s collection is profoundly marked by the great figures of European art, by **Expressionism**, **Cubism** and **Futurism**. From Argentina, for example, there are the painters Xul Solar, with his *Pareja* (Couple) (1923) and Emilio Pettoruti (*La Canción del Pueblo*, 1927). From Uruguay, there are Rafael Barradas (*Quiosco de Canaletas*, 1918) and Joaquín Torres-García, while the Brazilian Tarsila do Amaral revisits **Surrealism**, integrating it with the exoticism of his own culture (*Abaporu*, 1928).

During the 1930s, the social and political context of South America encouraged the birth of a movement with a very distinctive character, **Social Realism**. Its great proponents are clearly the Mexicans—Diego Rivera, David Alfaro Siqueiros and José Clemente Orozco—but the importance of the Argentinian Antonio Berni with, for example, *Manifestación* (1934) and the Brazilian Candido Portinari (*Festa de São João*, 1936-9) should also be highlighted.

Covering several decades from the 1920s onward, **Surrealism** mixed very well with Latin American culture, with its popular piety, its mystic legends, and even its exploration of the psyche and automatisms. The figurehead of this movement was, of course, the Mexican Frida Kahlo, whose *Autorretrato con Chango y Loro* (1942) is much admired. But one mustn't forget artists such as Antonio Berni, Alfredo Guttero, Roberto Matta and Wifredo Lam.

From the 1940s onward, Buenos Aires became an important place artistically in the emergence of **Concrete Art** and its variations, which played on lines, surfaces, colors, spaces, optic distortions and movement, real or imagined. The 1950s, which marked the end of the Modern period, corresponded with the appearance of very different styles. Artists no longer worked only with paint, but created montages, installations and performances. At the same time, the international trends of Pop Art, neo-Surrealism and neo-Realism prompted already established artists to explore new avenues. In this respect, Antonio Berni's career has much to teach us. The Colombian Fernando Botero (*Los Viudos*, 1968, and *El Domingo por la Tarde*, 1967), Antonio Dias, Jorge de la Vega, Antonio Seguí, Liliana Porter and Guillermo Kuitca should also be mentioned.

To finish, don't miss the latest acquisitions, such as Marcia Schvartz's *Batato* (1989), plus work from Guillermo Kuitca (Argentina) and Jose Bedia (Cuba), who also became active at the tail end of the 20C.

The museum also hosts many interesting temporary exhibitions, including some high-profile loans from other parts of the world, such as the first big display of Andy Warhol's work in Argentina. On the website are details of all

Travel Tip:
Saying Argentina is the country of *empanadas* is an understatement. *Empanadas* are a dime a dozen, found in many cafes on every street corner throughout the city. So if beef/chicken *empanadas* just aren't doing the trick, take a taxi ride to Palermo Hollywood and ask for Fierro Hotel, where head chef Hernan Gipponi will whip you up a special batch of his rabbit *empanadas*! *Buon Appetito*!

current exhibitions, plus a wide-ranging literary and film program. The museum has its own small cinema on site, which puts on art house features and cult classics.

As you leave, note the thermometer-like structure that's flashing red, green and yellow on the outside front steps—it looks pretty but it is also measuring the levels of noise from traffic. Just by its side is a lovely, modern café/restaurant, where you can sit outside and try to block out the sound of that traffic.

» *Cross over the road outside MALBA, and take the road in front of you that is slightly to your left, San Martín de Tours. Follow it until you hit Libertador at the end. Turn left and you will come to the next stop (10 mins).*

» *Note that if you turn left outside the museum and carry on walking down Libertador for another 5 minutes, you will be back to your starting point. If you still have energy, carry on down here for another 10–15 minutes and you will be able to enjoy some of the key sights of Recoleta (see p170).*

Museo de Arte Popular José Hernández

Map V, C2. ◗ *Allow 30mins. Libertador 2373.* ✆ *(011) 4803 2384. www.museohernandez.org.ar. Open Wed–Fri 1–7pm, Sat, Sun and public holidays 10am–8pm. 1 A\$. No charge Sun.* This museum is housed in a beautiful early 20C family residence, that of **Félix Bunge**, a boxing promoter in Argentina *(see below)*. It contains craft and popular art collections, representative of the country's various traditional and contemporary specialties (silverwork, leatherwork, woodwork, glass, textile art, basketmaking, etc.) It recently acquired a small collection of Carnival costumes from Corrientes province.

A great supporter of local artisans and budding artists, it also organizes concerts and various music, painting and weaving classes and workshops. The museum is named after **José Hernández**, an Argentinian literary hero for his epic poem about gauchos, *Martín Fierro*. As a celebration of *criollo* traditions and Argentinian crafts, it makes a good contrast to the Europe-centric collection at the Decorative Arts Museum.

FÉLIX BUNGE

Even more interesting than the exhibits in the Museo de Arte Popular is the story of the building's owner Felix Bunge. Born in 1894, Bunge came from a wealthy family of *estancieros* and ran with the city's aristocracy during the 1920s. Bunge was also a trainer for one of the top boxers Luiz Ángel Firpo and for a while the national boxing headquarters were in the stables of Bunge's house. More than just a boxing aficionado, Bunge also followed and gave his funds to tango, gaucho culture and reactionary politics. Bunge came to an untimely end when his butler *(mucamo)* murdered him in 1935. In the last room of the museum, you can see a small laminated book with newspaper clipping of Bunge's life.

Parque Tres de Febrero★★

Map V, BC 1–2.

The veritable green lung of the capital, this huge park (80ha/198 acres), also known as the **Bosques de Palermo**, occupies the whole northern section of the district and is the biggest public garden in Buenos Aires. Opened in 1875, it is one of the major works of Franco-Argentinian landscape artist Carlos Thays *(see p170)*. Its vast grassy expanses dotted with monuments and statues and criss-crossed with shady footpaths and flower-lined walkways is the ideal place to enjoy some green without leaving the city. Locals come here to picnic, run, cycle or take a boat out on the artificial lakes. The park also contains a racecourse, velodrome, polo field and golf course. In the southern part of the park, at the intersection of *avenidas* Santa Fe and Sarmiento, the exhibition center La Rural hosts many international trade fairs and shows every year.

Jardín Botánico Carlos Thays★

Map V, B2. ◗ *Allow 30mins. Entrance via Av. Santa Fe (no 3951), Las Heras and República Arabe Siria.* ☏ *(011) 4831 4527. www.jardinbotanico.gov.ar. Open daily 8am–7pm (6pm in winter); Guided tours (in Spanish, 1hr 30mins) Fri 10.30, Sat–Sun 10.30am and 3pm.*

Designed in 1898, this botanical garden covering more than 7ha/17 acres exists to contribute to the conservation of plant biodiversity, notably that of Argentinian flora, which includes more than 10,000 species, 2,000 of them endemic. Punctuated with fountains, sculptures and five lovely greenhouses, these gardens are home to more than 6,000 species from every province in the country *(ombú, ibirá pitá, pindó, yatay, jacarandá…)* and from the world at large (including French, Roman and Japanese gardens). Don't miss the little interpretative trail to discover Argentinian flora *(trail guide in Spanish and English is available at the park reception).*

Jardín Zoológico

Map V, B2. ◗ *Allow 2–3hrs. On the corner of Sarmiento and Las Heras.* ☏ *(011) 4011 9900. www.zoobuenosaires.com.ar. Open Tue–Sun 10am–6pm (last entry 5pm). 22.50 A$ (without attractions), each attraction (boat crossing, reptile house, aquarium and tropical rain forest): 11 A$, daily pass*

Location:
Between Libertador and Las Casares.
Subte: Palermo, Plaza Italia and Scalabrini Ortiz (line D).
Bus nos.: 10, 34, 37, 57, 128, 130, 152, 160, 161, 166.

ASK PETER...

Q: What is the best value way to visit the zoo?
A: Within the Bosques de Palermo lies the 18ha/45-acre Buenos Aires Zoo, containing 89 species of mammals, 49 species of reptiles and 175 species of bird; for the best value, purchase the Pasaport Ahorro for 34 A$, which allows you to visit every exhibit, including the aquarium. The park is a great day for families as well, but should be avoided at night.

ARGENTINIAN WINES

Wine has become so popular in Argentina that in 2010, the Argentinian government declared wine to be the national liquor. It's easy to see why; Argentina is now the fifth-largest wine producing nation in the world.

Many of the vineyards and wineries have Spanish origins and were brought over during the Spanish colonization. The vines were originally brought to Santiago del Estero in 1557 and expanded slightly to neighboring regions before spreading out to other parts of the country. Spain also produced the Torrontes grape, which makes great white wines. However, it's not just about Spain. The French introduced Argentina to the Malbec grape and Italy is responsible for the Bonarda grape, which are unlike their ancestors and produce fruity and light wine.

Note, under Argentinian wine laws, if the name of a particular grape appears on the wine label, at least 80 percent of that wine must have been made from the grape on the label. Argentina has many different types of grapes found all over the country; Malbec grapes make a red wine with intense fruity flavors and a soft, velvety texture; the Pedro Gimenez grape is the most popular white wine grape and creates wines high in alcohol content. Other popular varieties include Torrontes, Chardonnay and Sauvignon Blanc.

Argentinian wine is just starting to be internationally recognized. Prior to 1990, Argentina winemakers were more interested in making large quantities, but not necessarily wine that could compete on an international scale. More than 90 percent of the wine during this time was consumed inside the country.

Argentina's answer to the Napa Valley is in Mendoza, which is about 700 miles west of Buenos Aires. It's home to as many as 800 wineries which have been gaining recognition particularly for their premium Malbec wines. But even if you can't make it to Mendoza, you can taste incredible Argentine wines in Buenos Aires. Gran Bar Danzon *(see p250)* has one of the more extensive wine menus in the city—and they serve by the glass, so you can mix and match to create your own tasting.

including attractions: 34 A$ (under 12s free).
This zoo, which was opened in 1875, contains more than 2,500 animals of 350 different species in over 18ha/44.5 acres. Aside from offering the chance to discover certain species that you won't have been able to see during your trip to Argentina, its originality lies above all in the architecture of its buildings, which reproduce structures from around the world: the Arch of Titus in Rome, the temple of the goddess Nimaschi in Mumbai, a French-style palace, a gothic pavilion…

There is a farm where visitors can feed the animals, while more exotic residents include jaguars, red pandas, elephants, hippos and giraffes.

Museo Evita★

Map V, B2. ◗ *Allow 1hr. Lafinur 2988. ℘ (011) 4807 0306. www.museoevita.org. Open Tue–Sun 11am–7pm, 15 A\$. Guided tour (1pm–7pm) 25 A\$.*

The wife of the former President Juan Domingo Perón, Eva Duarte Perón, known as Evita, is one of the country's most memorable figures *(see p42)*. The museum devoted to her life and social and political work tells the incredible story of this still much-adulated woman, who was in every way a legend, from her early years of poverty and career as a film star to her marriage and her premature death.

Converted from the women's shelter of the social aid foundation that she created in 1948, the museum contains a huge collection of photographs, videos, press articles and personal items, including some pieces from her wardrobe. There is also archive footage of the streets of Buenos Aires when her funeral was held and over a million people flocked onto the streets. The museum also has an attractive cafe/restaurant with an inviting outdoor patio on a sunny day.

Jardín Japonés

Map V, C2. ◗ *Allow 30mins. On the corner of Figuero Alcorta and Casares. ℘ (011) 4804 4922. www.jardinjapones.org.ar. Open daily 10am–6pm. 8 A\$.*

Created in 1967 as a gift from the Japanese community, this cultural complex offers various exhibitions and activities relating to Japanese culture. With its lake, little wooden

Travel Tip:
To see more influential places in Evita's life, Argentina Travel has a half-day tour that departs each Tuesday at 2pm. The tour includes a stopover at the Presidential Palace and Casa Rosada. *Booking: ℘ 770 891 7510; argentourism@ gmail.com.*

FLOOD PLAIN

If you would have wanted to build a city on the land where modern day Palermo now sits back in the 16C, the local inhabitants probably would have laughed at you. The area was and still is to this day, notorious for flooding. An Italian farmer named Giovanni Domenico Palermo was the one who originally bought the flood plains to the north of Buenos Aires in the 16C, drained them and turned it into prosperous orchards and vineyards. Palermo still gets hit hard by storms and due to an underground river lower Palermo still floods a couple of times a year.

GRAND ARCHITECT

We have a Frenchman to thank for most of Buenos Aires' green spaces. Charles Thays (1849-1934), renamed Carlos once naturalized, was in fact a Parisian architect and landscaper who decided to settle in Argentina in 1889. Having fallen in love with the country and its flora, he brought back trees and plants from his trips to Argentina's different provinces and was able to show off their beauty to best advantage in parks, gardens, squares and along the capital's avenues. Appointed director of parks and gardens to the city of Buenos Aires in 1891, he left a heritage of beautiful "compositions." While his major works are undoubtedly the **Parque Tres de Febrero★★** and the **Jardín Botánico★**, he was also the grand architect of the *plazas* de Mayo, de los Dos Congresos and de la Constitución, as well as the parks of Barrancas de Belgrano, Colón, Lezama, Patricios and Pereyra.

bridges, pavilions and tea house, it is a refreshing oasis in the heart of the city. It's also one of the largest overseas Japanese gardens in the world and contains numerous species brought from the Far East. Sushi and various traditional dishes are served in the restaurant.

Planetario Galileo Galilei

Map V, C1. ❍ *Allow 40mins. On the corner of Sarmiento and Figueroa Alcorta.* ✆ *(011) 4771 9393. www.planetario.gov. ar. Open Tue–Fri 4.30pm; Sat, Sun and public holidays hourly from 2–6pm. 6A$ (exhibitions) and 10 A$ (shows). Telescope: Sat and Sun 7.30–9pm.*
Opened in 1966, the Buenos Aires planetarium seems rather outdated, but it offers lots of activities and projections during the week and free sky-watching sessions during the summer. Three metallic meteorites that were discovered in the north of Argentina are exhibited at the entrance.

Museo de Artes Plásticas Eduardo Sívori

Map V, B1. ❍ *Allow 30mins. Infanta Isabel 555.* ✆ *(011) 4772 5628. www.museosivori.org.ar. Open Tue–Fri 12–8pm; Sat, Sun and public holidays 10am–8pm. 1 A$ (free Wed and Sat).*
This fine arts museum exhibits a wide panorama of Argentinian works from the first half of the 20C, all styles mixed together. Find it within the Parque Tres de Febrero, just opposite the bridge of the Rose Garden.

NIGHTLIFE
...LIKE A LOCAL

If you're looking for a night out, Palermo lets you experience how locals go out on the town. The night is never ending in Buenos Aires and is especially hot in Palermo, starting with dinner and drinks and ending well into the following morning. Many people don't even arrive at the nightclubs until 2am.

Niceto Club *(Niceto Vega 5510)* has dominated the club scene for almost a decade. With two different DJs and dance floors—this is the place to go dancing. Go on a Thursday and dance the night away to a soundtrack of pop, rock, reggae, hip hop, electro, funk, and tango. Know that this dance club can get very busy and isn't for the faint of heart. It tends to really kick up around 3am.

If you're looking for a more upscale and reserved night of drinks and dancing, Belushi Martini Bar *(Honduras 5333)* is your spot. This nightclub brings out some of the best-dressed crowds. Belushi features three rooms, each with its own style, ambiance, and music. Start the night at the sushi bar on the first level. Then enjoy one of the best martinis in town on terrace before gathering your strength to go inside and dance. Know that the dance floor doesn't heat up until around midnight. General admission translates into US$30, but also includes your first drink.

Mundo Bizzaro *(Serrano 1222)* is an off-beat alternative. The bohemian bar with enough risky artwork on its wall to merit the name has more than 50 cocktail options. After 1am the music changes and the dancing starts. Some of the most eclectic beats can be heard here.

Congo *(Honduras 5329)* is another popular after dinner spot that features a back garden and outdoor booths and cobblestone courtyards. It's considered one of the city's best outdoor drinking areas. While the cover charge is a little steep (10 A$ for ladies and 30 for gentlemen), they give you drink coupons at the door.

LAS CAÑITAS

Las Cañitas is a small subdivision of the Palermo neighborhood, roughly contained by avenues Luis María Campos and Libertador. It is named after a small country estate that used to reside on the spot at the beginning of the 20C. Predating that, the area was mainly swampland; in the 19C, its southern edge was Buenos Aires' cutoff point, as the wetlands around the Maldonado stream were considered unhygienic. These days, the Maldonado river runs mostly underground, much of it following the trajectory of Avenue Juan B. Justo. Over the years, a rather sleepy residential area gradually replaced the wide open spaces of the district, until the 1990s, when it suddenly became the place to be seen. Towering apartment blocks sprang up, and its core streets became lined with lively pubs, restaurants and nightclubs. Some of this spirit lives on, however Palermo Viejo has long-since usurped as the city's hottest area for a night out. Las Cañitas today has a safe, mainstream feel and has little in common with more gritty parts of town. By day or by night, it remains a nice place for a stroll.

Travel Tip:
El Hipodromo Argentino de Palermo is one of Argentina's most prestigious racecourses. Over 120 race meetings are held every year, including November's Gran Premio Nacional. Turf, as it is known in Argentina, is an alternate activity on a visit to Buenos Aires. The first-class racecourse is open Monday through Thursday from 2–10pm (times vary Friday through Sunday), and women usually get in for free.

Centro Cultural Islámico Rey Fahd

Map V, B2. ❍ *Allow 1hr–1hr 30mins for tour. Avenida Intendente Bullrich 55.* ✆ *(011) 4899 1144. www.ccislamicoreyfahd.org.ar. Guided tour Tue, Wed, Sat 11.45am.*

Seeing two minarets rise above a huge supermarket can take visitors by surprise. Opened in 2000 and occupying 3.5ha/8.6 acres, it holds conference rooms, a library and a school. There is capacity for worship for 1,200 men and 400 women. Designed by Saudi Arabian architect Zuhair Faiz, it is the biggest Islamic temple in Latin America, usurping the previous titleholder in Caracas, Venezuela.

Museo Nacional del Hombre

Map V, off map. ❍ *Allow 30mins. 3 de Febrero 1370/78.* ✆ *(011) 4783 6554. www.inapl.gov.ar. Open Mon–Fri 10am–6pm. 1 A$.*

Right on the border with Belgrano, this is Argentina's national museum of anthropology. The collection of 500 pieces includes archaeological findings, aboriginal crafts and a collection of masks from across the continent. The museum pays homage to the often-overlooked indigenous communities still living in Argentina today, plus it also includes archive photos of groups that were tragically eradicated by European colonizers.

Palermo Viejo

Map V, B3.

Palermo Viejo (Old Palermo) is the area that has evolved the most over recent years. It is a very pleasant residential area with roads lined with elegant early 20C houses, none more than two stories high. As a result of a housing boom, many of these homes have been restored, and an astounding number of designer stores, cafes and restaurants have sprung up, making this undoubtedly the trendiest part of town. The train tracks by the side of Avenida Juan B. Justo—along which the new Metrobús now runs—are often seen as the rough dividing line between the areas the have been nicknamed Palermo Soho to the east and Palermo Hollywood to the west. You can have a very pleasant few hours wandering this small network of streets, making spontaneous pit stops en route.

Plaza Serrano

Map V, A3. ◗ *Allow 20–30mins. Honduras and Serrano.*
You will always see this on maps under its official name, **Plaza Julio Cortázar**, however, it is still known commonly as Plaza Serrano, because it is bordered on one side by Avenida Serrano. It's not the most attractive plaza in the city— a children's playground is caged off in the middle and the bars that surround it all seem to blend into one—yet it's a good place to soak up a bit of Palermo Viejo's laidback atmosphere. On a mild winter's day, these open-fronted bars are just as busy as in mid-summer. At the weekend, there's a small craft market.

Palermo Hollywood

Map V, A2. ◗ *Allow 1hr. Between Juan B Justo, Dorrego, Santa Fe and Córdoba.*
The area situated to the west of the railroad is usually known as Palermo Hollywood, after various television companies and film studios set up here in the early 2000s. A few years ago, it was notably less developed than the so-called Palermo Soho area, but this is fast changing. There are now plenty of chic cafes, cocktail bars and boutique hotels here too.

Location:
Roughly contained by avenues Santa Fe, Scalabrini Ortiz, Dorrego and Córdoba. To find its core, arrive at Plaza Italia and walk southwest.
Subte: Ministro Carranza, Palermo, Plaza Italia (D line). The Metrobús also cuts through its middle, via Juan B. Justo (Stations: Pacífico, Guatemala, Honduras).
Bus nos.: 34, 39, 55, 57, 93, 108, 111, 140, 151, 166, 168.

In every neighborhood of Buenos Aires, you can find locals at work or at play. But Belgrano is where the locals actually live. That is not to say the neighborhood is without places to visit—on the contrary, Belgrano has several excellent museums and a Chinatown.

Belgrano is the most populous of the city's many *barrios*. Situated to the north of ritzier Palermo, Belgrano is a residential neighborhood with a suburban feel. Named after Manuel Belgrano, the designer of the Argentinian flag, Belgrano is split into four sub-neighborhoods: Belgrano C, Belgrano R, Belgrano Chico and Bajo Belgrano.

Belgrano C is the most interesting of the districts for tourists. It is where you will find most of the borough's museums and the Barrancas de Belgrano, another of French landscaper Charles Thays' designs. The promenade at Barrancas de Belgrano is a local favorite, and you'll often find families gathered there on weekends. Just east of Belgrano C in Bajo Belgrano, you can visit the tiny Barrio Chino, a Chinatown made up of mainly Taiwanese immigrants. If you're looking for some variety, the area has the city's most authentic Asian restaurants.

Belgrano is also home to the arch rivals of the Boca Juniors, the River Plate soccer club. River Plate's home stadium is the largest stadium in the country, the Estadio Monumental Antonio Vespucio Liberti also known as "El Monumental."

While you're here you'll also want to take a look at the Museo Historico Sarmiento and the Museum of Spanish Art. The Museo Historico Sarmiento holds books, furniture, diplomas, letters, miniatures and other personal items belonging to writer and former president Domingo F. Sarmiento. A visit to these museums is like taking a trip through the most important decades of 19C Argentina. Near the Museo Historico is the Larreta Museum of Spanish Art. Housed in the former home of writer Henry Larreta, the museum was designed to resemble a Renaissance palace, and has an Arabian-style garden surrounding it.

Larreta formed his collection in the early 20C, and it includes polychrome wood sculptures, and Renaissance and Baroque altarpieces and paintings.

PETER'S TOP PICKS

 CULTURE

The Museo de Arte Espanõl Enrique Larreta houses a remarkable Spanish art collection. **Museo de Arte Espanõl Enrique Larreta (p 201)**

 HISTORY

Learn about the history of Argentina through its former president Domingo F. Sarmiento. **Museo Histórico Sarmiento (p 202)**

 ENTERTAINMENT

You can tango throughout Buenos Aires, but to get down with the locals check out La Glorieta's weekend Tango *milonga*.
For the soccer fan, El Monumental is home to one of the city's most popular teams and it is large, which means visitors can usually score tickets. **La Glorieta (p 202) El Monumental (p 200)**

 **GREEN SPACES**

A weekend stroll along the promenade at the Barrancas de Belgrano is a must. **Barrancas de Belgrano (p 200)**

 SHOP

As this is a local *barrio*, the crafts at the weekly market in Plaza Belgrano are not your average tourist trinkets and are real local goods. **Plaza Belgrano (p 200)**

EL MONUMENTAL

Estadio Monumental Antonio Vespucio Liberti or El Monumental, as it is commonly known to sports fans all around the world, is the biggest football stadium in all of Argentina. It is considered the national stadium and is home of one of the biggest soccer teams in the country, River Plate.

In 1934, the already very successful team purchased the land to start construction for its home stadium. By May 1935, the cornerstone for the stadium was in place and the building committee started construction of the stadium with a substantial loan from the government. Architects Jose Aslan and Hector Ezcurra created the design and led the construction team in a three-year process.

Exactly three years to the date that the first brick was laid, the stadium opened to 8,000 people who witnessed the placement of the Argentinian and team flags on the grounds. The next day, the city hosted a festival which brought together 120,000 people to watch the first official game at the stadium. The home team hosted Penarol from Uruguay and happily, they won the match 3–1.

In 1978, the stadium was completely remodeled for the World Cup and expanded to be able to seat up to 70,000 fans. Matches at the stadium are a riot of fans in red and white cheering for their favorite team. It is definitely an experience for everyone, football fan or not!

The stadium is not only for football. In addition to hosting the home games for River Plate, El Monumental is also the main stadium for other national and international sporting events, including the Argentina National Football Team, the FIFA World Cup qualifications and various rugby matches. El Monumental was the first host of the Pan American Games' closing ceremony in 1951. As one of the city's largest arenas, it's also been home to sold out shows by Madonna, Michael Jackson, Bon Jovi and other major acts.

Plaza Belgrano *and Around*

Map I, B1.

If you arrive on public transport, by bus or subway, your first impressions of Belgrano won't do justice to this pretty, affluent residential district in the north of the capital. Steer clear of Avenida Cabildo, the busy main shopping street, and get to Plaza Belgrano, where you will find a little craft market at weekends and a rather more "authentic" at-

mosphere. The square is dominated by the Iglesia de la Inmaculada Concepción (Church of the Immaculate Conception), an imposing Renaissance-style building that is also known as *la Redonda* (the round). Farther west, on a little hill, the public park **Barrancas de Belgrano** is where the district's inhabitants go to walk. Its pretty pavilion, **La Glorieta**, is taken over at weekends by tango dancers for a *milonga (see Tango p253).*

Museo de Arte Españöl Enrique Larreta★

Map I, B1. ◯ *Allow 1hr. Juramento 2291. ☎ (011) 4784 4040. www.museolarreta.buenosaires.gob.ar. Open Mon–Fri 1–7pm; Sat, Sun and public holidays 10am–8pm. 1 A$ (free Thu). Guided tour Mon, Wed and Fri 5pm; Sat, Sun and public holidays 4pm and 6pm. Guided tour of the garden the first Sat of the month at 3pm and 5pm.*

To the northwest of Plaza Belgrano, the former Andalusian-style residence of the writer **Enrique Larreta** (1873-1961) houses his superb Spanish art collection: furniture, paintings, decorative arts, religious art. Among the remarkable objects, note the beautiful sculptures in polychrome wood and the altarpieces from the Renaissance and Baroque periods. The house is surrounded by a fine garden *(entrance on de Obligado, 2155).*

Museo Histórico Sarmiento

Map I, B1. ◯ *Allow 30mins. Juramento 2180. ☎ (011) 4782 2354. www.museosarmiento.gov.ar. Open Mon–Fri 1–6pm; Sat–Sun 3–7pm. 5 A$, Wed free. Guided tour Sun 4pm, book in advance.*

Founded on the fiftieth anniversary of the death of the writer and former president Domingo F. Sarmiento, this museum celebrates his life through a collection of his

PARQUE TIERRA SANTA

As the most populous of the Buenos Aires *barrios*, it only makes sense that Belgrano would house a large theme park for the masses to go and enjoy. But those who have Disneyland in mind will be in for a surprise. Located at Avenida Rafael Obligado 5790 is the popular—and controversial— Tierra Santa, the self-proclaimed "first" Christian themed amusement park. The park is a loosely based reconstruction of ancient Jerusalem and houses animatronics, actors and everything in between.

Location:
Demarcated by Juramento, Cuba, Echeverria, Vuelta de Obligado.
Subte: Juramento (line D).
Bus nos.: 15, 29, 41, 42, 44, 57, 59, 60, 63, 65, 67, 68, 80, 107, 113, 114, 133, 152, 161, 168, 184, 194.

ASK PETER...

Q: I'm craving Chinese food; can I get it in Buenos Aires?
A: You can. Chinatown began forming in Belgrano back in the 1980s, when an influx of Chinese immigrants settled in the area that is now the intersection of Arribenos and Juramento and a few blocks farther. You will find multiple stores and restaurants that provide authentic goods from the Far East. The biggest celebration in Barrio Chino is of course Chinese New Year (Jan/Feb), where a plethora of reds and golds decorate the streets accompanied by parades, performances and good food.

Travel Tip:
Looking for a free **tango** lesson? Every Friday, Saturday and Sunday night at La Glorieta in the Barrancas de Belgrano locals of all ages gather to dance under the stars in one of the city's lovelier parks. The serious dancing starts at 8pm, but show up an hour early and get tango tips from veteran dancers eager to share their moves.

BELGRANO THROUGHOUT HISTORY
Established in 1855, the village of Belgrano rapidly developed to attain the status of a town. In 1880, the governor of the province of Buenos Aires, beaten in the presidential elections, decided to oust the national government. Belgrano was thus designated as the federal capital, while Buenos Aires remained the capital only of its province. This lasted only seven years as in 1887 Belgrano was annexed and became simply a district of Buenos Aires.
Today, Belgrano is a wealthy neighborhood, with tree-lined streets and some enviable family homes. The British-built railway bolstered an Anglo-Argentinian community in the area in the late 19C and the influence can be seen in its houses, some of which have Mock Tudor stylings. The area is known for its little China Town, **Barrio Chino**, which arose with Taiwanese immigration in the 1980s. Its entrance *(Juramento and Arribeños)* is marked by a dragon-topped gate, donated by the Chinese Embassy, and behind it are a few streets of Asian supermarkets and restaurants.

possessions accumulated by state acquisition and family donations. It is housed in an ornate building, in Italian neo-Renaissance style. Built between 1869 and 1874 and one of the first buildings in Belgrano, it was used as the seat of government for a brief period *(see below)*.

Museo Casa de Yrurtia

Map I, B1. ▶ Allow 30mins. O'Higgins 2390. ✆ (011) 4781 0385. www.casadeyrurtia.gov.ar. Open Tue–Fri 1–7pm, Sun 3–7pm. 1 A$. Guided tour Tue and Fri 3pm, Sun 4pm.
The Argentinian sculptor **Rogelio Yrurtia** (1879-1950), who is to thank for some of the monumental sculptures on display in Buenos Aires—*Canto al Trabajo* (on the Plaza Coronel Manuel de Olazábal, San Telmo), *Monumento a Manuel Dorrego* (on the corner of *calles* Viamonte and Suipacha) and *La Justicia* (in the courthouse)—lived in this beautiful Colonial house with his wife, the painter Lía Correa Morales. The house's different rooms are cluttered with projects, studies and statues created by the artist.

ICE-CREAM
...LIKE A LOCAL

Buenos Aires is a hub of multifaceted cultures, all with a Latin American twist and the Italian presence in Argentina comes alive with the *heladeria* or ice-cream parlor. Argentine's love their ice-cream and it's a must-have if you want to experience all the goodness this city has to offer.

The ice-cream in Buenos Aires is as diverse as its people, ranging from sweet, light sorbets to *dulce de leche* (a sweet, sticky caramel-type spread turned into a deliciously sweet ice-cream). This has become one of the most popular forms of ice-cream in the city and is a South American delicacy that should not be passed up by tourists. *Dulce de leche* ice-cream takes a traditional local sweet (usually in the form of a jam) and turns it into a frozen scoop with intense flavor. Many of the ice-cream parlors in the city carry up to 10 different types of *dulce de leche*.

Since ice-cream is such an important part of Latin American culture, most ice-cream parlors stay open late—opening mid-morning and staying open well into the night (midnight or sometimes even later!). Check out some of these local shops:

Helados Scannapieco
Av. Corodova 4826.
Palermo is famous for its cool treats and Helados Scannapieco is the place to go for some of the most traditional ice-cream you can get. The shop is more than 70 years old and remains family owned. It boasts 50 flavors and has been featured on many top 10 ice-cream lists around the world.

Persicco *Salguero 2591.*
Palermo hosts one of the most popular ice-cream chains in the city. The family-run business is an experience in itself—from the modern parlor to the famous chocolate-flavored scoops. This ice cream shop also sells pastries, cakes, coffee, and breakfast

Un'Altra Volta
Santa Fe 1826 & Callae and Melo, Recoleta.
Another one of Argentina's most famous ice-cream chains, Un'Altra Volta is in constant competition with Persicco to make the best ice-cream and attract the most people. This parlor takes a lot of its inspiration directly from Italy, offering some of the best gelato in the city. These shops encourage you to sit down inside to enjoy your ice-cream .

Cadore *Corrientes 1695.*
Located in San Nicolás, this shop offers some of the best dulce de leche in the city. It is known for this particular style of ice cream and offers many different homemade flavors of the frozen treat. This is a nonchain parlor, so if you're looking for something unique, this one is for you.

If you want an escape from the touristy center of the city, Buenos Aires is surrounded by outer neighborhoods that radiate from the inner *barrios* to the city limits. These areas don't attract many tourists, but are what most locals call home.

To the south of Buenos Aires, you'll find *barrios* Nueva Pompeya and Barracas. These are working-class neigborhoods, but they have a few surprises. Nueva Pompeya, for example, is home to one of the city's most unusual attractions, a bird market called the Feria de los Pajaros. Every Sunday morning throughout the year pet sellers come to Sáenz Avenue and Perito Moreno to sell companion birds and goldfish. The fair is also a great place to try out Argentinian street food. To the west of Buenos Aires are the very suburban and middle-class neighborhoods of Balvanero, Caballito, Mataderos and Chacarita.

The gaucho *barrio* Mataderos is especially worth visiting for its weekly fair. For those who would like a taste of Pampas culture, but don't have the time to venture beyond Buenos Aires, the Feria de los Mataderos *(see p206)* is held every Sunday. This weekend fair is based on the gaucho culture, and you can buy typical Pampas crafts, meats, cheeses and sausages there. The fair also has a selection of traditional street foods from open-air vendors. You can sample freshly made *empanadas*, *tortillas* and *humitas*, a type of *tamale*. The people of Mataderos are proud of their gaucho culture, so you might see everyday residents (not actors) showing their cultural pride in full gaucho costume.

To the North of Buenos Aires are the districts of Núñez and Villa Crespo. Villa Crespo is sometimes referred to as "Palermo Queens," which the locals aren't crazy about, since they pride themselves on being their own neighborhood outside of Palermo. Villa Crespo, like Queens in New York, has an industrial background, but that is where the comparisons stop. The *barrio* is traditionally known for its Jewish community and it's also is a good place for bargain hunters, with outlet stores from brands like Lacoste, Puma and Cacharel.

Feria de los Mataderos on Sunday Photo: © Bertrand Gardel/hemis.fr

PETER'S TOP PICKS

 CULTURE

Consider the new media installations at the Galleria Arte x Arte and visit the distinctive La Calle de los Colores. **Galleria Arte x Arte (p 212) La Calle de los Colores (p 209)**

 GREEN SPACES

Parque Rividada combines local bargain shopping with outdoor green space. This open park filled with historic sculptures has a second life as a counterfeit entertainment market. **Parque Rivadavia (p 210)**

 HISTORY

Before there were subways, there were trams. Take an historic ride on the Tranvía Históric, which is kept up and running by local tram enthusiasts. The tomb of Carlos Gardel in the cemetery is also a big attraction in the neighborhood. **Tranvía Históric (p 211) Cementerio de la Chacarita (p 208)**

 SHOP

You might not be in the market to bring home a pet canary, but the Feria de los Pajaros is an unforgettable spectacle. Plus the local food stalls associated with the market are a street food experience not to be missed. **Feria de los Pajaros (p 214)**

 EAT

Head a little out of the main city, and then you eat at an authentic *asado*. Or, for one better, take a cooking class and learn to make your own. **Teresita (p 207)**

Location:
In the city's north;
neighboring
Belgrano.
Train: Nuñez,
Rivadavia (Mitre line
—overground,
not *subte*).
Bus nos.: 15, 28, 29,
57, 117, 130, 152.

Núñez

Map I, B1.

This northern *barrio* takes its name from its founder, local politician Don Florencio Emeterio Núñez, who donated land for the railroad station in 1873. It has a similar feel to neighboring Belgrano, with leafy streets and attractive homes. On its east side, the River Plate runs at its side and a portion of the Parque de los Niños (children's park), has been turned into a summertime city "beach" since 2009. It also contains soccer and volleyball pitches. Find it where avenue General Paz ends. River Plate soccer club is generally associated with Núñez, even though their stadium—Monumental Antonio Vespucio Liberti, also known simply as El Monumental—is technically based in Belgrano.

Escuela de Mecánica de la Armada (ESMA)

Map I, B1. ◗ *Allow 3hrs. Libertador 8151.* ✆ *(011) 4704 7538. www.espaciomemoria.ar. Guided tours (book in advance) Mon, Wed, Fri 10am, noon, 2pm; Sat 11am, 1pm. English available on request.*

During the country's so-called Dirty War in 1976-83 *(see History p36)*, this military school was used as clandestine prison, where thousands were tortured and killed. Since 2004, it has been a museum, dedicated to the memory of victims.

FERIA DE MATADEROS

Right on the city's western limits, Mataderos *(45mins by bus from the center—less in a taxi)* is where a traditional gaucho fair takes place on weekends *(every Sunday afternoon, except in the height of summer when it moves to Saturday evenings)*. The word *mataderos* refers to the slaughterhouses that once stood here, but these days, the old buildings are used to house market stalls. Over 300 of them are put up every week, selling traditional foods, such as homemade *dulce de leche* and *empanadas*, plus country clothing, including ponchos and silver-buckled belts. There is typically live music and folk dancing, with some participants dressed up in full gaucho regalia. You can often catch displays of horsemanship too. *Av. Lisandro de la Torre and Av. De Los Corrales.* ✆ *(011) 4323 9400. www.feriademataderos.com.ar. Apr–mid-Dec, Sun 11am–8pm. Mid-Jan–March, Sat 6pm–1am.*

Travel Tip:
To get to this fair west of the city center you can take buses nos 55, 63, 80, 92, 103, 117, 126, 141, 155, 180. If you are driving, take Av. Rivadavia until Av. La Plata, then Highway 25 de Mayo until the exit at Calle Escalada. Continue to Av. Eva Perón, then Lisandro de la Torre.

ASADO ...LIKE A LOCAL

Do you know what an *asado* is? If not, now is the time to learn!

An *asado* is a weekly occurrence for *porteños*. It's a time to gather with friends and family and enjoy great food. Argentina and beef go hand in hand and the *asado* is a celebration of succulent cuts of meat and slow cooking. The meat is cooked on an Argentinian *parrilla* (grill) that might measure up to 6m/20ft in length. Using natural wood to warm the *parrilla* for short periods of time, several cuts of beef, sweetbreads, sausages and chicken are slowly grilled (between 45 minutes to a couple of hours) creating a delicious three-course meal.

The first course is *picada*, a spread of dried/cured meats and cheeses served with wine. The second course is *achuras*, which include *chorizo*, *molleja* and French bread topped with *chimichurri* (a marinade that originated in Argentina). The third course is comprised of *papas fritas*, **salad** and *bife de chorizo*, *vacio*, *entrana*, *lechon*, *pollo* or ribs *(see p243 for translations.)*

To learn how to make authentic Argentina *asado*, take a cooking class with Teresita. Cooking with Teresita has become such an institution she's now shed her last name like Madonna. Teresita is an expert in Latin-American cooking and uses those skills to show both locals and tourists how to create authentic meals using the freshest ingredients. Teresita attended the Aileen Bovio Cooking School in the 1970s and has traveled to remote villages ever since, learning the best local techniques. She later opened a kitchen in Argentina to show others various techniques of Latin-American cooking.

As part of the class you are taken to the butcher shop to see the different beef cuts and learn which ones to choose for the absolute best *asado*. Next, you will go back to Teresita's kitchen to learn how to grill the meat to perfection. You will also prepare other classic Argentinian dishes to compliment your meat.

Once all the hard work is complete, sit down and enjoy the meal! Pair the *asado* with some local Malbec and you will be enjoying a true Argentinian meal. The location is 30-40 minutes south of Buenos Aires; consult the website for directions. Cooking with Teresita starts at 11am and goes until 4pm for US$110. *(Spiro 456, Adrogue, CP 1846; (011) 4293 5992; www.try2cook.com/cooking-classes-in-buenos-aires.html).*

In a deliberate move, barely any modifications have been made—just a few signs have been added, while some of the rooms are kept empty.

Location:
In the city's west, neighboring Palermo and Villa Crespo.
Subte: Dorrego, Federico Lacroze (B line).
Train: Federico Lacroze (Urquiza).
Bus nos.: 19, 39, 42, 44, 47, 63, 65, 71, 76, 78, 87, 93, 108, 111, 112, 123, 127, 140, 168, 176, 184.

Chacarita

Map I, B2.

The name Chacarita comes from *chacra* meaning "small farm," dating back to when the area was run by Jesuits in the 18C. Nowadays, the center of the *barrio* is busy with commuters who swarm in and out of busy Federico Lacroze station, where a network of overland routes meets the *subte*. At the weekends, there is a small organic food market, El Galpon, in the old railway sidings, which has a bohemian vibe and its own informal restaurant with outdoor seating (*Federico Lacroze 4171; ✆ (011) 4554 9330; www.elgalpon.org.ar; Wed and Thu, 9am–6pm*).

Cemententerio de la Chacarita★

Map I, B2. ◗ *Allow 1hr. Guzmán 780. ✆ (011) 4553 9338. www.cementeriochacarita.com.ar (unofficial site). Open 7am–6pm.*

At 70ha/175 acres, this is the biggest cemetery in Argentina and was created for the yellow fever victims that Recoleta would not accept. On initial entry, it bears resemblance to the higher-class necropolis across town, with rows of elaborate tombs, set out in block formation. Beyond this, there are rows of simple white crosses for the poor. The main attraction for many is the tomb of **Carlos Gardel**

Travel Tip:
When you're headed out of town, you might be tempted to hop on the train. Trains in Buenos Aires aren't always the peaceful experience you might expect. Many trains are not well-maintained, which can mean an unpleasant experience and delays. If you do travel by train, know there are four classes, but you'd do well do avoid the *tourista* class as it is the most overcrowded.

BARRACAS GENTRIFICATION

Like the famous Caminito area located in La Boca, Barracas is another *barrio* that has been pegged as a "tougher" area and has undergone some gentrification in recent years. But what draws most people to the area is its reputation of being as beautiful and diverse as el Caminito, just without all the tourists. Barracas even has its own famous street of brightly painted houses called Calle Lanin. But unlike its La Boca counterpart, which is mainly defined by its solid-colored houses, Calle Lanin is known for the striped and swirled designs that cover the walls of the houses that stretch down the street.

(see p54), which includes a large bronze statue, where devotees leave offerings throughout the year, including lit cigarettes that are rested between his fingers. The tomb of faith healer **Madre María Salomé Loredo** also draws a stream of devotees, as did the tomb of Juan Domingo Peron, until his remains were transferred to his former home in the provinces in 2006. The other most interesting part is the Recinto de Personalidades (celebrities' enclosure), in the cemetery's seventh sector, where the resting places of various entertainers are marked by kitsch statues recreating the act they were most famous for, such as playing the accordion or the piano.

Barracas

Map I, C3.

The area takes its name from the shacks and warehouses *(barracas)* that lined the waterside in the 19C. Like many of the southern *barrios*, things were all going well here, until the yellow fever outbreak caused the wealthy residents to abandon their homes and the area to fall into decline.

Recently, things have been looking up and the neighborhood has been given a boost as the government seeks to turn it into a design district. Some old warehouses and factories have been transformed into loft apartments, such as the French-style Barracas Central building at the corner of Lanin and Feijóo. The transformation is in its early days though, so be extra streetsmart if you come to this area.

Location:
In the city's south. West of La Boca, south of San Telmo.
Bus nos.: 12, 17, 20, 22, 25, 45, 51, 59, 60, 79, 95, 98, 100, 102, 129, 133, 134, 148, 154, 195.

Centro Metropolitano de Diseño

Map I, C3. ● *Allow 40mins for tour. Algarrobo 1041.*
℘ (011) 4126 2950. www.cmd.gov.ar. Guided tours Fri, 11am. Book ahead by emailing visitasguiadascmd@gmail.com.

Housed in a converted fish market, this high-tech design center was created as part of the government plan to inject more investment and opportunity into the city's south. Covering 14,000sq m/151,000sq ft, it is used by small and medium design companies. Buenos Aires has long been recognized for being a leader in design and in 2005 it was named one of (then) only three UNESCO-appointed Cities of Design, alongside Berlin and Montréal. Now it has its own dedicated nucleus, which also acts as a focal point for the Buenos Aires International Design Festival every October. It is worth visiting if you are a design enthusiast and book the guided tour.

La Calle de los Colores
Map I, C3. ◗ *Allow 15mins. Lanín 1–200 (between Brandsen and Suarez).*
Close to boarded-up buildings and an austere-looking psychiatric hospital, this hidden backstreet comes as a welcome contrast, injecting color into the working-class *barrio*. In 2001, a *porteño* artist, Marino Santa María, decided to give his street a lift by painting the frontages of the houses. The result is a two-block splash of color, using distinctive swirling mosaics. Santa María—whose workshop is at number 33 (📞 *(011) 5728 3364)*—specifically said he was not trying to produce another el Caminito *(see p163)* or create any specific purpose, other than simply joining creativity and everyday life, and opening up art to people who would not normally go to museums. There are sporadic street fairs here, but generally this is a residential road with none of the tourist circus you find in La Boca. You may want to go to take some photos, but if you do, don't walk around the surrounding area displaying an expensive camera.

Location:
In the city's west; past Balvanera.
Subte: Puan, Primera Junta, Acoyte, Rio de Janeiro (line A).
Metrobús: Donato Alvarez, San Martín.
Train: Caballito (Sarmiento line).
Bus nos.: 2, 5, 15, 24, 25, 26, 36, 42, 55, 65, 71, 76, 84, 85, 86, 88, 92, 96, 99, 103, 104, 105, 112, 124, 132, 135, 141, 146, 172, 181.

Caballito

Map I, B2.

The name of this *barrio* means "little horse" and it is said to come from the horse-shaped weather vane on a neighborhood *pulpería* (gaucho bar). It's a low-key, middle-class area, which is at its most lively on its portion of Avenida Rivadavia, one of the capital's most important arteries, extending a remarkable 35km/22mi. Caballito is blessed with two large green spaces, Parque Rivadavia and Parque Centenario. The latter was created by renowned French-Argentinian urbanist Charles Thays *(see p194)*, who completed the project in time for the 1910 centenary of the May Revolution.

Museo Argentino de Ciencias Naturales
Map I, B2. ◗ *Allow 1–2hrs. Angel Gallardo 490.* 📞 *(011) 4982 0306. www.macn.secyt.gov.ar. Open daily 2–7 pm. 5 A$.*
Situated on the edge of pleasant Parque Centenario, this natural history museum has been in its current location since 1937, having previously occupied a variety of spaces around town since its foundation in 1812. It holds a huge collection, focusing on botany, paleontology and geology. Generally, the setup is very traditional (stuffed animals and fossils behind glass cases), but there have been attempts to modernize it with some interactive displays. The main floor includes skeletal reconstructions of giant dinosaurs found in Patagonia.

Parque Rivadavia

Map I, B2. ◯ *Allow 30–40mins. Rivadavia 4800.*
Covering 6ha/15 acres, this park has a small lake, an amphitheater and a children's play area. There are also two notable sculptures, a large stone arch with South American Independence leader Simón Bolívar riding through, dating from 1942, and *Fuente de la Doncella*, a fountain by Barcelona artist Josep Limona I. Bruguera, inaugurated in 1931. The latter was removed in the 1970s after conservative locals complained about the female figurines nudity. She was moved back in 2003 when the park underwent substantial renovation. On Sundays, the park has a fair selling books, CDs and records. After the 2001 crisis, the numbers of vendors selling secondhand and pirate goods shot up from 90 to 900, and the park's makeover project was instigated to bring these swelling numbers back under control.

Tranvía Histórico★

Map I, B2. ◯ *Allow 20–30min. Emilio Mitre 500.* ✆ *011 4114 5791. www.tranvia.org.ar. Open Sun 10am–7pm. Sat–Sun 4–7.30pm (until 8.30pm Dec–Feb).*
This small section of historic tramway is kept open and running every weekend by a group of enthusiasts, the *Asociación Amigos del Tranvía* (Friends of the Tram Association) since 1980. Anyone is welcome to hop on its 2km/1.2mi loop as it runs between *calles* Emilio Mitre, Rivadavia, Hortiguera and Directorio. The trip takes around 15–20 minutes, with trams leaving from Emilio Mitre 500 at 20-minute intervals. The route skirts along the edge of so-called "Barrio Inglés"—Emilio Mitre and Valle—known for its English-style houses.

Villa Crespo

Map I, B2. Map V, A3-B3.

The Palermo effect is starting to creep over peaceful Villa Crespo's borders, with cute cafes, trendy bars and the odd boutique hotel opening their doors. Yet it still retains a residential feel, with some of its bars, such as 878 *(see p250),* **hidden behind deliberately unmarked frontages. At one point, real-estate agents started to label it Palermo Queens, but residents didn't take kindly to it. Like New York's Queens, Villa Crespo has**

Travel Tip:
The farther you get from the city center, the more authentic your experience can get and the *barrio* of Mataderos is about as authentic as they come. Located about an hour outside of the city, the *barrio* was founded on the site of old turn-of-the-20C slaughterhouses and is today home to the lively Feria de Mataderos.

Location:
South-west of Palermo.
Subte: Angel Gallardo, Malabia, Dorrego (B line).
Metrobús: Aguirre, Corrientes, Honorio Pueyrredón, San Martín.
Bus nos.: 15, 19, 36, 57, 92, 99, 106, 109, 110, 127, 140, 141, 151, 160, 168.

Travel Tip:
The neighborhood
of Villa Crespo has
discounts on leather
goods on Murillo
Street, especially one
flagship store called
Murillo666. Also, a
section of Cordoba
Avenue is known
for its factory outlet
stores.

an industrial heritage and originally grew up around a 19C shoe factory. The area is known for its large Jewish community and it is also a good place to pick up a bargain, from the outlet stores just west of Avenida Córdoba—Lacoste, Puma, Cacharel—to the leather specialists on Murillo Street.

Galeria Arte x Arte

Map V, B3. ◗ *Allow 30mins. Lavalleja 1062.* ✆ *(011) 4773 2738. www.galeriaartexarte.com. Open Tue–Fri 1.30–8pm, Sat 11.30am–3pm. Closed Jan–Feb.*

There are plenty of small galleries tucked away on the streets in this part of town (see *gallery-nights.com.ar* for details of *barrio*-wide open days), but this is a standout choice. It is deceptively big *(1,800sq m/1,9375sq ft)* and well equipped. The specialism is new media, with video installations and photography displays. It has six exhibition halls, a video room, a reading room and a library.

Location:
In the city's south.
West of Barracas and
La Boca.
Bus nos.: 6, 9, 15, 28,
32, 42, 44, 46, 70, 75,
76, 85, 91, 112, 115,
128, 135, 150, 158,
160, 165, 177, 178,
179, 188, 193.

Nueva Pompeya

Map I, B3-C3.

This southern neighborhood is strongly associated with tango. Along with neighboring Parque Patricios, it has the nickname *barrio de las ranas* (neighborhood of frogs), because there was once a huge waste dump here and those who sifted through the trash in the notoriously boggy ground, which was prone to severe flooding, were known as the "frogs." Its most recognizable landmark is the neo-Colonial José Félix Uriburu Bridge, also known by its former name, Valentín Alsina. This is another neighborhood where visitors should exercise great caution and preferably visit with a local.

Iglesia de Nuestra Señora del Rosario de Nueva Pompeya

Map I, B3. ◗ *Allow 20mins. Esquiú 974.* ✆ *(011) 4919 0772. www.pompeya.parroquia.org. Open daily 7.30am–noon, 3–8pm.*

This Buenos Aires *barrio* seems to have little in common with the Roman city of Pompeii that it takes its name from, but the connection stems from this church. The story goes back to a reformed Satanist in Italy, Bartolo Longo (1841-

GAUCHOS

Traveling north to the outer neighborhoods of Buenos Aires, you might come across gauchos, a term used to describe wanderers of the Pampas and other Argentinian grassland areas. These hardworking horsemen, commonly referred to as "South American cowboys," are known for their notoriously free lifestyle.

The gauchos spent many years herding cattle and working ranches in the vast plains of northern Argentina. They made their living riding horses and keeping the cattle in order. Many gauchos spent so much of their lives on horseback that they became bow-legged from so little walking. Many times a horse was a gaucho's sole property. Much like North American cowboys, in the past gauchos had a reputation for being strong and silent types who weren't immune to using violence if threatened. If you want to see how close the gauchos are to cowboys, check out the 1952 film *The Way of the Gaucho* staring Gene Tierney and Rory Calhoun.

As you'll see in the film, gaucho dress is very distinctive. A traditional outfit includes a poncho, which is also used as a saddle and sleeping blanket; a facon (large knife); a rebenque (whip); bombachas (loose fitting pants); a wide-rimmed hat; and a tirador (a belt used with the pants). The Gaucho "facon", or large knife, is usually tucked into the back of the gaucho sash. The facon is legendary not just as a weapon and ranch tool, but also as the main food utensil carried around. It's fitting considering that the gaucho diet is said to consist entirely of beef and yerba maté.

Don't expect to see modern gauchos in this outfit; instead they are likely to be found wearing overalls and boots. Whatever the outfit, gauchos remain an essential part of ranching in Argentina. Gauchos still live on rural farms and practice many of the same traditions, including riding horses, herding cattle and playing their traditional music. In fact the gaucho's horse skills remain legendary and are considered some of the best roping and riding skills in the world. Most gauchos are found in the Northern and Eastern Pampas region.

1926) who, to save his sinful soul, dedicated his life to promoting the Virgin of the Rosary. His devotion led to a church in this name being built in Pompeii, as well as various others around the world, including this one, inaugurated in 1900 in neo-Gothic style. After his death, Longo was beatified by the Pope and this church is highly significant to the country's Catholic majority.

Feria de los Pajaros
Map I, B3. ❷ *Allow 30mins. Perito Moreno and Sáenz. Open Sun 8am–2pm.*
Dating back 50 years, this bird market is an unusual and little-known weekly event, drawing very few tourists. It consists of a few stalls selling birds—namely canaries. Cages, feed, toys and accessories are also on sale, as well as other pets and snacks for hungry shoppers.

Location:
Just west of center; south of Palermo.
Subte: Carlos Gardel, Pueyrredón, Pasteur, Callao (B line); Plaza de Miserere, Alberti, Pasco, Congreso (line A); Corrientes, Once, Venezuela (line H); Callao, Facultad de Medicina (D line).
Train: 11 de Septiembre (Sarmiento line).
Bus nos.: 6, 10, 12, 17, 24, 26, 29, 37, 39, 41, 50, 60, 61, 62, 64, 68, 71, 75, 95, 99, 101, 106, 108, 109, 111, 115, 118, 124, 132, 140, 146, 168, 150, 152, 180, 188, 194.

Balvanera

Map 1, B2-C2 and Map II, A2–4.

Once and Abasto, as well as Congreso *(see p126)*, **are unofficial neighborhoods that fall into the center-west** *barrio* **of Balvanera. Once (pronounced "on-say") centers around the 11 de Septiembre railroad station, named after an 1852 battle, and Plaza Miserere, also called Plaza Once. It's known for having a large immigrant population and plenty of cheap, quantity-not-quality shopping. Abasto is a strong tango neighborhood and was once home to the genre's biggest legend, Carlos Gardel. The dashing performer remains omnipresent, from his statue on an alley that bears his name (Pasaje Carlos Gardel 3200) to the series of wonderful murals on Pasaje Zelaya, depicting him in his trademark hat and painted by Marino Santa María** *(see La Calle de los Colores p210)*. **Pasaja Zalaja also has lyrics of Alfredo La Pera's most famous tango songs painted on its walls. For more street art, see Calle Jean Jaure** *(700)*, **which pays homage to the** *porteño* **style of** *fileteado*. **Aside from its tango heritage, Balvanera is also known for having a large Peruvian community, so there are plenty of no-frills** *cantinas* **for getting a fix of** *ceviche* **(seafood "cooked" in citrus) and** *Inca Kola* **(a Peruvian soft drink).**

Palacio de las Aguas Corrientes★★
Map II A2–3. ❷ *Allow 40mins. Riobamba 750.* ✆ *(011) 6319 1104. Open (museum) Mon–Fri 9am–1pm. Guided tours every Mon, Wed and Fri, 11am.*
This 1887 building sums up Buenos Aires' extravagant Belle Époque better than any other. Filling up an entire block, the Water Palace is one of the city's most beautiful buildings, built in high Victorian style, its façade covered with

300,000 glazed Royal Doulton bricks, all shipped over from Britain. Yet, despite all this extravagance, it was never more than a folly, built to disguise water tanks. Today it houses a peculiar museum, **Museo del Patrimonio Aguas Argentinas**, which displays a collection of toilets through the ages, among other water-related objects.

Museo Casa Carlos Gardel

Map I, B2. ❍ *Allow 30–50mins. Jean Jaurès 735.* ✆ *(011) 4964 2015. www.museocasacarlosgardel.buenosaires.gob.ar. Open Mon, Wed, Thu, Fri 11am–6pm, Sat–Sun 10am–7pm. 1 A$ (free Wed).*

The far-fetched legend says that tango superstar **Carlos Gardel** (1890-1935) *(see p54)* bought this house five times having repeatedly sent his tour money back to a friend, who kept losing it at the horse races. Gardel lived here with his mother from 1927 to 1933, before moving to New York to work with NBC and Paramount. It is a traditional *casa chorizo*, shaped long and thin, like a sausage, and visitors can explore four rooms containing memorabilia and belongings related to the star. There is also a TV that constantly loops his films.

The back two rooms relate to his death, aged 44, in a plane crash while touring in Colombia. The dramatic newspaper headlines, calling the date the "Blackest Day in Argentina," show the impact he had on his country.

Mercado de Abasto★ and Museo de los Niños

Map I, B2. ❍ *Allow 1hr. Corrientes 3247.* ✆ *(011) 4959 3400. www.abasto-shopping.com.ar, www.museoabasto.org.ar. Open daily 10am–10pm. Children's museum Tue–Sun 1–8pm. 40 A$ children (weekends 45 A$), 20 A$ adults.*

This fabulous Art Deco building was finished in 1934, designed, in part, by Slovenian architect **Viktor Sulčič**, who was also responsible for Boca Juniors' stadium *(see p167)*. It was originally a food market, but in the late 1990s it was turned into a shopping mall, with a multiscreen cinema, food court and an array of chain stores. It now lays claim to the only kosher McDonalds outside of Israel.

Upstairs is the children's museum, with plenty of educational and inspirational games for the under 12s. Experiential exhibits allow kids to step into the shoes of a doctor, banker, actor or journalist, among other professions. Next door is a small fairground, Neverland, complete with mini Ferris wheel.

Travel Tip:
Walking the streets of Buenos Aires you're sure to spot posters with Carlos Gardel's image splattered on random street corners. Carlos Gardel is *the* Tango Maestro of Argentina, being the first to introduce the world to tango.

ASK PETER...

Q: Are there any evening activities you'd recommend in the outer neighborhoods?
A: It's a Monday night, you either stay in and rest from your trip or decide to go to a bar, or you might decide to join the 3,000 Argentinians who gather every Monday to listen to 17 musicians and drummers performing. Ciudad Cultural Konex *(Sarmiento 3131)* is an old oil factory in Abasto, and the giant fiesta is led by creator and leader Santiago Vazquez. La Bomba is from 8pm to 10pm, but be sure to be early—lines go all the way around the block.

If you have the time, get away from the bustle of Buenos Aires to get a sense of life outside of the city and a taste for the rest of Argentina... and even Uruguay.

Just a few kilometers north of the city there is the Paraná Delta, a region that is a favorite weekend getaway for city dwellers. The Delta is also home to around 3,000 islanders who live in stilted houses. Following the Delta can take you only a few kilometers short of the border of Uruguay and into a tropical terrain that seems almost Amazonian.

Northwest of Buenos Aires, you'll find a completely different landscape but one that has become the emblem of Argentina, the wide grassy plains of the pampas. Save a few days to stay in San Antonio de Areco, which is considered the home of the gaucho culture. Here you can stay on an *estancia* (working farm), and see modern-day gauchos performing farm tasks and herding cattle. In some *estancias*, you can even participate in chores and try your hand at being a gaucho for the day.

South of San Antonio de Areco is another Pampas town, the country town of Los Lobos. Los Lobos is most famous for its lakes, known as the Lagunas Encadenadas, the chained lakes. They are great for water sports; especially fishing which is bountiful in the area.

While you're in Buenos Aires, it's also worth getting another stamp on your passport by visiting neighboring Uruguay. An hour by catamaran and three hours by ferryboat across the Río de la Plata takes you to the historic town of Colonia del Sacramento in Uruguay. This little town was founded by the Portuguese and is reminiscent of historic sectors in Lisbon. Colonia del Sacramento is renowned for its historic quarter, a World Heritage Site. The quarter has the oldest church in Uruguay, the Iglesia Matriz, which dates back to 1680. The historic center also offers panoramic views of the town from El Faro, the white lighthouse constructed in 1857 from stones from the ruins of the convent.

Boats at Tigre, the Panará Delta Photo: © Christian Guy/hemis.fr

PETER'S TOP PICKS

 CULTURE

Take a trip across the water to Uruguay, to experience a different culture to that of Buenos Aires. See if you can spot the Portuguese influence.**Colonia del Sacramento (p 230)**

 GREEN SPACES

Isla Martín García is my pick for lush forests and an isolated beach experience. **Isla Martín García (p 221)**

 HISTORY

If you're Catholic, you might have heard about the pilgrimage to Lujan. Try to visit in October when almost a million devotees make the trip from Buenos Aires on foot. **Basílica de Nuestra Señora de Luján (p 225)**

 STAY

Get away from it all, camping on the Paraná Delta. **Paraná Delta (p 218)**

 ENTERTAINMENT

Check out the stadium in La Plata for football as well as concerts. Newly opened, it's one of the country's most high-tech stadiums. Another recommendation would be to take to the water-wa0ys by boat in the Paraná Delta. **La Plata (p 227)**. **Paraná Delta (p 218)**

Location:
Tigre is situated
28km/17mi north
of Buenos Aires.
The Paraná Delta's
waterways are
scattered with
numerous recreation
areas, which offer
many different
activities and
have beaches for
swimming. See
Getting There and
Getting Around,
opposite.

ASK PETER...

Q: What is your
recommendation
for getting out on
the Delta?

A: There are plenty
of luxury cruisers
leaving from here, but
the cheapest options
are the pleasant river
taxis that locals take
to get from island to
island. Some of these
operators have deals
with local restaurants
and will drop you off
somewhere for lunch,
picking you up again
an hour or so later.
You can also explore
the waters by kayak.
(Try El Dorado Kayak,
www.eldoradokayak.
com; ✆ 15 6503
696 cell.)

Tigre and the Paraná Delta★★

**Formed at the confluence of the Paranaíba and Grande
rivers, the Río Paraná travels more than 4,000km/
2,485mi through Brazil, Paraguay and Argentina, before flowing into the Atlantic Ocean.**

**In the last part of its Argentinian run, it divides into
several arms and forms the Paraná Delta, a swampy
plain that stretches over a length of 320km/199mi
and reaches up to 60km/37mi wide. This interlacing
of waterways and small islands, which has been declared a Biosphere Reserve by UNESCO, is a favorite
weekend getaway for the inhabitants of Buenos Aires,
and many parts of it are accessible only by boat.**

**Some of the most beautiful houses have their own pri-
vate docks, or even little private beaches, and many
have been converted into hotels or guesthouses.**

Your starting point will be the town of **Tigre★★**, which is
so-named because of the "tigers" (jaguars) that were once
hunted here. Spend some time enjoying the town's waterfront, visiting the museums or just soaking up the atmosphere.

The English-style rowing clubs and Victorian mansions
date back to the area's brief Belle Époque in the late 19C–
early 20C, before it fell out of favor with high-society *porteños* as they headed to the coastal resort of Mar del Plata
instead.

EXCURSIONS ON THE PARANÁ DELTA

To taste the magic and intimacy of the Delta, you need
to travel around the labyrinth of its waterways by boat.
Leaving from the *estación fluvial* (river station), boats of all
kinds—*lanchas*, private and tourist yachts, rowing dinghies,
motorboats, Zodiac—offer trips on the river. A cheaper
option than the tourist excursions is to take one of the ferries
(see Practical Information) that travel up the river and get off
at one of the waterside cafes or recreation areas. Ideally, push
on as far as the Zona **Tres Bocas** *(Interisleña company, get off
at the Muelle Santa Rosa; allow 30mins journey time; 17 A$)*, or
get off and go for a walk, taking the **circuito del Bigua** *(2hr
round trip.)*

GETTING THERE

BY CAR – From Retiro, take the Avenida del Libertador as far as General Paz, then the Autopista del Sol (Panamericana Acceso Norte). On arrival at San Isidro, follow directions to Tigre Centro. Allow about 30mins.

BY BUS – Take line no. 60 that departs from Constitución and travels via *calles* Constitución, Salta, Humbertoler, Luis Sáenz Peña, the *avenidas* de Mayo, Rivadavia, Callao, Lavalle, Ayacucho, Las Heras, then Plaza Italia and avenida Santa Fe *(allow 1hr 30mins)*. Some faster buses, marked Panamericana, take the expressway.

BY TRAIN – The town of Tigre has two stations: Tigre *(Av. Int. Ricardo J. Ubieto)* and Delta *(c. Vivanco)*.

TBA provides a direct service between the Retiro railroad station and Tigre *(Mitre line)*. Trains run every 10–15mins on weekdays and every 30mins on Sat and Sun *(journey time 50–55mins)*. You must buy your ticket from the ticket office *(nos 10–13)*, before boarding. The train departs from platform 1, 2 or 3 *(1.35 A$)*. You can also take the faster *(25mins)* and more picturesque **Tren de la Costa**, which connects Maipú station to Delta, Tigre. Trains leave

approximately every 20mins *(from 7.10am to 11pm on weekdays, midnight on Fri, and from 8.30am to midnight on Sat and Sun; return from 6.40am to 10.30pm on weekdays or 11.30pm on Fri and from 8am to 11.40pm on Sat and Sun)*. Leaving from Retiro station, take the Mitre line with TBA *(see above)* and get off at Mitre station. Once there, cross the bridge on Av. Maipú to reach the Tren de la Costa station *(www. trendelacosta.com.ar;16A$)*. Or if you staying in Palermo, you can catch bus, or a taxi, from Av. Santa Fe to the Tren de la Costa station at Maipú 2300 *(Av. Santa Fe turns into Cabildo then Maipú)*.

GETTING AROUND

BY BOAT – Ferries provide a service to the main waterways, departing from the river station. They stop on request, as they're also used by people going to the delta hotels or to their second homes. **Interisleña** ☎*(011) 4749 0900*; **Jilguero** ☎*(011) 4749 0987*; **Líneas Delta** ☎*(011) 4749 0537.*

BY WATER TAXI – There is also a *lanchas taxis* (water taxi) service, but it's of course more costly. **Marili** ☎*(011) 4749 5076 or 15 4413 4123*; **Giacomotti** ☎*(011) 4749 1896*; **Julia María** ☎*(011) 4749 2325.*

Museo Naval de la Nación

◗ *Allow 30mins. Paseo Victorica 602.* ☎ *(011) 4749 0608. Open Mon 2.30–5.30pm, Tue–Fri 8.30am–5.30pm, Sat, Sun and public holidays 10.30am–6.30pm. 3 A$.*

This large museum has an old-fashioned charm and tells the story of navigation, from the first sailing logs to the latest developments in naval instruments and arms. To follow in a chronological progression, start with the Leban room, on the left. Models, maps, paintings, engravings, photographs and sculptures illustrate, more specifically, Argentina's maritime and naval history. The museum's most-prized exhibit is the remains of the frigate captained by Independence hero Admiral Guillermo Brown. Some planes and cannon are also on display outside.

Travel Tip:
Cross the main bridge facing Tigre station. Follow Avenida Lavalle north along the riverfront to reach the confluence with Río Luján and **Paseo Victorica**, a lovely promenade that is lined with restaurant terraces and rowing clubs (as well as the Museo Naval de la Nación and Museo de Arte Tigre).

ASK PETER...

Q: How would you advise getting about?
A: The best and easiest way to get around Argentina is by the comfortable and frequent long-distance buses *(see p91)*. It is recommended to opt for these over the trains, except when heading to Tigre and San Isidro. Note that for some of these places you could also organize a *remis* (long-distance taxi), which can be quite reasonable for small groups. Ask your hotel to book you one and agree a price before setting off. If you are heading out to an *estancia (see Planning Your Trip p70)* in any of these destinations, they will typically arrange transportation for you. When you book, ask if transfers are included in the rate.

Museo de Arte Tigre★

◐ *Allow 1hr. Paseo Victorica 972. ℘ (011) 4749 4528. www.mat.gov.ar. Open Wed–Fri 9am–7pm (last entry 6.30pm), Sat and Sun 12–7pm. 5 A$. Guided tour Wed–Fri 11am and 4pm, Sat and Sun 1pm, 3pm and 5pm.*

Located in the historic Tigre Club, this is an unmissable stop—if only to walk along the fabulous raised walkway overlooking the river. After years of neglect, this huge French-Italianate building, with Doric columns and ornate turrets, was carefully restored over a lengthy period in the late 1990s/early 2000s. Removing, polishing and restoring the 100,000 hexagonal marble tiles that make up the now-splendid walkway took two years alone. The nominal entrance fee allows you to explore the equally elaborate interior, featuring marble staircases, huge chandeliers and ornamental motifs, which could easily be found in one of the palaces of Buenos Aires' Avenida Alvear. Indeed, one of the architects, **Paul Pater**, was also behind the city's French Embassy *(see Recoleta p170)*.

The museum's seven rooms contain a beautiful collection of Argentinian figurative art from the 19C and 20C. The country's greatest artists are represented here, including cartoon gauchos of **Florencio Molina Campos** *(see p233)*.

Museo del Maté

◐ *Allow 20mins. Lavalle 289. ℘ (011) 4506 9594. www.elmuseodelmate.com. Open Wed–Sun 11am–6pm (summer 7pm). 10 A$.*

This quirky little place claims to be the only *maté* museum in the world, and it is probably right. It proudly contains a 2,000-piece collection of apparatus used to make Argenti-

THE TIGRE CLUB

Today, the Tigre Club houses the Tigre Art Museum, but it was once a meeting place for the rich and famous of the area. The club was originally built next to the Tigre Hotel (destroyed in 1940), financed by Ernesto Tornquist and officially opened in 1912. The building is famed for its large mezzanines and windows, marble staircases and Venetian mirrors. It also housed a casino until 1933 when a law was passed that prohibited casinos so close to Buenos Aires. After the demolition of the Tigre Hotel, the Tigre Club remained as a restaurant with live shows, but never again regained its former glory. It was declared a National Historic Monument in 1979.

na's beloved national tea. If you are a novice, this is a good way to be introduced to the tradition and find out the rights and wrongs of preparation. Onsite there is a small "maté bar," where you can refresh yourself with unlimited rounds of the drink and put your own technique to the test. There are *yerba maté* cakes to try too.

Museo de la Reconquista

 Allow 30min. Liniers 818. *(011) 4512 4496. Open Wed–Sun 10am–6pm.*
On August 4, 1806, this house, which belonged to the Spanish merchant Martin José Goyechea, welcomed the troops that were going to win back Buenos Aires, then in the hands of the English. The modest museum is dedicated to this episode in particular and, more widely, to the history of Tigre. On display are various weapons and documents dating from the time.

Isla Martín García

 Allow 1 day. Tours Cacciola. *(011) 4749 0329. www.cacciolaviajes.com. Tue, Thu, Sat–Sun at 9am. Returning to Tigre at approx 8.30pm. 140 A$ (return).*
This 168ha/415-acre island is officially part of Argentina, even though it is practically touching the coast of Uruguay and 33.5km/21mi from Tigre. It was discovered in 1516 by Spanish explorer Juan Díaz de Solís, who named it after a crewmember who died there. Over the years, it has served as a holding place for political prisoners, a naval base and a home for Nicaraguan poet Rubén Darío. It's relaxing place to wander around the scattered historical sites and sandy beaches *(no swimming)*. Around 150 people live here year-round.

Travel Tip:
Tigre is the perfect opportunity for *porteños* to practice/learn wakeboarding, wakesurfing, and waterskiing. If pressed for time while on your trip, take a *paseo* (round-trip boat tour) lasting an hour and giving you a little taste of the river; if possible, go on weekdays when it is less crowded.

San Antonio de Areco★

San Antonio de Areco, one of the oldest towns in the Pampas, was founded in 1730 in honor of Saint Anthony of Padua. It owes its fame to the writer Ricardo Güiraldes, author of a bestselling gaucho novel, *Don Segundo Sombra* (1926), which describes the rustic life of a gaucho in the Argentinian Pampas.

This peaceful market town, with its beautiful Colonial architecture and unique atmosphere, is a perfect illustration

Location:
San Antonio de Areco is situated 111km/69mi northwest of Buenos Aires. See Getting There p223.

TIGRE AND THE PARANÁ DELTA

Locals escape to the Paraná Delta to get a taste of a less hectic way of life. Many of the people who have made this place home live permanently in wooden houses raised up high above the water on stilts. The most populated area is Tigre, the transportation hub of the Delta and a picturesque town in its own right. Tigre has some quaint features including museums, bars, and riverside restaurants that allow you to enjoy the slow-moving everyday life. Also on the to-do list should be exploring the local homes, from smaller ones all the way up to Belle Époque mansions.

The British influence is seen in the rowing clubs that populate the Delta. Starting in the 1800s, rowing fuelled the boom and growth of the area. In 1873, rowing moved from the city to the Delta and there was the first regatta, which was so successful that all the city's regattas moved there. In keeping with the time, buildings are in the grand Belle Époque style. In its heyday, there were over a dozen rowing clubs on the Delta including the Tigre Boat Club, the Rowing Club Argentino and the Club San Fernando. You can see all the historic clubs names and dates on the Rowers Monument on the waterfront along Paseo Victorica. One of the most impressive rowing clubs on the waterfront is on the opposite bank to the monument: the **Club de Regatas La Marina**.

Tigre is also a popular destination for those looking to explore areas around Buenos Aires that are not necessarily on the tourist map. It is the starting point for those looking to penetrate deeper into the Delta and offers many ways to do it—vintage mahogany commuter launches and motorboats are some favorites.

Another interesting aspect of the Paraná Delta and the surrounding areas is the way the houses are described—instead of numerical addresses, each residence has its own unique name to distinguish it from the others.

Joining the locals are some of the exotic (and endangered) species who call this mild, humid jungle home. Due to the low altitude, the Delta has slightly warmer temperatures than other areas of Argentina and is a perfect place for particular species to live and thrive, such as jaguar, coypu, river otter, red-faced guan and capybara.

of a certain gaucho lifestyle. It includes some noteworthy places, in particular many leather and silver workshops, where superb gaucho items, equipment for horsemen and utensils for life in the *campo* are still produced. Moreover, the area around the river is delightful and perfect for walking or just lazing around.

Historic Center

The historic center *(casco histórico)* is roughly demarcated by the *calles* Guido to the south, Del Valle to the west and Rivadavia to the east, as well as by Boulevard Zerboni, which runs alongside the peaceful Río Areco to the north. You can start your walk at pretty Plaza Arellano, where the **Church of San Antonio de Padua** is dedicated to the town's patron saint.

Next, take the time to stroll along the lovely shady lanes and visit the many workshops, which are continuing a gaucho tradition that goes back more than a hundred years, including **Museo-taller Draghi** *(Lavalle 387; ☎ (02326) 454 219; www.draghiplaterosorfebres.com; open Mon–Sat 9am–1pm, 4–8pm, Sun 10.30am–1pm; 10 A$)* which includes superb items that have been created or collected over nearly 45 years: *maté* gourds, knives and lassos, horse decorations. Other workshops will introduce you to different aspects of the gaucho tradition, such as its textiles and costume and leatherwork.

The town also has several little museums, such as the **Museo Municipal de Artes Plásticas Juan B. Tapia** *(Lavalle 377; open Sat, Sun and public holidays 9am–8pm)* and the **Centro Cultural** and **Museo Usina Vieja** *(Alsina 66; open Tue–Sun 11am–5pm; 1.50 A$)*, which has a bric-à-brac collection of old objects (radios, cash register, agricultural material, airplane, etc.). One of the best museums in town for getting to grips with gaucho culture has sadly been closed for quite some time following severe flood damage. At the time of writing its opening date was unknown but, if you feel like a stroll, you can give it a try by crossing the bridge over the river and walking for 10 minutes up the dusty road. On your left will be **Parque Criollo y Museo Gauchesco Ricardo Güiraldes** *(☎ (02326) 455 839; www.museoguiraldes.com.ar)*. Its previous opening hours were Wed–Mon 11am–5pm.

Museo las Lilas

Moreno 279. ☎ (02326) 456 425. www.museolaslilas.org. Open Thu–Sun 10am–6pm (summer 8pm). 20 A$.

This is certainly the most fun museum in town. Located in a bright, newly renovated building, it is dedicated to the work of cartoonist **Florencio Molina Campos**, who is known for his humorous portrayals of gauchos

Travel Tip:
Lindblad Expeditions *(www.expeditions.com)* sails on the National Geographic Explorer on a 14-day tour of Antarctica departing from Buenos Aires. What's neat about this company is that its tours have flexible schedules, so they can take advantage of the unexpected. Plus, you've got access to a fleet of Zodiacs and kayaks, and will travel with a team of experts: we're talking naturalists, marine biologists, polar historians and even a National Geographic photographer. Rates start from about US$10,580.

GETTING THERE
BY CAR – San Antonio de Areco is situated 111km/69mi northwest of Buenos Aires via *rutas* 9 and 8. Allow 1hr 30mins.
BY BUS – Several buses go to San Antonio de Areco, leaving from Retiro railroad station *(30–40 A$)*. Nuevo Chevallier *(www.nuevachevallier.com, ℘(011) 4000 5255)* provides around 14 connections a day from Retiro to San Antonio.

and country life. The *porteño* artist (1891-1959) became a household name through designing popular calendars and, in later life, was a consultant for Disney. The museum's admission fee includes a complimentary coffee and *medialuna* (croissant) from the onsite café.

Location:
67km/42mi west of Buenos Aires.
Bus no.: 57 from Plaza Miserere in Once (Jujuy and Riverdavia). 1hr 20mins. Buses run every 30mins at quarter to and quarter past the hour. If you are staying in Palermo, you can pick up the same route in Plaza Italia, just in front of the La Rural conference centre. *10.50 A$.*

Luján

Lujan is a hugely important town for Argentina's devout Catholics. Every October, around one million people make a pilgrimage here with many traveling the 68km/42mi from Buenos Aires on foot. They come for the huge neo-Gothic basilica standing in the center of the town's main plaza. Whether you are religious or not, visiting Lujan makes a nice day trip from the capital. At the weekend, there's a chance to indulge in innocent pleasures, such as visiting its Coney Island-style fairground, browsing the kitsch souvenir stalls or taking a stroll along the riverside boardwalk, past locals sitting at picnic benches sipping maté.

Nearby—and accessible by bus *(infrequent)* or taxi *(10mins)*—is the old railway village of **Carlos Keen**. When the trains ceased operation, the town turned into a ghost town and was only recently given a new lease of life as restaurants sprang up in its corners, turning it into a "slow food" destination. There is nothing much to do here except eat and drink. Expect to be served *picadas* (platters of cheese and meats), *empanadas* and sizzling platters of barbecued meat, along with plenty of Malbec to wash it all down. All the restaurants in town do the same menu, so just take a wander around the expansive central green and pick the one that takes your fancy. **Angelus** *(www.angelusrestaurant. com.ar)* was one of the first restaurants to take a gamble on this sleepy village and it remains one of the best.

Basílica de Nuestra Señora de Luján★

◐ *Allow 30mins. San Martín 51. ℘ (02323) 420 058. www.basilicadelujan.org.ar. Open 7am–8pm.*

Started in 1889 and finally finished in 1937, this striking basilica was designed by French architect Ulderico Courtoisand. Its twin towers stand 106m/348ft high and can be seen for miles around. An impressively huge French organ sits in the gallery, but most visitors come to see the tiny 38cm/15in statue of the Virgin Mary, later named the Virgin of Luján after an intriguing incident in the mid-17C. The story goes that when a wealthy merchant was trying to transport his possessions, his cart got stuck here in the mud and his horses would not budge. He tried removing some of the heavy load, but it didn't work.

The only thing that made it start again was taking off one of his two statues of the Virgin. After taking the figurine on and off several times, and stopping and starting accordingly, he declared a miracle. A makeshift chapel was made to house the Virgin in her chosen resting place until this grander monument was erected. The Virgin of Luján became the patron saint of Argentina and you can see her image on Catholic iconography across the country.

Complejo Museográfico Enrique Udaondo

◐ *Allow 40mins. Lezica and Torrezuri 917. ℘ (02323) 420 245. Open Wed 12.30–5pm. Thu–Fri 11.30am–5pm, Sat–Sun 10.30am–6pm. 3 A$.*

This museum, charting local history and early transport, is housed in various Colonial buildings, including the town's late-19C *cabildo* (town hall). Part of the building was once used as a prison for English military captured during the failed invasions of 1806. Various artifacts on display include art, silverware and military uniforms. The transport section holds the first hydroplane to cross from Europe to Argentina and La Porteña, the country's first steam train.

San Isidro

This riverside town on the outskirts of the capital is the place to mix with the area's most well-heeled residents and gaze longingly at their mansions. The area makes a nice stop en route to Tigre, when taking the Tren de la Costa *(see p219)*, **which drops you off at the British-**

Travel Tip:

Don't pass on taking a day trip to Luján. Behind the museum, there's an old-fashioned board-walk with fairground rides, similar to Coney Island. Come to experience the culture of this amazing city, but don't miss out on the fun. You can even rent a paddle boat and enjoy Luján from the water.

Location:
24km/15mi north of central Buenos Aires.
Train: Tren de la Costa *(20mins)* or the Mitre line from Retiro *(35mins)*. See Tigre Getting There and Getting Around.
Bus no: 60. (1hr 20mins.) See Tigre Getting There and Getting Around.

Travel Tip:
The charming city of San Isidro is halfway to the very popular Tigre. This well-heeled town has some great restaurants and bars on the main strip, as well as beach-front locations to enjoy a relaxing, quiet day outside the craziness of the city. You can't miss the San Isidro Cathedral, built in 1898, and standing in the center of town.

style railroad station in the historic center. Here you are just a couple of minutes away from Plaza Mitre and the late-19C cathedral. Just in front of the cathedral is Plaza de San Isidro, home to one of the country's oldest artisan fairs. The town is also known for its huge 1930s-style hippodrome (*Márquez 504*) and **Museo Histórico Municipal General Pueyrredón**, which was once owned by the eponymous 19C military leader (*Rivera Indarte 48; ℘ (011) 4512 3131; www.museopueyrredon. org.ar; open Tue, Thu 10am–6pm, Sat–Sun, 2–6pm*). To get to the museum from the cathedral, follow Av. Libertador five blocks, turn left on Peña and after two blocks turn right onto Rivera Indarte.

Villa Ocampo★

◐ *Allow 1hr. Elortondo 1837. ℘ (011) 4732 4988. www.villaocampo.org. Open Thu–Sun 12.30–7pm. 12 A$ (18 A$ Sat–Sun). Guided tour Thu–Fri, 2.30pm, 4.30pm; Sat–Sun 2.30pm, 3.30pm, 4.30pm. Catch a taxi, the number 60 bus or the train to Beccar (Mitre line), plus a seven-block walk.*

Originally the summer residence of one of Argentina's most famous writers, **Victoria Ocampo** (1890-1979), this Belle Époque property was in 1973 donated to UNESCO by the owner herself, and turned into a cultural center for the public. Walking around its library and expansive grounds, you are treading in the footsteps of the hostess's most distinguished guests: Graham Greene, Federico García Lorca, Albert Camus and Antoine de Saint-Exupéry.

As the founder of esteemed literary magazine *Sur*, Ocampo also entertained Argentinian writers here, including Jorge Luis Borges and Adolfo Bioy Casares, who married her sister, Silvina. Note that the house is quite far out of the center.

Location:
56km/35mi southeast of Buenos Aires.
Train: Approx 1hr from Constitución station in Buenos Aires. Avoid this station at night.
Bus: 1hr 15mins from Retiro bus station, Buenos Aires. La Nueva Metropol; ℘0800 222 6798. 1888 (www.metropol. com.ar). 15 A$. Every 10 mins.

La Plata

This city, characterized by its linden trees and diagonal roads, is the capital of the Province of Buenos Aires, an area around the size of Italy. It's a planned city and was the first in Latin America to have electric street lighting. Sites to see are the Paseo del Bosque park; Plaza Moreno; the Catedral de la Inmaculada Concepción de la Plata, which took over a hundred years to complete and is the largest church in Argentina; and the Museo

de Arte Contemporáneo Latin Americano *(Calle 50 between 6 and 7; ℘(0221) 427 1843; www.macla.laplata. gov.ar; open Tue–Fri 10am–8pm, Sat–Sun 2–9pm winter, 6pm–10pm summer).* **A new high-tech stadium** *(Av. 32 and 35)* **opened here for the 2011 Copa América soccer tournament and now hosts some of the country's biggest music events as well.**

Museo de La Plata★

❍ *Allow 1–2hrs. Paseo del Bosque, no number. ℘(0221) 425 7744. www.fcnym.unlp.edu.ar. Open Tue–Sun 10am–6pm. 6 A$ (Tue free).*

The original collection for this natural history museum was based on donations from the founder, Patagonian explorer **Francisco Pascasio Moreno**. It opened in 1888 and has continued to expand, with exhibits covering botany, zoology, geology and paleontology. Housed in a Grecian-style building guarded by two stone saber-tooth tigers, it has a collection of some three million fossils and relics, including replicas of dinosaur skeletons found in Patagonia. It's a good place to get in touch with Argentina's prehistoric period, when it was home to the biggest mammals the world has ever seen.

Lobos

With most of its residents making a living off the surrounding rural plains, this is a fairly typical Pampas town, with characteristically quiet roads and traditional, low-rise houses. Although popular with Argentinian tourists, you are quite unlikely to hear a foreign accent here, especially off-season.

The pretty lake, 15km/9mi out of town, is used for fishing and water sports, such as wakeboarding, kitesurfing and rowing. Equipment can be hired on the lakeside and there are also several good picnic spots. There is a big polo scene in the area, with many local *estancias (see Planning Your Trip p70)* offering the chance to watch a match or attend a practice session.

Three-times president of Argentina **Juan Domingo Perón** was born in Lobos in 1895. His family home *(Buenos Aires 1380)* has been restored and houses a collection of Perón's possessions, including a letter he wrote to Evita when he was imprisoned on Isla Martín Garcia *(see p221).*

Location:
100km/62mi southwest of Buenos Aires.
Bus: 1hr 40mins from Retiro bus station, Buenos Aires. www.lobosbus.com.ar. ℘(011) 4381 6000. 29 A$. Every hour on the half-hour.

Location:
120km/75mi south of Buenos Aires.
Bus: 2hrs 30mins from Retiro, Buenos Aires to Chascomús.
www.condorestrella. com.ar. ☎0810 666 266 367. 46 A$.

VICTORIA OCAMPO

Described by famous author Jorge Luis Borges as the quintessential Argentine woman, Victoria Ocampo was most famous for creating the literary magazine *Sur*. The magazine featured many important writers, including Borges, Albert Camus, and Ernesto Sabato. She was one of the most influential and well-known women in South American during the early to mid-20C and was briefly imprisoned for her opposition of Argentine leader Juan Domingo Perón. She won many awards and honorary degrees during her lifetime, including Commander of the Order of the British Empire, and honorary degrees at both Columbia University and Harvard University.

Chascomús

Most tourists—again mainly Argentinian—come to Chascomús for its lake and narrow cobblestone streets. In the height of summer (Jan–Feb), the camp-sites become crammed, an all-consuming smell of barbecued beef wafts through the air and a non-stop *cumbia* soundtrack puts paid to early nights. Many visitors come to fish and practice other recreational sports, such as yachting, or to simply cycle along the shoreline.

Off-season, it's sleepy, but local authorities have been trying to attract visitors with events and festivals, such as tango week in April and the theater festival in August *(www.chas-comus.gov.ar)*. The historic center of town, expanding from Plaza Independencia, and the late-19C Iglesia Cathedral, are also worth a look. At weekends, there are small crafts fairs at Costanera and Perón, and Constanera and Lastra.

Uruguay

Just a short ride across the River Plate by ferry lies peaceful Uruguay (population 3.4m), a country that is often overshadowed by its huge, extrovert neighbors, Brazil and Argentina. Tourism here is developing fast,

IGUAZÚ FALLS
...LIKE A LOCAL

If you are looking to get even farther out of town, one option is to hop a quick flight to what is often considered one of the natural wonders of the world—Iguazú Falls. It's about 90 minutes from Buenos Aires' local airport, El Aeroparque Jorge Newbery, to the Iguazú Falls International Airport, which takes you to the Argentinian side of this national wonder. Once you land at the airport, you can take a bus or a taxi directly to the national park. And if you're looking to spend the night you can stay at the Sheraton Iguazú, which is within the boundaries of the park, or in Puerto Iguazú.

The falls themselves touch the borders of Argentina, Paraguay and Brazil. All three countries have built healthy businesses bringing travelers to the land-mark, though Argentina is often thought to have the best views.

We're not talking about just looking at one waterfall. Iguazú Falls is actually a group of many separate falls—locals have cited from 75 to over 200—which go from the cliffs of the Río Iguazú Superior to the Río Iguazú Inferior below. Lush jungles surround the falls and the view is incredible, but don't forget to listen as well. The falls are known to produce steam-engine sound effects!

The border between Argentina and Brazil runs through the Devil's Throat, which is one of the park's main landmarks and one of the most dramatic views. Check out the Devil's Throat in the afternoon because the morning sun often blocks the full view.
The national park is open from 8am and usually does not close until after 6pm. However, visitors have been know to jump over the barricades for early ac-cess and to beat the crowds in the morning. Also some companies do operate moonlight tours for a different view of the park a few nights a month during full moon.

If you do consider taking a tour of the falls, there are many companies based out of Puerto Iguazú that offer a range of experiences for different price points. Don't get upsold to the jungle safaris. It may sound like a cool concept, but few exotic animals have been spotted in the area. Instead, consider a boat trip under the falls. And if you travel to Paseo Inferior, which is the area below the cliff-edge, you will see signs that direct you to a free ferry ride that takes you to Isla San Martín, a rocky island in the middle of the river. Note that the last ferry leaves at 3:45pm.

Location: Across the Río de la Plata.

By ferry: Two ferry operators offer a regular service between Buenos Aires and Uruguay: **Buquebus** *(Antártida Argentina 821; ℰ (011) 4316 6500; www.buquebus.com)* and **Colonia Express** *(Pedro de Mendoza 330; ℰ (011) 4317 4100; www.colonia express.com.ar).* A fast ferry to Colonia del Sacramento takes around 1hr; the slow service takes 3hrs. To get to Montevideo, Buquebus' direct ferry takes 3hrs, while Colonia Express offers ferry-and-bus combos *(approx 4hrs).*

By car: From Colonia, Montevideo is a 2.5hrs drive along Ruta 1. For car hire in Colonia, try Europcar *(Avenida Artigas 152; ℰ (00598) 4522 8454; www.europcar.com.uy).*

Travel Tip:
Colonia del Sacramento is the perfect getaway from the bustling city of Buenos Aires, just be sure you don't miss your ferry back home; tourists forget the one-hour time difference between Colonia and Buenos Aires.

with a growing number of visitor-friendly *estancias* **and high-end hotels. There is even an emerging wine industry, specializing in the Tannat varietal. For a daytripper, the most notable difference between here and Argentina is the more evident relationship with the water. Suddenly, you'll see fish and seafood starting to appear on menus, and people making a conscious effort to get a river view, from a boardwalk or restaurant terrace.**

Colonia del Sacramento★★

Surrounded by river on three sides, this UNESCO World Heritage Site is all cobblestone streets, walled ramparts and charm as sweet as *dulce de leche*. There are plenty of restaurants and cafes too, many with atmospheric outdoor seating.

Colonia, as it is known for short, may be quiet now, but it has seen its fair share of conflict. From the late 17C to early 19C, control of the town was batted between Spain and Portugal during multiple invasions, and the nation's joint influences can be seen in its architecture.

The town's historic center is very compact, making it easy to get around on foot or hired bicycle. You can pick up a map at the **tourist office** *(Manuel Lobo 224).*

El Portón del Campo, a mid-18C stone gate and drawbridge, marks the entrance to the old town *(10–15min walk from the ferry terminal).* Walk straight and you will hit Plaza Mayor. On your left, look out for a small sidestreet, Calle Los Suspiros (street of sighs), which has some of the oldest examples of Portuguese influence. A little further ahead is the lighthouse, which you can climb for a good **panorama**.

The historic center's other main square is Plaza del Gobernador, which contains the remains of the house and gardens of the governor of Río de Janeiro, who founded the town in the name of Portugal in 1680. The church, **Basílica Matriz del Santísimo Sacramento**, dates from that time, although it has undergone substantial renovations.

The town has seven little museums in old Colonial houses. An all-inclusive pass costs US$50. The museums open from 11.15am to 4.45pm, with each one closing on a different day of the week.

The riverside beaches on the outskirts are a far cry from the Caribbean, but their mud-colored waters can looks surprisingly attractive when backed by a blue sky and when the sun catches them during one of the frequently wonderful sunsets.

Montevideo★

▶ *Allow 1 day.*

The Uruguayan capital (population 1.3m) can have a sleepy feel at times, especially at the weekend when few residents seem to frequent the center. The city sprawls 20km/12mi west to east and, for daytrippers, the most interesting part of town is surely the **Ciudad Vieja**, the historic center, although be very wary of walking around here after dark.

The main square is **Plaza Independencia**, which is a mishmash of architectural styles, some fabulous, some less so. Its highlight is the eclectically styled **Palacio Salvo**, a captivating skyscraper that was once the tallest on the continent and is sister to the **Palacio Barolo★★** in Buenos Aires *(see p113)*. The statue in the middle of the plaza is of José Artigas, the Independence hero and so-called Father of Uruguay, whose remains are in the permanently guarded crypt below.

Busy shopping street 18 de Julio runs off Plaza Independencia to the east, while pedestrianized Sarandí runs west and leads you farther into the old town. A visit to Mercardo del Puerto (Piedras and Pérez Castellano), close to the waterfront, is a highlight to any visit to Montevideo. Built in the style of a British railroad station with a huge iron roof, this indoor market is full of open-plan restaurants, with giant *parrillas* (grills) loaded with meat and roasting vegetables. Fish and seafood are also available. Go on a very empty stomach.

From Monday to Saturday, there is an indoor artisans' market at Plaza Cagancha, six blocks from Plaza Independencia *(18 de Julio and Gutiérrez Ruiz; 10am–8pm)*.

On Sundays, don't miss the flea market, **Feria Tristán Narvaja**, which is a little farther afield, where the street of the same name bisects 18 de Julio *(9am–3pm)*.

The city's *rambla* (promenade) wraps around the coastal edge for 27km/17mi, makes it one of the longest esplanades in the world. Locals come here to jog, drink *maté* and have romantic moments as the sun sets.

ASK PETER...

Q: Is it necessary to convert Argentine pesos to Uruguayan pesos for my day trip? **A:** Millions of Argentines flock to the beaches of Uruguay during the summer season, and there's really no need to change your currency. The Argentinian peso and the US dollar are both widely accepted.

YOUR STAY IN
BUENOS AIRES

Hipodromo de Palermo
Photo: © Pietschmann/Alamy

Where to Stay

ASK PETER...

Q: My travel budget is limited; do you think I can find hotel savings in Buenos Aires?

A: Although the dollar goes far in Buenos Aires, that's not especially true in its hotel rates. The major, well-known hotels charge comparable world capital city rates. But here's an option: consider a vacation rental. There are a variety of US and local companies that rent rooms, such as ApartmentsBA. com. Caution, before you sign up for an apartment, make sure you specify exactly what you are receiving and have a mutually agreeable definition of terms, for example define 'bathroom'—it is just a toilet, or a toilet, bath and shower? Are you sharing it with another apartment or bedroom? Make sure that the detail is not lost in translation.

When choosing a base, most people opt for the city center, Recoleta, Palermo or San Telmo, with some also picking Puerto Madero for its high-end hotels. Palermo and San Telmo are the most atmospheric picks, with bars, stores and restaurants all within walking distance. Recoleta also has some standout hotels and is a classic choice. All hotels accept credit cards and include breakfast and Wi-Fi in their rates, unless otherwise stated.

Centro *Map II.*

Microcentro is packed with every sort of establishment, particularly plenty of business hotels. You are certainly in the city's busiest shopping district with the pedestrian streets of Florida and Lavalle, but this is not the place to find the either the nicest places to stay or the best restaurants. The district is particularly congested during the daytime and less animated in the evening, with the notable exception of Corrientes, where all the theaters are.

$ Hostel Suites Florida – *Florida 328 (subway line B, Florida); (011) 4325 0969; www.hostelsuites.com;* ▤; *320 beds: 65–70 A\$/dormitory of 4–6 beds, 30 rooms: 300 A\$ double ensuite room; Internet access.* Kitchen, launderette, cinema, bar, all the advantages of a youth hostel, but more comfortable… the new generation of hostels are now as good as classic hotels. Ideally situated on Florida, this place is perfect for those who want to shop. Rooms are modern and well equipped. If this hostel is fully booked, try the other Microcentro address: Hostel Suites Obelisco *(Corrientes 830;* (011) 4328 4040).

$$ Facón Grande Hotel – *Reconquista 645 (subway line B, Florida or L.N. Alem);* (011) 4312 6360/69; www.hotelfacongrande.com; ▤ ✕ ▣; *97 rooms; Internet access.* A business hotel that manages not to be too impersonal, thanks notably to its great decor, which pays tribute to gauchos. Sunny, comfortable and very pleasant rooms.

$$ Gran Hotel Hispano – *Mayo 861 (subway line A, Piedras); (011) 4345 2020; www.hhispano.com.ar;* ▤; *60 rooms; Internet access.* Located a stone's throw from Café Tortoni *(see p112),* this pleasant family-run establishment is one of the few cheap hotels on the avenue that isn't depressing. Its Spanish-style inner courtyard, around which the rooms are arranged, and its terrace are even quite appealing. A good place, well maintained, and appreciated by those on a tight budget.

$$$ Dazzler Tower San Martín – *San Martín 920 (subway line C, Gén. San Martín);* ℰ*(011) 5256 7700; www.dazzlertowersanmartin. com;* 🖃 🅿*; 88 rooms; Internet access.* Ultramodern and very comfortable, this international hotel is impeccably situated near the city center's main pedestrian street. It provides spacious rooms, a heated swimming pool and a good, hearty breakfast. Attractive special offers on discount websites.

$$$ Esplendor – *San Martín 780 (subway line C, Gén. San Martín);* ℰ*(011) 5256 8800; www.esplendorbuenosaires.com;* 🖃 ✗*; 51 rooms; Internet access.* Behind the classic façade of a listed building hides a very trendy hotel, which charms from the outset thanks to its spaciousness and its designer decor. Everything in of the best taste and the former patio now houses an art gallery. The rooms, all very original, enjoy every comfort, and some even have a jacuzzi.

$$$ Rooney's – *Sarmiento 1775, 3rd floor (subway line B, Callao);* ℰ*(011) 5252 5060; www.rooneysboutiquehotel.com;* 🖃*; 14 rooms.* This superb "boutique hotel" is a really unique place, decorated in a wonderful Belle Époque style. Rooms and suites are all personalized and in exquisite taste, with period furniture and artifacts. Free tango lessons are regularly organized on the pretty patio. There are also some apartments.

$$$$ Casa Calma – *Suipacha 1015 (subway line C, Gén. San Martín);* ℰ*(011) 5199 2800; www.casacalma.com.ar;* 🖃*; 18 rooms; Internet access.* This hotel, entirely devoted to wellbeing, is an oasis in the heart of the city. The immaculately white rooms open out, via wide picture windows, onto a mass of greenery. Each of these spacious rooms has its own individual spa with sauna, jacuzzi, hydromassage bathtub and organic beauty products *(massages available on demand, 200 A$).* Even the breakfasts have been thought out to provide fitness and energy with a selection of fresh products and lots of little extras for your greater pleasure.

Puerto Madero *Map III.*

This district, which has had a trendy makeover, attracts upwardly mobile types. Its hotels are all expensive and rather impersonal. But check discount sites on the Internet, where you may find attractively priced special offers.

$$$$ Faena Hotel – *Martha Salotti 445 (subway line A, Plaza de Mayo);* ℰ*(011) 4010 9000; www.faenahotelanduniverse.com;* 🖃 ✗ 🅿*; 108 rooms.* El Porteño is a very fine red-brick building, a huge mill transformed into a luxury hotel, under the creative direction of Philippe Starck. The result is a place of refined elegance, mixing the exuberance of the Belle Époque with leather, wood and brick. The outdoor pool is the place to be seen (in designer swimwear, of course) and the most surreal aspect is the decorative unicorn heads in the dining room. As a whole it's a success, but the prices are prohibitive and the atmosphere is *very* exclusive.

Travel Tip:
Here's a scam to be aware of: Watch out for the currency when you book a hotel room. Known as "the stupidity tax," some hotels and businesses charge English speakers more as a matter of policy. But get this, the hotel might quote their rate to you in US dollars, but at checkout you'll be charged substantially more in pesos. Know your rights and your currency before you book.

$$$$ Hilton Hotel – *Macacha Güemes 351 (subway line B, L.N. Alem);* 📞*(011) 4891 0000; www.hilton.com;* 🖥 ✖ 🅿*; 400 rooms; Internet access.* With its glass lobby as big as a cathedral, this jewel in the crown of the well-known chain has adopted the same style as its American big brothers. Resolutely modern, it has the advantage of being in the center of the neighborhood and the nearest to the subway *(15mins on foot)*. There is a 16m/ 52ft outdoor pool with sundeck.

$$$$ Madero Hotel – *Rosario Vera Peñaloza 360, Dique 2 (subway line A, Plaza de Mayo);* 📞*(011) 5776 7777; www.hotelmadero.com;* 🖥 ✖🅿*; 197 rooms; Internet access.* Contemporary design, spacious, sunny and peaceful: all the signs of a luxury hotel, with a business clientele. Heated indoor pool, spa and fitness center.

San Telmo *Map III.*

Located to the south of the center, the district of San Telmo preserves a certain charm with its old, crumbling buildings that today are gradually being restored. It has to be said that lots of stores, hotels, bars, restaurants and tango rooms have opened over the last ten years, guaranteeing that the area is lively at all hours of the day and night. San Telmo also has the city's greatest number of youth hostels.

$ Ayres Porteños – *Perú 708 (subway line C, Independencia);* 📞*(011) 4300 7314; www.ayresportenos.com.ar; 20 beds: 47–60 A$ in dormitories and 180 A$ for a double room; Internet access; kitchen, launderette, baggage checkroom.* This "thematic" hostel (their own claim) flies the colors of Buenos Aires with some 60 colorful frescoes, depicting famous local figures, plus decorative landings, walls and doors. The rooms are clean, although the furniture is rather old fashioned. And there's a little roof terrace (although it's somewhat unappealing) where you can sunbathe.

$ Hostel Inn Tango City – *Piedras 680 (subway line C, Independencia);* 📞*(011) 4300 5764; www.hitangocity.com;* 🖥 🍽*; 90 beds: dormitories of 4–8 beds (50–58 A$/pers.), mixed or single sex, and some double rooms (175–200 A$); Internet access; kitchen, launderette, baggage checkroom, terrace.* This place benefits from the know-how of the Hostel Inn chain, which is always a good option for backpackers. It's quite a party place, so to be avoided if you're after some peace and quiet.

$ Ostinatto – *Chile 680 (subway line C, Moreno);* 📞*(011) 4362 9639; www.ostinatto.com;* 🖥*; 80 beds: from 46 A$/bed (dormitory of 12 beds) to 60 A$/bed (dormitory of 4 beds), and 230–250 A$ for a double room; Internet access.* Most of the hotels now have a "concept". Ostinatto's was to take over an old building in the district and to redesign its spaces to give it a design edge. Add to that a huge modern kitchen, a terrace with a pool in which to take a quick dip, a piano-bar, a small cinema and a few yoga and tango lessons, and you have one of the coolest hostels in San Telmo.

$ Tanguera Hostel – *Chile 657 (subway line C, Independencia); ☎(011) 4361 9147; www.tanguerahostel.com.ar; 8 rooms: 35 beds; 45 A$ in an 8-bed dormitory; 130 A$ for a double room; Internet access; kitchen and barbecue.* A small peaceful hostel, a long way from neighboring "factories," and where you'll soon feel at home. Housed in a beautiful, large bourgeois-style apartment, it has eight basic rooms that share a modern, clean bathroom. There is even a little terrace.

$$ Posada de la Luna – *Perú 565 (subway line C, Moreno); ☎(011) 4343 0911; www.posadaluna.com; ▦; 6 rooms; Internet access. Two nights minimum.* A charming guesthouse, hidden from the street. Don't hesitate to ring the bell for someone to open the door to you on this superb 19C residence. The rooms look onto a lovely, sunny, Colonial-style patio and have lots of character, with their parquet floors and brick and wood ceilings. Another little secret is a little garden surrounded by plants that has a barbecue and its own spa (well, a hydromassage bathtub).

$$$ Mansion Dandi Royal – *Piedras 922–936 (subway line C, Independencia); ☎(011) 4361 3537; www.hotelmansiondandiroyal.com; ▦; 30 rooms; Internet access (Wi-Fi only).* This smart hotel, entirely dedicated to tango, is organized over five floors, with salons, courtyard gardens, a swimming pool, solarium and fitness center. Not all of the relatively small rooms have the elegance of the lobby (far from it), but they are comfortable nevertheless. L'Academia de Tango Dandi, which is an integral part of the hotel, offers courses every day, which are also open to non-residents.

$$$ Telmho – *Defensa 1086 (subway line C, San Juan); ☎(011) 4116 5467; www.telmho-hotel.com.ar; ▦; 9 rooms; Internet access.* Ideally situated at the heart of San Telmo, on the picturesque Plaza Dorrego, this contemporary-style "boutique hotel" has nine sunny suites, decorated in very pale tones, with mezzanine bedrooms and, in some cases, a balcony opening onto the square. There's a sun terrace on the roof.

Recoleta *Map II.*

Very central and fairly tranquil, this affluent district includes some of the most luxurious hotels in Buenos Aires and offers little choice for travelers on a more limited budget.

$$$ Art Hotel – *Azcuenaga 1268 (subway line D, Pueyrredón); ☎(011) 4821 4744; www.arthotel.com.ar; ▦; 36 rooms; Internet access.* The beautiful architecture is highlighted by the use of natural materials, soft tones and elegant furniture. The originality of the place lies in the work of Argentinian artists—paintings, engravings and photos—that decorate the walls of the lobby, salon and bedrooms. The exhibitions change monthly, so you will no doubt feel that you are discovering a new place every time you stay here.

$$$$ Alvear Palace Hotel – *Alvear 1891 (subway line D, Pueyrredón);* ☎*(011) 4808 2100; www.alvearpalace.com;* 🍽 ✖ 🅿; *195 rooms; Internet access.* The grand dame of all Buenos Aires hotels, this sumptuous establishment has hosted presidents, diplomats and A-list movie stars. Decorated in an Imperial style, rooms mix antique French furniture with modern luxuries, so you can expect to watch a flat-screen television in your marble bath. Inaugurated in the 1930s, you get caught up in the history as soon as the smartly dressed bellboys guide you through the wooden revolving door. It's worth entering the lobby just for a look, or for its famed afternoon tea. There is an indoor pool and spa.

Palermo *Map V.*

With its wide, shady streets lined with low-rise buildings and century-old residences that have been admirably restored, Palermo Viejo is the nicest district in which to stay in Buenos Aires. In addition, it's packed with designer boutiques, inventive restaurants and hip bars.

$ Casa Esmeralda – *Honduras 5765 (subway line D, Ministro Carranza);* ☎*(011) 4772 2446; www.casaesmeralda.com.ar;* 🚿; *4 rooms; 20 beds; 70 A$ in dormitories; 210 A$ for a double room; Internet access (Wi-Fi only); kitchen.* This hostel does not fall into the new wave of boutique-like properties, but if your priority is an intimate, home-from-home atmosphere, it's a good choice. Bathrooms are shared and rather old-fashioned, but the ultra-friendly staff and small garden—complete with shaded hammocks—make up for it.

$ Hostel Suites Palermo – *Charcas 4752 (subway line D, Palermo);* ☎*(011) 4773 0806; www.hostelsuites.com;* 🍽; *40 beds, 9 rooms: 70–80 A$ in dormitories, 248 A$ for a double room; Internet access; kitchen, launderette.* Housed in a beautiful early 20C residence that has been completely renovated, this stylish hostel enjoys all the comfort of the "new generation" of hostels. Dormitories and double rooms have their own private bathroom and lovely furnishings. As a little extra, there's a patio where you can eat breakfast and a big sun terrace on the roof.

$$ Hotel Costa Rica – *Costa Rica 4137 (subway line D, Scalabrini Ortiz);* ☎*(011) 4864 7390; www.hotelcostarica.com.ar;* 🍽; *25 rooms; Internet access.* A charming hotel with reasonable prices—quite a rarity in this district. The decor is contemporary, with a very soft tonal range, and the rooms are all different. The upstairs ones that look onto the lovely, huge terrace share a bathroom. The place wins out, too, with the extremely friendly reception you get from the team.

$$$ Fierro Hotel – *Soler 5862 (subway line D, Ministro Carranza);* ☎*(011) 3220 6800; www.fierrohotel.com;* 🍽 ✖; *27 rooms; Internet access.* A stylishly modern hotel, with a highly regarded onsite restaurant ran by chef Hernán Gipponi, who has trained at Michelin-starred establishments in Europe. The multi-course, and somewhat quirky, breakfast makes an interesting start to the day. There's a small plunge pool on the roof.

$$$ Home – *Honduras 5860 (subway line D, Palermo);* ℘*(011) 4778 1008; www.homebuenosaires.com;* 🍽 ✗; *20 rooms; Internet access.* Home sweet home… an expression very appropriate here. Everything here is in exquisite taste: the rooms, along contemporary lines, are enhanced with touches of color; the comforting cocoon of the spa; and the square garden with its refreshing swimming pool. The hotel also has a trendy bar and a fine restaurant.

$$$ – 1555 Malabia House *Malabia 1555 (subway line D, Scalabrini Ortiz);* ℘*(011) 4833 2410; www.malabiahouse.com.ar;* 🍽; *15 rooms; Internet access.* A very comfortable house, more than 100 years old, which is enveloped in soft lighting come nightfall. Inside, everything is orderly, elegant and calm. There are three categories of room: the least expensive have a private bathroom on the landing, while some have a balcony looking out onto the street.

Excursions

The Paraná Delta has numerous campsites, *cabañas* and hotels of all categories. You will find complete listings, with addresses and telephone numbers, at the tourist information office. Book ahead as it a very popular weekend spot for *porteños*. San Antonio is also a popular place for a getaway, with numerous *estancias* in the surrounding countryside.

Tigre

$ Tigre Hostel – *Libertador San Martín 190;* ℘*(011) 4749 4034; www.tigrehostel.com.ar;* 🍽 🛏 🅿; *20 beds, 2 rooms: 70 A$ for a single room, 160/180 A$ for a double room with/without ensuite; Internet access (Wi-Fi only); kitchen, launderette.* An extremely good hostel, located in a beautiful 1860 *posada*, which is surrounded by a large park. Everything here exudes freshness, cleanliness and calm. Communal rooms and bedrooms are well equipped and very appealing.

$$$ Villa Julia – *Paseo Victorica 800 (on the corner of Maschwitz);* ℘*(011)4749 0642; www.villajuliaresort.com.ar;* 🍽 🛏 🅿; *6 rooms; Internet access (Wi-Fi only).* This elegant 1913 riverfront building has been superbly restored and houses a friendly hotel, which preserves many of the building's original features. A lovely park surrounds the house and there's even a swimming pool.

San Antonio De Areco

$ Hostel El Puesto – *Belgrano 270;* ℘*(02326) 453 148; www.hostelel puesto.com.ar;* 🛏; *65 A$ in an 8-bed dormitory, 80 A$ in a 2-bed room; Internet and Wi-Fi.* Situated just three blocks from the main square, this new hostel is in one of the characteristic low-rise houses that are found in small Argentinian towns. There's a garden with a swimming pool and staff can also arrange polo lessons.

$$ Hotel Antigua Casona – *Segundo Sombra 495; ☎(02326) 456 600; www.antiguacasona.com;* 🖥 🛏 🅿; *5 rooms; No internet access.* A traditional building that has been converted into a fine guesthouse. The rooms, nicely done out with antique furniture, are arranged around a charming patio. A peaceful place.

$$ Hotel San Carlos – *On the corner of Zerboni and Zapiola; ☎(02326) 453 106; www.hotel-sancarlos.com.ar;* 🖥✖🅿; *29 rooms; Internet access.* Situated a stone's throw from the river, this place is quite charming, with its neat little rooms, lovely patio, swimming pool and spa.

$$$ Patio de Moreno – *Moreno 251; ☎(02326) 455 197; www.patio demoreno.com;* 🖥 🛏 ✖; *11 rooms; Internet access.* San Antonio's most fashionable designer establishment. Located in a beautiful historic building, it has been give a complete makeover in a very contemporary style. Its lovely covered patio and its pleasant garden, with a refreshing pool, add to its charm.

Where to Eat

Porteños eat late. Those that don't want to be rattling around in an empty dining room should aim to arrive after 9pm and recognize that it is not uncommon to see people taking their seats post-midnight. Not all restaurants accept bookings; in these cases, turn up early, before 1pm for lunch or before 9pm for dinner, or expect to wait.

All across town, you'll find no shortage of pizzerias, cafes and *parrillas* (grills), but in the last decade, there has been an explosion of new restaurants, serving more creative cuisine and fusion food. Most of these are in Palermo Viejo, with a handful in the center of town and San Telmo.

Buenos Aires also has a big delivery culture—anything, from hot meals to ice-cream, can be brought to your door. If you have trouble with the language, you can order from various places across the city via English-language site www.buenosairesdelivery.com.

Monserrat *Map II.*

The San Telmo effect is moving into neighboring Monserrat, as restaurants open to catch wandering tourists.

$$ Status – *Virrey Cavellos 178 (subway line A, Sáenz Peña); ☎(011) 4382 8531; www.restaurantstatus.com.ar;* 🛏; *open Mon–Sun noon–4pm, 8pm–midnight.* This family-owned Peruvian *cantina* makes a welcome change when you have had your fill of steak. Try the *ceviche* (raw fish "cooked" in citrus juice) and *papas a la huancaina* (potatoes in a creamy sauce). Cheap prices and a relaxed atmosphere make it popular with office workers and members of the local Peruvian community.

$$$ Aldo's – *Moreno 372 (subway line E, Bolivar); ℰ(011) 5291 2380; www.morenobuenosaires.com; open Mon–Sun 7am–midnight*. Housed in the Moreno Hotel and with some big-name backers, the menu here encompasses international food with an Argentinian twist. The best part: an expertly curated wine list, which lists items at cost price. You can buy bottles to go.

Centro and Retiro *Map II.*

Be warned: while most of Microcentro's restaurants are full of office workers at lunchtime, lots of them are closed in the evenings. Most of the cuisine is very classic, at fairly reasonable prices.

$$ La Rienda – *Paraguay 716 (subway line C, San Martín); ℰ(011) 4313 1524; open Mon–Sun 7am–midnight*. A bistro-style restaurant with very efficient service and a menu that focuses mainly on pasta and grilled dishes, which are cooked on the huge grill behind the bar. A tip: even the mini *bife* is a very substantial steak.

$$$ Dadá – *San Martín 941 (subway line C, San Martín); ℰ(011) 4314 4787; open Mon–Sat noon–3am*. This lively little bistro, with its Surrealist-inspired decor, is a top choice. The bar's specialty is different vodka-based cocktails, while on the menu, there is a selection of inventive, tasty and well-presented dishes made with fresh, good-quality ingredients. The desserts are huge and mouthwatering. The ambiance—jazz, rhythm & blues—is very congenial.

$$$ Tancat – *Paraguay 645 (subway line C, San Martín); ℰ(011) 4312 5442; open Mon–Sat from noon*. A Spanish restaurant with an intimate and friendly atmosphere, and a regular clientele. Try the tortilla with a glass of wine, or go for one of the main dishes *(allow 60 A$)*, which focus especially on seafood. If you want a table in the evening, it's best to book. At the bar, it's simpler, but always busy.

San Telmo and Puerto Madero *Map III.*

The popular district of San Telmo offers a large range of restaurants of very varying quality. Although some fashionable (and thus, of course, more expensive) establishments are thriving in the area, most places, not least the ubiquitous *parrillas*, are content to carry on as they always have, offering, all in all, good value for money. The docks are lined with restaurants, mainly on the west side, with large terraces facing onto the river. Lunchtime menus are

Travel Tip:
The price ranges here include an appetizer, main course and dessert for one, excluding drinks, taxes and tips. Note that they are only a guideline.

ORDERING A STEAK

If you think you can come to a Buenos Aires *parrilla* (grill) and just order "one steak, please." you're very much mistaken. An Argentinian meat menu is long, including most parts of the cow, and can seem quite daunting for a newcomer. These are the main cuts you need to know: *bife de chorizo* is sirloin, *bife de lomo* is tenderloin, *entraña* is skirt steak, *vacío* is flank steak and *asado de tira* is ribs. If you're hungry (and brave), order a *parrillada*, a hefty platter of meat, including *morcilla* (blood sausage) and *chinchulines* (small intestines).

Ask for your steak *bien cocida* (well done), *a punto* (medium) or *jugoso* (medium rare). Note that different chefs have a different take on these standards, but owing to Argentinian tastes, meat is generally more likely to be overcooked than undercooked. Note also that *carne*, which means all meat in other Spanish-speaking countries, is here often synonymous with beef, as if nothing else matters.

often good value *(around 50–60 A$)*, but eating here à la carte or in the evening is more expensive.

$ Abuela Pan – *Chile 518 (subway line E, Independencia); ☎(011) 4361 4936; www.abuelapan.com; open Mon–Fri 8am–7pm, Sun 9am–4pm.* Now in more spacious premises, this vegetarian restaurant offers special breads, tarts and delicious patisseries, as well as a choice of three menus at 28 A$, made with fresh produce. The menu changes daily and includes a low-calorie option.

$$ Desnivel – *Defensa 855 (subway line C, Independencia); ☎(011) 4300 9081; ✉; open lunchtimes and evenings; closed Mon lunchtimes.* This is the *parrilla* of the district, a no-frills cafeteria that is always full. It should be said that while the food here is standard fare, the dishes are more than substantial, the meat is tender and the prices very low.

$$ i Central Market – *On the corner of Pierina Dealessi and Macacha Güemes (subway line B, L.N. Alem); ☎(011) 5775 0330; www.icentral market.com.ar; open 8am–midnight.* An original concept that allows you to dine at any price range, depending on where you choose to sit. Snack on a salad or a sandwich, or sit down in a more traditional dining room or at a table on the terrace. There's focus on fresh, feelgood foods, plus a tempting selection of more sinful pastries. There's a lovely view over the most aesthetically appealing part of the docks.

$$ 70 Living – *Defensa 714 (subway line C, Independencia); ☎(011) 4362 2340; open lunchtimes and evenings. Happy hour 7–10pm*. A "three-in-one" place, as pleasant for an apéritif or dinner as for a drink at the end of an evening. It is set out on three floors, each with its own ambiance and—the cherry on the cake—there's a little terrace on the top floor. The food focuses on fresh ingredients and is well put together and nicely presented. At lunchtimes, there's a choice of three, well-priced set menus.

$$$ Amici Miei – *Plaza Dorrego (subway line C, San Juan); ☎(011) 4362 5562; www.amicimiei.com.ar; Open Tue–Sat noon until close; Sun lunch only*. Located on the first floor, this stylish place goes almost unnoticed, and yet its four tables on the terrace enjoy the best view there is of the very lively Plaza Dorrego. The food is not to be outdone, with delicious and substantial Italian specialties along with risottos, pizzas and pasta dishes.

$$$ Bahía Madero – *Alicia Moreau de Justo 430 (subway line B, L.N. Alem); ☎(011) 4319 8733/34; www.bahiamadero.com; open Mon–Sun noon until late*. A lovely terrace facing the docks and a classic menu of grilled meat and pasta dishes. The three-course special menu costs from 115 A$, including half a bottle of wine.

$$$ Café San Juan – *San Juan 450 (subway line C, San Juan); ☎(011) 4300 1112; ⌷; open Tue–Sun noon–4pm, 8pm–close*. On the rather unprepossessing Avenue San Juan, there hides a modest cafe that is a cafe only in name and modest only in size. This appealing restaurant uses market-fresh ingredients in an inspired way. The menu—with dishes ranging from tapas to braised rabbit—is scrawled on a chalkboard and changes according to the mood of the chef. A family business where reservations are advised.

$$$ Siga la Vaca – *Alicia Moreau de Justo 1714 (subway line B, L.N. Alem); ☎(011) 4315 6801/02; www.sigalavaca.com; open noon until late*. Located near the university buildings, this big and popular—it's often packed out—*parrilla* offers an appealing all-inclusive, all-you-can-eat menu. The price of the set menu is more in the evenings and at weekends.

La Boca *Map IV.*

Although the district is touristy and there are plenty of restaurants, menus tend to offer standard fare with nothing too inventive.

$$ Barberia – *Pedro de Mendoza 1959; ☎(011) 4303 8256; open summer: lunchtimes and evenings; winter: 11am–6pm*. A little away from the crowds of Caminito, this pasta and grill restaurant caters mainly for tourists. The food is certainly unremarkable, but the service is attentive and guest can enjoy a tango show during their meal.

$$ El Obrero – *Agustín R. Caffarena 64; ☎(011) 4362 9912; www. bodegonelobrero.com.ar; ⌷; open Mon-Sat noon–4pm, 8pm–late*. *Obrero* means worker in Spanish and this was originally a working

Travel Tip:
In a city heavily influenced by its Italian heritage, something unique to Argentinians is the tradition of eating a slice of *faina*; *faina* is a very thin chickpea-based pizza that sits on top of your standard pizza slice, acting as a second crust on top. For locals, it is customary to enjoy your *faina/pizza* combo with a couple glasses of cheap Moscato.

man's *parrilla*. It now adds plenty of the tourists to the mix, along with visiting A-listers, who favor its down-to-earth style. Take a taxi, as the surrounding streets have a reputation.

$$ Il Matterello – *Martín Rodríguez 517; ☏(011) 4307 0529; open Tue–Sat lunchtimes and evenings, Sun lunchtime*. You certainly won't come here by chance. This excellent Italian restaurant is hidden away in a quiet alley, four or five streets away from Caminito. A family place with a friendly atmosphere.

Recoleta *Map II.*

This high-end neighborhood can offer high-end prices too, but more affordable restaurants, including pizzerias, can be found on Av. Santa Fe.

$$ Artesano – *Mansilla 2740 (subway line D, Pueyrredón); ☏(011) 4963 1513; open Mon–Fri 8am–10pm, Sat 9am–8pm*. This excellent vegetarian restaurant does not lack followers, because it carefully selects its produce and everything is homemade: salads, sandwiches, savory and sweet tarts, and bread and Viennese pastries made with wholemeal flour, but also hot dishes, cooked in the oven or steamed. There are also delicious fruit juices and a breakfast menu.

$$ Cumaná – *Rodríguez Peña 1149 (subway line D, Callao); ☏(011) 4813 9207; ☐; open noon–1am*. This fun restaurant, which specializes in food from the north, has built itself a good reputation for its excellent *empanadas* (savory and sweet) and its pizzas (around 30–40 A$). Friends often meet here from 4pm to 7pm, to share a *maté* accompanied by some biscuits. It's relaxed and there are crayons on the tables for children. The only downside is the wait for a table, which can sometimes be rather long.

$$$$ Sirop Restaurant & Sirop Folies – *Vicente López 1661, Pasaje del Correo (subway line D, Callao); ☏(011) 4813 5900; www.siroprestaurant.com; Sirop Folies: open Tue–Sun 10am–midnight (Fri–Sat 12.30am). Sirop Restaurant: open Mon–Sat noon–3.30pm, 8pm–midnight*. Two addresses in one, nestled at the end of a quiet no-through road. On one side is the elegant restaurant-cum-tearoom, with its neo-Baroque decor, which serves breakfasts, brunches *(Sat and Sun 11am–5pm)* and an excellent daily menu; on the other is an equally refined restaurant, serving "modern," more sophisticated cuisine *(main course around 55 A$)*.

Palermo *Map V*

Palermo Viejo is home to some of the trendiest restaurants, as well as the best accommodation. Restaurants here are often high quality and serve food that, if not cheap, is certainly more inventive than most places in Argentina.

$$ Oui Oui – *Nicaragua 6068, Palermo Viejo (subway line D, Ministro Carranza);* ☎*(011) 4778 9614; www.ouioui.com.ar;* ✉*; open Tue–Fri 8am–8pm, Sat–Sun 10am–8pm.* This French-style cafe is exceedingly popular, especially for weekend brunch and its cute decor that has inspired plenty of local copycats. You can't go wrong with a plate piled with eggs, mixed leaves and thick potato wedges. Homemade lemonade is also highly recommended. In true Buenos Aires style, there is no cutoff point for late risers, but expect to wait 20–30 minutes for a table. No reservations.

$$ El Preferido de Palermo – *Jorge Luis Borges 2108, on the corner of Guatemala (subway line D, Plaza Italia);* ☎*(011) 4774 6585; open Mon–Sat noon–4pm, 8pm–late.* In line with old traditions, it is half grocery store, half bar. Walls are lined with rows of old-fashioned cans and bottles, with bar stalls and tables for those wanting to sample the deli-style menu. Alternatively, you can opt for one of the well-laid tables in the more formal adjoining restaurant. Its reputation for classic, hearty food has turned it into a local institution.

$$$ Bio – *Humboldt 2199 (subway line D, Palermo);* ☎*(011) 4774 3880; www.biorestaurant.com.ar; open daily 9am–5pm, Tue–Sat 8pm–1am.* Despite its meat-crazed reputation, there are a handful of good vegetarian restaurants in the city and this is one of the best established. It uses only organic products and adopts a country kitchen style. Special world cuisine menu on Mon evenings.

$$$ La Cabrera & La Cabrera Norte – *Cabrera 5099 and 5127 (subway line D, Plaza Italia);* ☎*(011) 4831 7002; www.parrillalacabrera. ar; open 12.30pm–4.30pm, 8.30pm–1am (Fri–Sun 2am).* This restaurant is considered by many, quite justifiably, as one of the best in Buenos Aires. The meat is not only extremely tender, but the portions are gargantuan and served with several side dishes. It's not uncommon to have to wait more than an hour on the sidewalk before you can be seated (they'll serve you a glass of champagne for your patience). Reservations are taken, but only for sittings at 1pm or 8.30pm.

$$$ Café des Arts – *Near Figueroa Alcorta 3415;* ☎*(011) 4808 0754; open 9am–9pm.* MALBA's *(see p188)* fine restaurant is in the hands of a French chef. The decor is minimalist, overlooking greenery, there's a nice terrace, and the cuisine is light (salads, tarts, seafood…).

$$$ El Trapiche – *Paraguay 5099 (subway line D, Palermo); ☎(011) 4772 7343; open noon–4pm, 8pm–1am.* This lively *parrilla* is typical of the district. Its simple setting, with tables laid with white tableclothes, its somewhat old-fashioned waiters and its irreproachable grilled meats, served in generous portions, have made this restaurant a huge success. A great wine list and a well-priced lunch deal.

$$$$ Osaka – *Soler 5608 (Metrobús Guatemala); ☎(011) 4775 6964; www.osaka.com.pe; 🍴; open Mon–Sat 12.30-4pm, 8pm–1am.* A trendy fusion of Peruvian and Asian cuisine, with an open kitchen so you can see the sushi chefs at work. Years after opening, it is still one of the hottest places in town and reservations are recommended with one week's notice.

$$$$ Tegui – *Costa Rica 5852; ☎(011) 5291 3333; www.tegui.com. ar; open Tue–Sat, 12.30–3.30pm, 8pm–late.* This high-end restaurant tries to play down its credentials by hiding behind a wall covered with (specially commissioned) street art. Inside the decor is highly contemporary, as is the food, which inventively mixes Argentinian traditions with international trends. Some of the dishes verge on molecular cuisine (i.e. there's foam). Pricey.

Belgrano and the Outer Neighborhoods *Map V*
There are plenty of options—local favorites and new openings—in *barrios* that don't receive so many tourists. Belgrano has its own Chinatown, which is good for a quick bite or a takeaway *(see p201)*. Villa Crespo also has a number of interesting restaurants, as it benefits from young, creative residents.

$$ Almacen Secreto – *Aguirre 1242, Villa Crespo (Metrobús Aguirre); ☎(011) 4854 9131; www.almacensecretoclub.blogspot.com; 🍴; open Tue–Sat from 8pm.* Eating here really does feel like being let into a secret. Tucked away on a residential sidestreet, you feel like you've stepped into someone's front room, and that was the original idea of a place that falls into the city's in-home dining scene. This is where to come for a taste of food from across Argentina, from Patagonia to the Andes.

Excursions
In Tigre you will find several bars and restaurants, of very varying quality, along Paseo Victorica. In San Antonio De Areco, there are a handful of options around the square or close to the waterfront.

Tigre

$$$ Il Novo Maria Luján – *Paseo Victorica 611;* ☎*(011) 4731 9613;*
www.novomariadellujan.com; 🚗*; open 8.30am until close.* One of
Tigre's finest addresses, perfectly situated on the riverfront and on
the site of a grand family estate. There's a varied menu, with salads,
fish and meat dishes, plus some Italian options.

San Antonio De Areco

$$ Esquina de Merti – *Plaza Arellano, on the corner of Arellano and
Segundo Sombra;* ☎*(02326) 456 705; www.esquinademerti.com.ar;* 🚗*;
open 9am–midnight. Restaurant noon–3.30pm, 8.30pm–midnight.*
This skillfully restored *pulpería* (tavern) has preserved its original
architecture and its old-world charm, with its wooden bar, beautiful
cash register and fresco. The varied menu includes good, reasonably
priced salads and *parrilladas*.

Entertainment

Buenos Aires is a cultural city with active scenes for theater
and music lovers. Throughout the year many cultural centers present a range of activities encompassing all artistic
disciplines: theater, dance, concerts, film screenings, art
exhibitions, tango displays and various seminars and
workshops. The city offers a wide choice of theaters, from
the renowned international opera house to small experi-
mental theaters. A large number of them are grouped
on the lively Avenida Corrientes, the *porteño* Broadway,
where you can find classical and dramatic works, musicals,
contemporary theater and *revista* (revue).

Buenos Aires is well known for its lively nightlife, the famous *movida porteña*, with clubs and bars springing up
with changing fashions. There are plenty of opportunities to watch live music of all genres, including the local
specialties of tango, *rock nacional, cumbia* and folklore.

Performing Arts
Cultural Centers
Centro Cultural Borges – *Map II, C2; Viamonte 525 (on the corner
of San Martín), Retiro (subway line B, Florida);* ☎ *(011) 5555 5359;*
www.ccborges.org.ar.

Travel Tip:
The opera season
—which features a
program of operas,
ballets and classical
music concerts—
runs from March to
December.

Centro Cultural Plaza Defensa – *Map III, A2; Defensa 535,
San Telmo (subway line E, Belgrano);* ☏ *(011) 4342 6610;
http://plazadefensa.blogspot.com.*
Centro Cultural Recoleta – *Map II, B1; Junín 1930, Recoleta;*
☏ *(011) 4803 1040; www.centroculturalrecoleta.org.* Located in
a former (17C) Recollect monastery, this cultural center has
some 27 exhibition rooms.
Centro Cultural San Martín – *Map II, B3; Sarmiento 1551,
San Cristóbal, (subway line B, Uruguay);* ☏ *(011) 4374 1251;
www.ccgsm.gov.ar.*
Ciudad Cultural Konex – *Map II, A3; toward Sarmiento 3131,
Recoleta (subway line B, Carlos Gardel);* ☏ *(011) 4864 3200;
www.ciudadculturalkonex.com.*

Theaters
Teatro Colón – *Map II, B3; Libertad 621, San Nicolás (subway
line D, Tribunales);* ☏ *(011) 4378 7100 or 4378 7344 (booking);
www.teatrocolon.org.ar.* After extensive renovation,
Argentina's most traditional theater reopened to the public in
May 2010, with a great, eclectic program comprising opera,
dance and concerts.
Teatro Nacional Cervantes – *Map II, B2; Libertad 815,
Recoleta, (subway line D, Tribunales);* ☏ *(011) 4815 8883;
www.teatrocervantes.gov.ar.*
Teatro San Martín – *Map II, B3; Corrientes 1530, San Nicolás
(subway line B, Uruguay);* ☏ *(011) 4371 0111 and 0800 333 5254,
www.teatrosanmartin.com.ar; ticket office: open 10am–10pm.*

Travel Tip:
A strong tradition
of classical music—
orchestral and
choral—is alive and
well in the city. One
option that won't cost
you a peso is found
at the University of
Buenos Aires, which
hosts classical music
concerts on a nearly
weekly basis. For
more, call ☏ (011)
4809 5647 or check
out the schedule at:
http://www.derecho.
uba.ar/extension/
conciertos.php.

Teatro Alvear – *Map II, B3; Corrientes 1659, San Nicolás
(subway line B, Callao);* ☏ *(011) 4373 4245.*
Teatro Regio – *Map IV, A2; toward Córdoba 6056, Palermo
(subway line B, Dorrego);* ☏ *(011) 4772 3350.*
Teatro de la Ribera – *Map V, B2; Pedro de Mendoza 1821,
La Boca;* ☏ *(011) 4302 9042.*
Teatro Sarmiento – *Map II, A3; Sarmiento 2715, Palermo
(subway line H, Corrientes; B, Pueyrredón);* ☏ *(011) 4808 9479.*

Live Music
Boris Club de Jazz – *Gorriti 5568, Palermo Viejo (subway line
D, Palermo);* ☏ *(011) 4777 0012; www.borisclub.com.* With a
200-person capacity, this is a hip newcomer to the Buenos
Aires jazz scene, with near-nightly events (closed Monday).
El Empujón del Diablo – *Carranza 1969, Palermo Viejo
(subway line D, Ministro Carranza);* ☏ *(011) 4774 7354; www.
elempujondeldiablo.com.ar.* This intimate, down-to-earth
peña offers regular performances from a variety of folklore
performers. It can get lively.

Luna Park – *On the corner of Bouchard and Av. Corrientes, San Nicolas (subway line B, L.N. Alem);* ✆ *(011) 5279 5279; www.lunapark.com.ar.* This 8,000-capacity venue, built on the site of the former amusement park of the same name, is an iconic venue, not least for being the place where Eva "Evita" Duarte and Juan Perón first met. Past performers have included Frank Sinatra and Manu Chao. It also hosts boxing and basketball competitions.

Notorious – *Callao 966, San Nicolás (subway line B, L.N. Alem);* ✆ *(011) 4813 6888; www.notorious.com.ar.* Perhaps the most famous and established jazz venue in town.

La Trastienda – *Balcarce 460, San Telmo (subway line B, Belgrano);* ✆ *(011) 4342 7650; www.latrastienda.com.* An atmospheric, mid-sized venue for live bands, from funk to Argentina's own brand of *rock nacional*.

Nightlife
Bars

Dadá *(see Where to Eat p242)* – offers a fine selection of cocktails, in particular vodkas in various mixes. The ambiance is jazz-style, rhythm & blues.

Gibraltar – *Perú 895, San Telmo (subway line C, Independencia);* ✆ *(011) 4362 5310; Open 6pm–4am; happy hour 6–9pm.* More authentic than most English pubs abroad, this popular place always draws a crowd, with locals often outnumbering the expats. There's a variety of beer on tap, a pool room out back and a menu of good pub grub, including Thai curry and jacket potatoes. If you're a cigar aficionado, tell the barman and you may gain access to the small members' bar upstairs.

70 Living *(see Where to Eat p243)* – proves itself to be as good for an apéritif as for a late-night drink.

Gran Bar Danzón – *Libertad 1161, Recoleta (subway line D, Tribunales);* ✆ *(011) 4811 1108; www.granbardanzon.com.ar; open from 7pm (8pm on Sat and Sun); happy hour 7–9pm.* You have to climb a flight of stairs to get to the great industrial-style room of this stylish hangout. You'll find more than 200 examples of Argentinian wine here, most of them available by the glass, and a wide choice of original cocktails. Should you wish to dine here (the sushi is divine), the cuisine is quite creative and it has a good reputation, but the place is rather noisy.

ASK PETER...

Q: Is the music scene all about tango?
A: Far from it! Encompassing rock, pop, folk, R&B, dance, jazz and various Latin styles, the capital hosts a large number of concerts throughout the year, with an increasing tendency to draw in big international names. In addition, there are numerous bars with eclectic programs of live music, showcasing local groups and new talent. For something different, you could also try a *peña*, one of the small folk clubs that offers music from the country's north-west, where you can often sample regional food too.

Travel Tip:
Found on "quiet" Arevalo Street in Palermo Hollywood (home to the office of movie/TV producers) one can walk past the black metal door and easily overlook the small sign reading "Frank's." You see, Frank's is a throwback to the speakeasy revolution of the 1920s where a password was needed to a secret location in order to enjoy a few cocktails. In order to get into Frank's you must pass two tests: first you must get past the doorman (go with a big group and you won't be denied entrance) who will lead you to a smaller room filled with phone booths; second, you must enter the secret code into the phone which will then open a door and allow you to enter the bar (just ask the doorman for help with the code) where you're greeted by the swanky chandeliered bar.

Milión – *Paraná 1048, Recoleta (subway line D, Callao; ☎ (011) 4815 9925; www.milion.com.ar; open Mon–Wed 12pm–2am, Thu 12pm–3am, Fri 12pm–4am, Sat 7.30pm–4am, Sun 8pm–2am.* This chic, trendy bar-restaurant, which occupies the three floors of a superbly restored mansion, has been a stalwart of *porteño* nightlife for over 10 years. At the back, there is a delightful little garden and, on the first floor, a beautiful terrace on which to make the most of summer evenings. The musical atmosphere is eclectic, with a mixture of jazz, soul, funk, bossa nova, tango and electronic. In addition, art exhibitions and projections are regularly organized.

Antares – *Armenia 1447, Palermo Viejo (subway line D, Plaza Italia); ☎ (011) 4833 9611; www.cervezaantares.com; open from 7pm; happy hour 7–10pm.* This well-known brewery has its own bars, including in this huge industrial-style building, where it soon becomes impossible to hear yourself speak. There are seven varieties of traditional house beer and the tasting menu of mini glasses is good fun. You can also get a bite to eat here: the menu includes snacks and tapas.

Congo – *Honduras 5329, Palermo Viejo (subway line D, Palermo); ☎ (011) 4833 5857; open Tue–Sun 8pm–3.30am.* One of the classic attractions of Palermo Viejo nightlife, this bar owes its success especially to its superb garden, which is perfect for warm evenings.

Home *(see Where to Stay p239)* – on the sunny patio of this very trendy hotel, overlooking the garden and swimming pool, is a lovely cocktail bar where you can enjoy an apéritif accompanied by a few tapas. In summer, every Friday evening, a DJ takes to the decks for an eclectic evening.

878 – *Thames 878, Villa Crespo (subway line B, Corrientes; Metrobús stop Aguirre); ☎ (011) 4773 1098; open daily from 8pm.* This speakeasy-style bar is worth a slight detour from the center of Palermo Viejo. This converted woodshop has received a stylish makeover and boasts an outstanding range of whiskey.

Nightclubs
Asia de Cuba – *Pierina Dealessi 750, Puerto Madero; ☎ (011) 4894 1328; www.asiadecuba.com.ar.* A restaurant during the day, and an upmarket nightclub Wed–Sat.

Bahrein – *Lavalle 345, San Nicolás; www.bahreinba.com; open Tue–Sat.* Best known for its drum-and-bass nights on Tuesdays.

Crobar – *Passeo de la Infanta, Palermo;* ☏ *(011) 4778 1500; www.crobar.com.ar; open Fri–Sat.* DJ evening on Fridays, and a mix of electronic music, house, hip-hop, dance and techno on Saturdays.

Niceto Club – *Niceto Vega 5510, Palermo;* ☏ *(011) 4779 9396; www.nicetoclub.com; open Thu–Sat.* Famed for its Thursday night party hosted by drag queens, Club 69.

Pachá – *Rafael Obligado 6151 (Costanera Norte), Palermo;* ☏ *(011) 4788 4280; www.pachabuenosaires.com; open Fri–Sat.* Like its famous sister venue in Ibiza, this superclub has a musical identity based on electro, progressive and deep house sounds.

Travel Tip:
Although most nightclubs are open from midnight, you should be aware that most don't really get going before 2.30am. On the other hand, you will often enjoy a preferential price if you arrive earlier. Most nightclubs are located in the district of Palermo Viejo.

Tango

You can listen to and dance the tango in numerous venues around the capital, but the districts of San Telmo and Abasto remain the most traditional centers.

Tanguerías

Tanguerías present staged diner-shows featuring professional dancers. Many view them as "tourist factories," but the shows are generally of quite a high standard. Obviously, prices vary depending on the venue. Most include dinner, but you can pay less by just going to watch the show. Allow on average 360–600 A$ for the dinner-show and 200–350 A$ for just the show.

El Querandí – *Perú 302, Monserrat (subway line E, Belgrano);* ☏ *(011) 5199 1770; www.querandi.com.ar; open Mon–Sat 8.30pm (dinner) and 10pm (show).*

Bar Sur – *Estados Unidos 299, San Telmo (subway line C, Independencia);* ☏ *(011) 4362 6086; www.bar-sur.com.ar.* Nonstop show, from 8pm to 2am, in an intimate venue.

El Viejo Almacén – *Independencia 303, San Telmo (subway line C, Independencia);* ☏ *(011) 4342 3353; www.viejoalmacen. com; open 8pm (dinner) and 10pm (show).*

La Ventana – *Balcarce 431, San Telmo (subway line C, Independencia);* ☏ *(011) 4334 1314; www.laventanaweb.com; open 8pm (dinner) and 10pm (show).*

Travel Tip:
For more information on classes, shows or the *milongas*, consult the magazine *La Milonga Argentina*, which is distributed free at various places in the city, or the city's official tango website: www.tangobuenos aires.gob.ar.

Travel Tip:
Fernet is an Italian liqueur containing a mix of 40 herbs and spices usually served after meals to aid digestion. The dark, syrupy alcoholic drink has continually been described as a cross between cough medicine, crushed plants and bitter mud so don't be surprised if your first experience of Fernet is much like your first beer; it's an acquired taste (and very popular in Buenos Aires).

Bocatango – *Brandsen 923, La Boca;* ✆ *(011) 4302 0808; www.bocatango.com.ar.* Located in an old *conventillo.* Daytime and evening shows.

Milongas

If you're looking for something more authentic, try *milongas* instead, which is where the *porteños* normally come to dance. There are three types of dances here: the tango, the waltz and the milonga, an earlier form of the tango, which is simpler, with a more lively, upbeat rhythm. There are seats around the outside for those who prefer to spectate. Anyone with even the most vague interest in Argentina's famous dance should fit in a visit to a *milonga*, a true Buenos Aires experience.

Confitería Ideal – *Suipacha 380–384, San Nicolás (subway line B, C. Pellegrini);* ✆ *(011) 5265 8069; www.confiteriaideal.com.* Established in 1912, this is one of the top tango venues in Buenos Aires, less touristy than those previously mentioned. *Open Mon 3–9pm, Tue 10.30pm–3am, Wed 3pm–8pm, 10.30pm–2am, Thu 10.30pm–3am, Fri 3–9pm and 10.30pm–4am, Sat 2–8pm, 10.30pm–3am, Sun 3pm–3am; allow 30 A\$.*

El Arranque – *Map II, B3; Bartolomé Mitre 1759, San Nicolás (subway line A, Congreso);* ✆ *(011) 4371 6767; Mon–Tue, Thu, Sat 3pm–10pm.*

Centro Cultural Torquato Tasso – *Defensa 1575, San Telmo;* ✆ *(011) 4307 6506; www.torquatotasso.com.ar.* Behind its fine façade, painted by the artist Jorge Muscia, hides a truly authentic tango club, where concerts of a high standard are given in a very friendly atmosphere. *Milonga Sun from 10pm (20 A\$).*

Salón Canning – *Scalabrini Ortiz 1331, Palermo (subway line D, Scalabrini Ortiz);* ✆ *(011) 4932 8829; open Thu 8.30pm (lesson) and 10.30pm (dance), Fri and Sun 11pm–4am.*

La Viruta – *Armenia 1366, Palermo (subway line D, Scalabrini Ortiz);* ✆ *(011) 4774 6357; www.lavirutatango.com. Milonga* every evening from Wed to Sun, from 11pm (Thu), 11.30pm (Wed and Sun) or midnight (Fri and Sat).

La Glorieta – *On the corner of Etcheverría and 11 de Septiembre, Belgrano (subway line D, Juramento). Milonga* in the open air, at the old-fashioned bandstand of Barrancas de Belgrano, Fri–Sun from 7.30 or 8pm to 11pm to midnight.

TANGO LESSONS

Many of the capital's hotels offer tango lessons or can direct you to suitable venues, in particular *milongas* and cultural centers, where you can take your first steps. A lesson lasts on average 1–2hrs, and ideally you should take four or five lessons so that you can begin to put together several movements.

Private lessons are also easy to come by, although they can be pretty pricey *(around US$80 per hour)*. For more on tango history see p54–55 and for information about tango tours see p75.

Academia Nacional del Tango

Map III, A2; Mayo 833, San Nicolás (subway line A, Piedras). ✆ *(011) 4345 6968. www.anacdeltango.org.ar.* This center has a museum and offers classes, which take place from Mon to Fri at 6pm (2hrs).

Confitería Ideal

Map II, C3; Suipacha 380–384, San Nicolás (subway line B, C. Pellegrini). ✆ *(011) 5265 8069.* Group lessons: Mon noon–3pm; Tue noon–3pm, 3.30–6.30pm, 6.30pm–8pm; Wed 12–3pm, 4–6pm, 6.30–8pm, 9–10.30; Thu noon–2pm, 2–4pm, 4–5.30pm, 6–7.30pm, 9–10.30pm; Fri 12–3pm, 9–10.30pm; Sat 3–5pm, 5pm–7pm, 9–10.30pm; Sun 9.15pm–11.15pm, 30 A$.

Centro Cultural Torquato Tasso

Map III, A3; Defensa 1575, San Telmo (subway line C, Constitución). ✆ *(011) 4307 6506. www.torquatotasso.com.ar.* Tango lessons Mon–Wed 6.30–8pm, Sun 7–10pm, 25–30 A$.

Mansion Dandi Royal

Map III, A3; Piedras 922 936; San Telmo (subway line C, Independencia). ✆ *(011) 4307 7623. www.hotelmansiondandiroyal.com.* L'Academia de Tango Dandi, which is part of the hotel, offers daily lessons that are open to non-residents *(1hr 30mins, 20–35A$).* The full timetable is available on the website. Private lessons available too.

La Viruta

Map V, A3; Armenia 1366, Palermo (subway line D, Scalabrini Ortiz). ✆ *(011) 4774 6357. www.lavirutatango.com.* Lessons are available at all levels, every evening except Mon. They typically start at 6–7pm *(29 A$).* See the website for the timetable of classes. Rock and salsa are also offered.

Travel Tip:
The Campeonato
Argentino Abierto
de Polo in Palermo
is the culmination
of the annual polo
season as well as
one of the oldest
and most significant
annual events in
international polo.
Plus, it is also one of
the main social events
in Buenos Aires. There
are *abonos* which are
tickets for all seven
dates, but buy your
tickets fast. The main
matches sell out in
just hours.

Spectator Sports

Whether you want to sip champagne and clap politely at a polo match, or stamp your feet and sing your heart out at a soccer stadium, joining a crowd of *porteño* sports fans is guaranteed to be a memorable experience. Pick a sport and get involved.

Pato

A bizarre cross between polo and basketball, this horseback game is Argentina's official national sport, practiced since the beginning of the 17C. It sees players trying to throw a ball into a raised hoop by hand. Originally, that ball was a live duck, now it is a football with handles. Watching a live game is not a common activity and many Argentinians will have never seen one, but it is exhilarating to watch and entry costs just a few pesos.

From Mar to Oct, you can attend weekend tournaments at the Campo Argentino de Pato, 30km/18.5mi from Buenos Aires *(ruta 8, Campo de Mayo)*. Check times and dates in advance at www.pato.org.ar.

Polo

The polo field at Palermo is one of the most well known in the world and can hold up to 45,000 people. The season runs from September to December (spring in the southern hemisphere) and culminates with the Abièrto Argentino de Polo (from mid-Nov to mid-Dec), one of the most important sporting events of the year.

Campo Argentino de Polo de Palermo – *Map V, AB1; Libertador 4300, Palermo; ☎ (011) 4777 6444; www.aapolo.com.*

Horse racing

Races are regularly organized at the city's racetrack:
Hipódromo Argentino de Palermo *Map V, B1; Libertador 4101, Palermo; ☎ (011) 4778 2800; www.palermo.com.ar.*

Soccer

This is the nation's sport of choice and the fans *(hinchas)* have to be among most passionate on earth *(see opposite)*. Securing a ticket is easy enough if you are prepared to pay over the odds, but it is advisable to go with an established tour operator *(see p76)* and it is strongly recommended that you take no valuables to the stadium.

THE BEAUTIFUL GAME

Argentina may be a Catholic nation, but many would argue that the religion that truly glues the nation together is soccer, or *fútbol* (for more about the history of the game see p166). Playing in the same white–and-celeste colors as the national flag, Argentina has won the Copa América (the South American championship) 14 times and the World Cup twice, in 1978 and 1986. It was British immigrants who first introduced the game to the country in the late 19C. The first Argentinian league was founded in 1891, making it the world's third oldest, after England and the Netherlands.

Of the 20 clubs in the first division, 11 are in Buenos Aires. The season runs from August to June. For fixtures, see the official website of the Asociación del Fútbol Argentino (AFA): www.afa.org.ar.

Boca Juniors and River Plate

The two most famous teams in the country are historic rivals: Boca Juniors and River Plate. The enmity stems from when they were both based in La Boca; later, River won nickname *los millonarios* (the millionaires), after moving to the more affluent neighborhood of Nuñez.

The Superclásico is the fierce derby between the two but, in June 2011, the clubs' intertwined history received a shock when River Plate were relegated for the first time in history, having spent 110 years in the Premier League and racking up 33 titles. Other staunch rivals in Argentinian football are Independiente and Racing, which are said to have the second closest stadiums in the world, only around 300m/330yd apart.

Las barras bravas

Argentinian fans are known for being tough, passionate and, in the most extreme cases, forming an indomitable mafia. Each team has a nickname for its most loyal supporters. Boca Juniors' *hinchas* (fans) are known as *El Doce* (the 12th player). River Plate's are known, rather unpoetically, as *Los Borrachos del Tablón* (the drunkards of the stand).

Messi and Maradona

Worshiped in their homeland and across the world, Lionel Messi and Diego Maradona are the two biggest names to hail from Argentina. Maradona, probably the sport's most outspoken character, helped the nation win the 1986 World Cup and returned to manage the national team in the 2010 World Cup, albeit with disappointing results. Messi was a child prodigy, who was transferred to Barcelona aged 13. Messi wears the number ten jersey for his country, just like Maradona once did.

Shopping

ASK PETER...

Q: I'm interested in doing some upscale shopping. Any suggestions?

A: If you are searching for the Rodeo Drive of Buenos Aires look no further than Avenida Alvear, a street filled with haute couture boutiques stretching seven blocks. Locals might do more window shopping than actual shopping here but walking past the international boutiques and looking at the local fashions is always a thrill. And yes, pop into Patio Bullrich if you want the experience condensed into a mall.

For general browsing, the best areas for shopping are San Telmo and Palermo Viejo. Prices will be somewhat inflated for the clientele of tourists and style-conscious *porteños*, but you can still find good bargains and window-shopping can be just as enjoyable.

Art and Antiques

With more than 500 art and antique stores, the district of **San Telmo**, and in particular Calle Defensa *(Map III, A2–3)*, is one of the most well known in this field. It is difficult to recommend one store above another, as so much depends on what you're looking for, but you can easily spend two hours browsing on these streets. In addition, the big **Feria de San Telmo** *(see opposite)* is held every Sunday.

Bookstores

Ateneo Grand Splendid – *Santa Fe 1860, Recoleta;* ✆ *(011) 4811 6104; open Mon–Thu 9am–10pm, Fri–Sat 9am–midnight, Sun noon–10pm.* Located in a superbly restored former theater, this huge bookstore is not only one of the largest in South America, but is also without doubt one of the most beautiful. Definitely worth a detour.

Gandhi Galerna – *Corrientes 1743, San Nicolás;* ✆ *(011) 4874 7501; open Mon–Thu 10–10, Fri–Sat 10am–midnight, Sun 4–10pm.* One of the city's largest bookstores.

Libros del Pasaje – *Thames 1762, Palermo Viejo;* ✆ *(011) 4833 6637; www.librosdelpasaje.com.ar; open Mon–Sat 10–10, Sun 2–9pm.* A beautiful bookstore that is a pleasure to amble around, especially as it also has a lovely cafe. Includes some books in English and French, plus a small but interesting collection of CDs.

Walrus Books – *Estados Unidos 617, San Telmo;* ✆ *(011) 4833 6637; walrus-books.com.ar; open Tue–Sun noon–8pm.* A lovely little shop dedicated to English-language books, new and used. The collection spans fiction and nonfiction, modern and classic.

Fashion

Those with an interest in fashion should head to **Palermo Viejo**, and in particularl **Palermo Soho**, where the streets are packed with small boutiques, independent design stores and select chain stores. For high-end designer goods (Hermés, Armani etc.), you'll be better off on Avenida Alvear in **Recoleta**. For trendy, vintage and alternative clothes, there are an increasing number of stores around **San Telmo**. In all of these areas, there are plenty of cafes to stop for coffee and take a break.

For shopping malls, popular inner-city sites include **Alto Palermo** (Santa Fe 3253, Palermo, just outside Bulnes subway station) or **Shopping Abasto**, housed in a wonderful Art Deco building (Corrientes 3247, Abasto; subway line A, Carlos Gardel). You can find various outlet stores in **Villa Crespo**, around calles Aguirre and Gurruchaga.

Galerías Pacifico – On the corner of Florida and Córdoba, San Nicolás; ✆ (011) 5555 5110; www.galeriaspacifico.com. ar; open Mon–Sat 10am–9pm, Sun 12–9pm. This gallery is a must-see for its hall with large painted frescoes. You'll find all the big international brands, alongside Argentinian designers and emblematic national brands, such as La Martína, Cardón, Casa Lopez, Akiabara and Ayres.

Cardón – Alvear 1847; ✆ (011) 4804 8424; www.cardon.com. ar; Mon–Sat 9–30am–8.30pm, Sun 10.30am–7.30pm. Chic, traditional gaucho clothing made from ultra-supple unlined leather, cashmere, linen and cotton.

La Martína – Paraguay 661 (near Florida), San Nicolás; ✆ (011) 4311 5963; www.lamartina.com; open Mon–Sat 10am–8pm. Banking on the Argentinian passion for polo and horses, this brand revisits classics with an imaginative touch (appliqué, playing with logos, textures…). They make shirts for Argentina's national polo team. A rather expensive, chic and conservative style, but one that's becoming increasingly fashionable in Europe.

Travel Tip:
It is not customary to haggle, but many stores will give a reduction if you pay in cash. Foreign tourists can request the VAT (Value Added Tax) return for the purchase of products manufactured in Argentina for a value of not less than 70 A$ (about US$70). See Tax-free Shopping, p96.

MARKETS

The ferias (markets) of Buenos Aires are a great place for buying souvenirs and presents. Artisans and entrepreneurs come to display their wares, which include jewelry, children's toys and household decorations.

Feria de San Telmo Map III, A3; Plaza Dorrego and Calle Defensa, San Telmo; open Sun 10am–5pm. This big market brings together more than 250 craft and antique stalls every Sunday.

Feria Plaza Francia Map V, D2; plazas Francia and Alvear (avenues Libertador and Pueyrredón), Recoleta; open Sat and Sun 11am–8pm. The gardens of the plazas Francia and Alvear host a craft fair every weekend, giving the district a bohemian air.

Feria de Mataderos See Outer Neighborhoods p206.

Food and Drink

Oro & Cándido – *Guatemala 5099, Palermo Viejo; ℘ (011) 4772 0656; www.oroycandido.com.ar; open Mon–Sat 10am–midnight, Sun 11am–6pm.* A mouthwatering selection of delicacies from around Argentina: cooked and smoked meats (including rhea and llama), Patagonian trout, cheeses, as well as jellies and syrups, chocolate and wine… all perfectly packaged to withstand traveling.

Del Buen Vivir – *Scalabrini Ortiz 1687, Palermo Viejo; ℘ (011) 4831 9717; open 10.30am–8.30pm.* This local wine merchant offers a fine selection of Argentinian wines, as well as homemade cheeses.

La Cava de Vittorio – *Arenales 2321, Recoleta; ℘ (011) 4824 0647; open Mon–Fri 10am–8pm, Sat 10am–2pm.* A specialist selection of Argentinian wines sourced from *bodegas* throughout the country.

Interior Decoration and Design

Buenos Aires Design – *On the corner of Pueyrredón and Libertador, Recoleta; ℘ (011) 5777 6000; www.designrecoleta.com.ar; open Mon–Sat 10am–9pm, Sun noon–9pm.* Located in the former Recollect monastery, this themed shopping mall is entirely dedicated to design (household equipment, decoration, accessories, etc.).

Leather Goods and Silverwork

La Calle Florida – A section of this shopping street—closest to Plaza San Martín, and *calles* Paraguay and Tucumán—is where you'll find leather goods and traditional crafts (woven textiles, knives, silverwork…). Note that most will agree to give you a significant discount if you pay in cash.

La Calle Murillo – This road in Villa Crespo, at the cross-section with Avenue Scalabrini Ortiz, contains numerous leather stores. Fewer tourists go here than Calle Florida (which is swarming with Brazilians), so you're more likely to pick up a bargain.

Rosa del Inca – *Florida 971, San Nicolás; ℘ (011) 4313 3515; open Mon–Fri 9.30am–8.30pm, Sat 10am–8pm.* A store worth visiting, even if just out of curiosity, to see what can be made from rhodocrosite, a lovely pink stone that is symbolic of Argentina and seen as a stone of peace and serenity.

Artesanos de Argentina – *Defensa 1244–1251, San Telmo; ℘ (011) 4300 5791; www.artesanosdeargentina.com.ar; open 10am–6pm.* This cooperative brings together some 15 traditional craftsmen and women, all with different specialties and backgrounds, but all charging reasonable prices.

Artepampa – *Defensa 917 and Bethlem 421, San Telmo; ℘ (011) 4362 6406; www.artepampa.com; open 10.30am–7pm.* A store where you can unearth some beautiful accessories and decorative items inspired by Argentina's different indigenous cultures.

Music Stores

There are two friendly stores in the San Telmo district. On one side of the street is:
Body and Soul – *Defensa 1295, San Telmo;* ✆ *(011) 4307 9035; open Tue–Sun 10am–1pm, 2–6pm.* A friendly store, selling a good selection of tango, folk, jazz and rock CDs. And opposite there's a vinyl specialist:
Miles – *Honduras 4912, Palermo Viejo;* ✆ *(011) 4832 0466; www.milesdiscos.com.ar; open Mon–Thu 10am–9pm, Fri–Sat 10–10, Sun noon–8pm.* A wide selection of CDs and records, all genres mixed together: tango, folklore, pop, rock, world music….

Spas

The people of Buenos Aires—both men and women—are an image-conscious bunch, so there are plenty of opportunities around town for treatments and pampering. Prices are often much cheaper than in the US or Europe, but you'll pay a premium in top hotels.

The centrally located **Panamericano Hotel** has a fair-priced spa on the 23rd floor, with a pool that looks out over the Obelisco and Teatro Colón *(Carlos Pellegrini 551;* ✆ *(011) 4338 5322; www.panamericano.us; 215 A$ for a day pass).* Pool-and-spa packages can also be arranged at **Duque Boutique Hotel** in Palermo *(Guatemala 4364;* ✆ *(011) 4832 0312, www.duquehotel.com; from 290 A$, including a massage)* or at **Mansion Vitraux** in San Telmo *(Carlos Calvo 369;* ✆ *(011) 4878 4292; www.mansionvitraux.com; from 760 A$ for two people).*
Outside the hotel scene, **Ser Spa** has a varied selection of packages, all reasonably priced *(Cerviño 3626, Palermo;* ✆ *(011) 4807 4688; www.aguaclubspa.com),* or try **Espacio Oxyvital**, which also has very small pool for cooling off in *(Nicaragua 4959;* ✆ *(011) 4775 0010; www.espaciooxivital.com.ar).* If you simply want a massage, **Pranna Terapias Corporales** is a small, friendly studio in Palermo, where an hour costs from 100 A$ *(Scalabrini Ortiz and Charcas;* ✆ *(011) 3528 2429; prannaterapiascorporales.blogspot.com/).*
Like the rest of the world, Buenos Aires has gone mad for yoga in recent times. For English-language tuition, try **Happy Sun Yoga** *(www.happysunyoga.com)* or **Buena Onda Yoga** *(www.buenaondayoga.com).*

Travel Tip:
Since almost all flights to BA qualify as long haul, why not head to a spa the minute you clear customs? The best bargain is the Spa Urbano Grande Manzana in Recoleta. How about a 60-minute professional massage of your choice (deep tissue massage or hot rock therapy, among others) for just US$25? You won't find that price at a hotel spa. Open Monday through Saturday from 9am–9pm.

INDEX

INDEX

INDEX

MAP LEGEND

★★★ **Worth the trip**
★★ **Worth a detour**
★ **Interesting**

Sight Symbols

▭●━━━━ Recommended itineraries with departure point	
🏠 ♦ ⊡ Church, chapel – Synagogue	▬ Building described
○ Town described	▬ Other building
AZ B Map co-ordinates locating sights	▪ Small building, statue
▪ ▲ Other points of interest	◦ ∴ Fountain – Ruins
⚒ ⌒ Mine – Cave	🇮 Visitor information
⚐ ⚑ Windmill – Lighthouse	⬤ ⚓ Ship – Shipwreck
☆ ⛪ Fort – Mission	☀ Ψ Panorama – View

Other Symbols

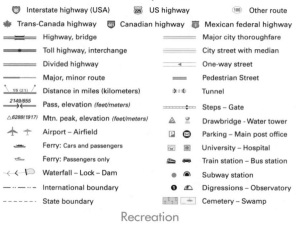

🛡 Interstate highway (USA)	🚩 US highway	⬭ Other route
🍁 Trans-Canada highway	Ⓐ Canadian highway	🛡 Mexican federal highway
═══ Highway, bridge		Major city thoroughfare
━●━ Toll highway, interchange		City street with median
═══ Divided highway		◄ One-way street
─── Major, minor route		═══ Pedestrian Street
15 (21) Distance in miles (kilometers)		⇥:⇤ Tunnel
2149/655 Pass, elevation *(feet/meters)*		╌╌╌ Steps – Gate
△6288(1917) Mtn. peak, elevation *(feet/meters)*		△ ⌷ Drawbridge - Water tower
✈ ✛ Airport – Airfield		🅿 ✉ Parking – Main post office
⛴ Ferry: Cars and passengers		🎓 ✚ University – Hospital
⛴ Ferry: Passengers only		🚂 🚌 Train station – Bus station
←←▷ Waterfall – Lock – Dam		● Ⓜ Subway station
─··─··─ International boundary		❶ 🔭 Digressions – Observatory
------ State boundary		▦ ◢ Cemetery – Swamp

Recreation

▪○○○○○● Gondola, chairlift	⟨===⟩ ⚑ Stadium – Golf course	
🚂 Tourist or steam railway	⊛ ▭ ▦ Park, garden – Wooded area	
⛴ ♌ Harbor, lake cruise – Marina	🦬 Wildlife reserve	
⚓ ☑ Surfing – Windsurfing	🦬 Ψ Wildlife/Safari park, zoo	
▦ ⚓ Diving – Kayaking	------ Walking path, trail	
⛷ ⚑ Ski area – Cross-country skiing	🚶 Hiking trail	

Sight of special interest for children

Abbreviations and special symbols

NP	National Park	NMem	National Memorial	SP	State Park
NM	National Monument	NHS	National Historic Site	SF	State Forest
NWR	National Wildlife Refuge	NHP	National Historical Park	SR	State Reserve
NF	National Forest	NVM	National Volcanic Monument	SAP	State Archeological Park

🛡	National Park	🛡	State Park	🛡	National Forest	🛡	State Forest

All maps are oriented north, unless otherwise indicated by a directional arrow.

MAPS

NOTES

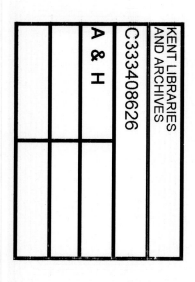

NOTES